TRUST NO ONE™ THE ⓍFILES™

OTHER X-FILES TITLES
AVAILABLE FROM HARPERPRISM

FICTION
THE X-FILES GOBLINS

THE X-FILES WHIRLWIND

THE X-FILES GOBLINS/WHIRLWIND

THE X-FILES GROUND ZERO

THE X-FILES RUINS

NONFICTION
THE TRUTH IS OUT THERE:
THE OFFICIAL GUIDE TO
THE X-FILES

THE X-FILES BOOK OF
THE UNEXPLAINED VOLUME ONE

THE X-FILES 1997 DESK DIARY

THE A-Z OF THE X-FILES

THE X-FILES POSTCARD BOOK:
THE CONSPIRACIES

THE OFFICIAL
THIRD SEASON
GUIDE TO

TRUST NO ONE™ THE ⓧ FILES™

Created by
Chris Carter

Written by
Brian Lowry

with research assistance
by Sarah Stegall

791.45
LOW

HarperPrism
An Imprint of HarperPaperbacks

HarperPaperbacks
A Division of HarperCollins*Publishers*
10 East 53rd Street, New York, N.Y. 10022-5299

We wish to acknowledge the following still photographers for their
photographic contributions to this book:
Michael Grecco, Chris Helcermanas-Benge, Jack Rowand, Ken Staniforth,
Marcel Williams, Graham Clegg, Bonnie Hay, and Patti McRenalds.
Special thanks to Angelo Vacco for his photographic contributions.

HarperPrism is an imprint of HarperPaperbacks.

HarperCollins®, ®, HarperPaperbacks™, and HarperPrism®
are trademarks of HarperCollins*Publishers* Inc.

HarperPaperbacks may be purchased for educational, business, or
sales promotional use. For information, please write:
Special Markets Department, HarperCollins*Publishers,*
10 East 53rd Street, New York, N.Y. 10022-5299.

ISBN: 0-06-105353-8

Printed in the United States of America

Front cover photograph courtesy of Fox Broadcasting Company
In-House Advertsing Department
Photography by Michael Lavine

First printing: November 1996

Designed by Paul Kepple

Library of Congress Cataloging-in-Publication Data
Lowry, Brian
    Trust no one : the official third season guide to the X-files /
created by Chris Carter ; written by Brian Lowry with research
assistance by Sarah Stegall.
            p.   cm.
    Sequel to: The truth is out there.
    ISBN 0-06-105353-8 (trade paperback)
    1. X-files (Television program) I. Carter, Chris. II. Stegall,
Sarah.   III. Title.
PN1992.77X22L72   1996   96-42078
791.45 72--dc20   CIP

Visit HarperPaperbacks on the World Wide Web at
http://www.harpercollins.com/paperbacks

❖ 10 9 8 7 6 5 4 3 2

ACKNOWLEDGMENTS

As with *The Truth Is Out There: The Official Guide to The X-Files,* this book could not have been written without the tremendous cooperation, patience, and helpfulness of the program's cast and crew in Los Angeles and Vancouver, who were extremely generous with a lurking figure who came to be known around the set as "the book guy." Thanks especially to Joanne Service, who lived up to her name in going well beyond the call of duty to help an outsider navigate around Vancouver; and Mary Astadourian, who somehow manages to juggle books along with everything else she does.

Belated thanks as well to Jennifer Sebree of Twentieth Century Fox licensing, who had the faith to let me do the first book; *Daily Variety* editor Peter Bart, who provided initial permission to take on such a project; and Fox Broadcasting's publicity department, as well as everyone at Twentieth Century Fox Television. Also, my gratitude to the new boss, the *Los Angeles Times*, for their flexibility and patience. And at the risk of being redundant, special appreciation (again) to Chris Carter, who provided an ink-stained wretch with free reign around the set and office. If this sort of behavior persists he may even have to retire the expression "Trust No One."

On a personal note, my eternal gratitude to my mother, Doris, who not only helped sustain me through the writing process with occasional high-carbohydrate meals but also doubled as the sort of loyal proofreader money can't buy; and all the friends who put up with this latest *X-Files*–induced disappearance. Finally, thanks to my sister Cathy and her family, who didn't let me hear the end of it after forgetting to acknowledge them in the first book.

CONTENTS

"The X Files"

9:00am
Crew call

Shoot call 9:30am
Sunrise 6:06am Sunset 8:16pm
Rain/Wind 90% H15 L7

NO FORCED CALLS WITHOUT PRIOR APPROVAL OF RROUCTION MANAGER

Producers	EXECUTIVE PRODUCER: CHRIS CARTER COEXECUTIVE PRODUCER: BOB GOODWIN PRODUCER: J.P. FINN				
Director	Bob Goodwin				

Scenes	Set	Cast	Pages	D/N	Location
10	Int Beach House - Foyer *Entering*	8	1/8	Day 1	2429 Christopherson Rd., Surrey
11	Int Beach House - Living Room *Looking*	8	2/8	Day 1	Same
24	Ext Beach House - Deck *Cancer Man*	1 11	1 7/8	Day 2	Same
22	Ext Beach House *Arrival*	1	2/8	Day 2	Same
25	Ext Beach House *Leaving*	1	1/8	Day 2	Same
23	Int Beach House - Living Room *Doors*	1	3/8	Day 2	Same
29 PT.	Int Beach House - Living Room *Seaching*	1	1 4/8	Night 2	Same

Total pages 4 4/8

CAST - Weekly and Day Players

Cast		Character	Status	Pickup	Makeup/ Wrdrobe	Set Call	Comment	NDB
DAVID DUCHOVNY	1	MULDER	SW	9:15a	10:30a	11:00a	HOME TO LOCATION	2
REBECCA TOOLAN	8	MRS. MULDER	SW		8:30a	9:30a	REPORT TO LOCATION	2
STEVEN WILLIAMS	11	X	SW	9:30a	10:30a	11:00a	HOTEL TO LOCATION	M

W = Work R = Rehearsal F = Finish S = Start H = Hold T = Test Tr = Travel

Atmosphere and Stand-Ins	Special Instructions
HMW SET REPORT TO LOCATION 11:00 AM MULDER STANDIN - JAAP	2ND UNIT SHOOTING 3X23 "WETWIRED" AT FORT LANGLEY - SEE 2ND UNIT CALLSHEET FOR DETAILS

Advance Schedule

Scenes	Set	Cast	Pages	D/N	Location
	Day 2 Tuesday 4/23				
13 PT.	Int F.B.I. - Directors Office *Serious Condition*	13	3/8	Day 1	Stage 4, North Shore Studios, North Vancouver
26	Int F.B.I. - Directors Office *Like A Dream*	2 4 7 13	1 3/8	Day 2	Same
31	Int F.B.I. - Directors Outer Office *Visitor*	1	2/8	Day 3	Same
32	Int F.B.I. - Directors Office *Cool Off*	1 2 13	1 6/8	Day 3	Same
17 PT.	Int Mulder's Office *Images*	1 2	2 0/8	Day 2	Stage 2

Total pages 5 6/8

Chris Carter, creator of *The X-Files*, has coined several memorable catchphrases that have made it into the national lexicon, with "The Truth Is Out There" perhaps foremost among them. Yet when he signs autographs, Carter usually writes the same rather stark inscription: "Trust No One."

These words, gasped by a dying Deep Throat to Agent Dana Scully in the first season's final episode, "The Erlenmeyer Flask," not only reflect the producer's own rather dark world view, but the show's continuing plot element of an intriguing and elusive conspiracy theory. They also represent the often unspoken but always present theme of skepticism and existential doubt that has elevated the series far beyond the realm of entertainment, and given it a place in the national consciousness.

One wouldn't necessarily expect such brooding strains to be found lurking inside Carter, with his blond ex-surfer, California good looks—unless one has paid close attention to the show itself. *The X-Files* viewers, who *do* pay close attention and who have learned that reality often masks mystery, can more easily accept that Carter's laid-back appearance serves to mask the uncanny combination of determination and creative intensity necessary to create one of television's most unique and popular series.

The X-Files is, more than anything else, the product of Carter's closely guarded vision—realized each week through the toil and dedication of a hand-picked staff that has the curious distinction of considering itself both uniquely privileged and severely overworked. Working under fierce deadline pressures, and booking long hours that often extend from dawn to dawn, these talented women and men spend more time on the show's set in Vancouver or within its tiny, cluttered bungalow on the Fox lot in Los Angeles than with their families, when the series is in production. (And the series is in production ten months of the year!) Like Carter, the staff is committed to a merciless but inspiring task: making *The X-Files* the best show possible, and then going just a little beyond....

Granted, in network television, what's desirable and what's possible often find themselves in conflict, as art struggles against the twin tyrannies of time and money. *The X-Files* crew, for example, has eight days to shoot each episode (viewed by the staff as a "minimovie"), compared to the many months and millions available for a feature film that is often far less ambitious. From that perspective, the Herculean effort that allows Carter and company to script and shoot two dozen meticulously crafted hours each season becomes all the more impressive, explaining why the coffee pots in *The X-Files* production offices are always warm.

As I wrote in *The Truth Is Out There*, virtually no one could have anticipated the show's eventual growth into such a phenomenon—generating both popular and critical acclaim, ranging from the die-hard fans who light up the Internet after each episode, calling themselves X-Philes, to a seat at the table alongside TV's most-honored dramas when the Emmys and other awards are presented.

Seen as a novelty when it premiered, *The X-Files* introduced television viewers to two FBI agents investigating the paranormal. One of the two, Fox Mulder, had his own personal tragedy to draw upon—the memory of having witnessed, as a boy, the abduction of his sister by aliens. The other, Dana Scully, was paired with a suspicious Mulder and approached his crusade skeptically, being predisposed by her training as a medical doctor to seek "scientific" explanations for the uncanny events and

Frank Spotnitz, Chris Carter Ken Horton, and Paul Rabwin.

strange connections they uncover.

Television executives (and even star David Duchovny himself, who saw the role as little more than a few weeks work before moving on to another movie) feared that the premise would be too confining, that the "alien of the week" concept would grow tiresome. Yet Carter quickly demonstrated that the show he envisioned would be much more than that, exploring not simply monsters and aliens but the deeper, still unexamined mysteries and nightmares of our postmodern society, many of them not even acknowledged until brought to the surface by *The X-Files*. In addition, Carter plotted a complex web of government conspiracies and secrets—the show's own "mythology," as he calls it—deeply intertwined with the two central characters' present and past.

Trust no one.

The same questioning of authority that prompted Carter to name a character Deep Throat after the Watergate scandal that shadowed his teens, struck a responsive chord with the public. So, too, did the show's leads, David Duchovny and Gillian Anderson. Duchovny had begun a promising movie career before making this foray into episodic television, while Anderson was a relative unknown who had worked mostly in theater before coming to Los Angeles to seek film work, receiving her final unemployment check the day she was chosen to costar in the series. Carter knew he had the right mix immediately, even though he had to fight to defend his casting decision, against the objections of some who wanted more overt sexuality from Anderson's role.

Trust no one.

The other star of *The X-Files* is the viewer. Carter knew that a significant sector of the viewing public would find the show and come to it, without pandering or "dumbing down," and he was right; even though the process was made all the more selective by the cryptic, never-quite-complete endings he insisted on providing, trusting viewers to "get it" despite the lack of a neat resolution. And get it they did.

Trust no one?

Even the romance has remained enigmatic and elusive. The at-times playful but always respectful interplay between the characters enthralled fans, while Carter has firmly held to his instinct to keep the relationship platonic and professional. Thus *The X-Files* has avoided the pitfall of a romantic entanglement that crippled a show like *Moonlighting* or resulted in a memorably awkward stretch on *Cheers*.

From the beginning, *The X-Files* distinguished itself by being flat-out scary. Initial perils included a variety of threats never seen before on television, including an Arctic space-worm that infected human hosts (the invader could be seen moving under the victim's skin), and a liver-eating mutant capable of wriggling through water pipes and heating ducts. Not since *The Night Stalker*, one of Carter's early inspirations, had such macabre images been seen on prime-time television. This highlighting of outright horror was extremely unusual in a show with such sophisticated characters and complex back story.

As this potent mix of qualities caught on, viewership of the show gradually snowballed. During the 1995–96 television season that officially ran from September through May (including repeats), the total audience grew by 7 percent, to more than 15 million people each week. Because of *The X-Files*'s dedicated upscale audience and the mysterious allure of Duchovny and Anderson, the series also became a major media darling—magazines like *Entertainment Weekly*, *Rolling Stone*, and *People* clamored to feature it in their pages. Then again, who can blame them, when a cover photo of Duchovny and Anderson in bed together became the bestselling issue in the history of Australian *Rolling Stone*, an immediate collector's item, and the first cover poached from that publication for the magazine's U.S. edition.

The program's commercial accomplishments hardly end there. The fX cable network bought rights to begin repeating the program Monday through Friday in September 1997, in a deal that allows for a simultaneous weekend syndication window on local TV stations. The success of *The X-Files* has also extended beyond the United States's borders, becoming the first U.S.–originated television program in years to achieve prime-time success in Japan, having already established itself as one of the most popular exports in countries like England and Australia. According to Associated Press, the last U.S. television show to have such an effect in Japan, perhaps appropriately, was *Twin Peaks*, whose brief run included a recurring role (albeit in drag) for Duchovny as well as roles for several other performers who have subsequently appeared as *The X-Files* guest stars.

Novels based on the stars and themes from the show began to appear on U.S. bestseller lists in 1994, and remain there today. Videos of early episodes immediately vaulted onto *Billboard*'s bestseller charts, and a CD featuring music by composer Mark Snow and other songs heard on the program released last spring became an immediate hit. Snow, for one, has savored the moment. "I've been doing this for twenty years," he says. "As a composer doing TV stuff, you inevitably think about moving up the ladder and doing features. But if it never happens, this is as good as it gets." Talk has even risen about marketing the five original themes Snow concocted for *The X-Files* before he and Carter settled on the by-now familiar six-note whistling sound.

For Carter, however, spin-offs and marketing, even of the most intelligent sort, are seen primarily as distractions. His focus, and that of the crew, remains fixed on the show itself—on balancing the requisite mix of thrills and humor, and providing the revelations that advance the show's mythology without ever revealing too much, too soon. "The truth," so often discussed on the series, thus stays tantalizingly "out there," just outside the audience's reach, providing ample room for speculation.

Carter's supervision of the show took on a new dimension, and a new degree of difficulty, during the third season. After three years of devoting himself exclusively to *The X-Files*, he found time while producing the series to develop, write, and produce the pilot episode for another Fox drama series, *Millennium*. With disarming simplicity, Carter explains that his involvement with the new entry—an eerie hour starring Lance Henriksen and Megan Gallagher—didn't split his focus, but merely required him to work twice as hard. The facts bear him out: While developing the second project, Carter didn't flag in his service to *The X-Files*, writing or sharing writing credit on seven episodes during the third season, and putting his unmistakeable creative stamp on all 24 of them.

With *The X-Files* moving to Sunday night—where Fox hopes even more viewers will be tempted to watch and expand their horizons—and *Millennium* inheriting the old Friday time slot, the network's fortunes clearly ride to some extent on Carter's shoulders. Still, if he feels pressure, the producer exhibits little sign of it, and his ability to shepherd both projects at once is, as Megan Gallagher told television critics, "an amazing juggling act to watch."

For all his own unremitting labors, Carter is the first to acknowledge that *The X-Files* is, above all else, a team effort. Though Carter remains the driving force behind the series, his unwavering commitment has filtered through the ranks: from the writers, who are urged to pursue their most fantastic and nightmarish ideas and then witness how they are realized; to the technical staff, constantly seeking new ways to capture the show's look and special effects in creatively cost-effective ways.

This commitment shows in little ways as well as big. The atmosphere around the sets and production offices speak more of perseverance and dedication than the show-business glitter one might expect. Most of the crew work in jeans and T-shirts, and days routinely run 12 hours or more. Nearly 200 people in Vancouver and Los Angeles take part in generating an episode of *The X-Files,* with Carter splitting his time between the two locales.

Physical production takes place in Vancouver, British Columbia, where the pursuit of excellence shines through despite the near-constant rain and frequent delays—a spirit that can be found in the shooting crew, the production office, and around the lot, as sets and props are quickly designed and constructed to accommodate the special needs of each new installment. Within the hectic but congenial environs of the show's tree-encircled lot, are many veterans of the TV industry who have worked on prime-time series before and seem to particularly savor their association with *The X-Files*. Many of these crew members recognize the rare opportunity afforded them being able to work on a program that pays more attention to detail, they agree, than programs they've been associated with before or are apt to work on in the future. Small wonder, then, that as crew members move on to new projects, Carter likes to talk about when (not *if*) they'll return—only half-kidding as he warns them about the cold, cruel entertainment world that awaits without.

Not quite 1,300 miles away, in Los Angeles, writers and postproduction personnel can be found in a casual, cluttered bungalow on the Twentieth Century Fox lot, working the same outlandish hours and indeed often "overnighting it" on a couch. Perhaps surprisingly, fewer of those associated with the series in L.A. have the television resumes of their Canadian counterparts; and indeed, for several of the writers, *The X-Files* represents their first television show. Tasks overseen in Southern California include writing and researching stories; adding sound effects, visual effects, and music; editing the raw footage from Vancouver; and painstakingly attending to the overall look and continuity of each installment. In all of these procedures, two words guide the process, often spoken in hushed reverence: "quality control."

Blue Duchovny.

Though Carter demands no more of the staff than he does himself, he also recognizes the devotion that goes into producing the show. With all the time spent in that Twentieth Century Fox bungalow or in Vancouver waiting for the next shot to be ready, a sense of extended family has not surprisingly developed. Duchovny's dog Blue and Anderson's daughter Piper are fixtures around the set, seeming to belong not only to the stars but to the crew as well. Such lighter moments, as Piper toddling about the set or Blue waiting patiently for her master, belie the darkness and gore often espied on-screen through those shrouded flashlight beams.

Although they remain constantly connected by phone coordinating each episode, the Vancouver and Los Angeles offices only get together when the season ends, attending the traditional "wrap party"—an event celebrating what's just been accomplished as well as heralding the much-needed break before the season to come. Yet even with the distance that separates them, there is a camaraderie between the Los Angeles and Vancouver crews, born of their common desire to produce a show they firmly believe is destined to with-

stand the test of time—a show people will be enjoying not only in a few weeks, but decades later. That understanding and pride infuse every episode, making the long hours, the rain-soaked location shoots, and the inevitable delays and hassles a whole lot easier to endure. These attributes are part of what makes *The X-Files* what it is, and an intangible but critical aspect of the show's success.

Because those elements are so particular to the series, Carter dismisses an alien invasion of a different kind—in the form of several prime-time imitators during the 1996–97 television season. And he vehemently rejects the notion that *The X-Files* in its third season became "a mainstream show," as some media analysts suggested.

"It didn't become a mainstream show at all," Carter stresses. "It was the same dark show—in fact, a darker show than it had ever been. It just gained a mainstream audience."

Indeed, the 1995–96 season represented foremost a growth year for *The X-Files* creatively, even in the face of the ongoing challenge that comes with an expanded audience base—namely, to satisfy those new viewers without alienating the core following. Duchovny and Anderson, for starters, continued to plumb the depths of their characters, the latter earning the Screen Actors Guild award and her first Emmy nomination—one of eight Emmy bids in all for the show, including recognition in such areas as writing, cinematography, art direction, sound, and as a candidate for outstanding drama series.

While *The X-Files* makes a point of avoiding formula, the third season again featured a potent mix of America's most potent nightmares and deepest myths, focusing on government intrigue surrounding agents Fox Mulder and Dana Scully, as well as its impact on their personal and family histories often told through epic two-part episodes. The monsters, too, were more developed and more varied. Consider the lightning-hurling teenager in "D.P.O." or the adipose-sucking predator who surfs the Internet in "2Shy"; psychic murderers, like the game-playing title character in "Pusher" or the amputee veteran in "The Walk"; and more earthly forms of evil, including the kidnapper of a young girl in "Oubliette," the serial killer in "Grotesque" or a body-parts selling ring in "Hell Money." As always, the monsters conveyed a deeper, even more frightening message—that the world we live in is stranger than we know, and more mysterious than we want to believe.

"In toto, I think it was a very high-quality season, perhaps our highest-quality season," Carter asserts.

Perhaps most notably, Season Three proved more eclectic in style than either of the first two years. Emboldened by the popularity of "Humbug," a darkly comic episode dealing with circus freaks written by Darin Morgan during the second season, the show returned to that genre on several occasions during 1995–96. Morgan's "Clyde Bruckman's Final Repose" (featuring a memorable performance by Peter Boyle, who also earned an Emmy nomination in the guest-acting category); "War of the Coprophages" (featuring memorable performances by a nauseating assortment of cockroaches); and "Jose Chung's *From Outer Space*" (a favorite among crew members that guest-starred Charles Nelson Reilly) continued the humor/horror as did Carter's darkly comic "Syzygy," where two teenage girls born the same day wreak havoc on their small town.

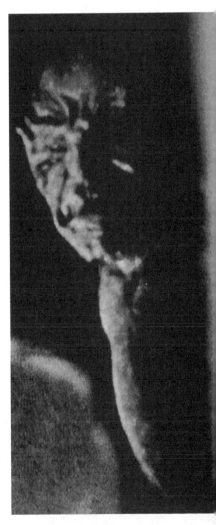

Cockroaches weren't the only earthly creatures highlighted in Season Three. Special guests also including the maggots in "The List"; the rats, cats, and jaguar spirit in "Teso dos Bichos"; an oddly situated frog in "Hell Money"; and, of course, an unfortunate Pomeranian named Queequeg who appeared in "Clyde Bruckman's Final Repose" and "Quagmire." Indeed, in the blur that follows producing two dozen episodes, one of Gillian Anderson's immediate reactions to the season was "lots of bugs." (Anderson actually garnered some attention for popping a cricket in her mouth during a scene in

"Humbug" the previous year, though contrary to the popular misconception, she quickly spit it out.)

Never one to settle for success, Duchovny—who continues to play an active role in the series's creative direction, working in concert with Carter and co-executive producer Howard Gordon on certain episodes—is pleased with the third season but looks forward to expanding the shows emotional range even further. Referring to one of the early second-season episodes, he notes, "I think when we did 'Duane Barry' the show became a really great show, and we maintained that level for a while, but we haven't gone beyond it. I'm waiting to go beyond it. We won't go beyond it technically, but we will go beyond it in terms of character, introducing a personal life of some kind. I think it's inevitable. You have to do it."

When it's pointed out that the show's most fervent loyalists, as well as Carter himself, have been especially vocal about not wanting to see Mulder and Scully romantically involved with anyone but each other, Duchovny simply shrugs and says the nuances he refers to don't necessarily have to involve *romance*. "Give Mulder a friend. Give him a squash partner," he suggests. "It's got to happen. I really don't care what anybody thinks we should or shouldn't do." Anderson remains more sanguine regarding such matters, though she indicates some interest as well in stretching the characters while understanding that such an evolution must occur within the show's parameters.

Carter continues to talk with the stars about such issues and pays attention to responses along the Internet, all with the understanding that his ultimately remains the final word. "I have very certain ideas about how I want the show to progress," he states. "I listen to these things—in fact, I listen to all ideas—and then I decide whether to incorporate them." In the near future, at least, it appears that the characters will remain, as Carter puts it, "consumed by the work," so Mulder probably won't have a lot of time to brush up on his squash game. (Carter and Duchovny are, in "real life," occasional squash partners, when time permits.)

"It's going to be hard to create any kind of real personal life for them," the producer concedes, "because it works against the kind of storytelling that we do. But I have some ideas ..." In keeping with his purposefully vague approach to any discussion of what's happening on the show next week, much less any long-term plans, Carter simply leaves that thought dangling.

Meanwhile, the elusive but omnipresent *X-Files* "mythology" continues to deepen. Season Three revealed more about a dark alien conspiracy as well as the personal history of its main characters. Mulder discovered in the season's opening two episodes, "Paper Clip" and "The Blessing Way," that his father had apparently made a "Sophie's Choice" in the abduction of his sister, Samantha; while Scully learned more about her own disappearance early in the second season and the murder of her sister Melissa, eventually apprehending the killer in "Apocrypha." As for the supporting players, FBI Assistant Director Walter Skinner, played by Mitch Pileggi, took a bullet for the cause (and a few beatings, prompting some good-natured grumbling from the actor) and was for the first time prominently featured in an episode which focused principally on him ("Avatar"). Renegade agent Alex Krycek (Nicholas Lea) turned up selling government secrets before receiving his comeuppance, while the Cigarette-Smoking Man (William B. Davis), X (Steven Williams), the Lone Gunmen (Dean Haglund, Bruce Harwood, and Tom Braidwood), and the members of the mysterious Shadowy Syndicate (among them John Neville as one of the show's more recent oddly named characters, the Well-Manicured Man) all continued to make their mark.

Beyond chronicling the ins and outs of the latest season and each individual episode, this book—based on my own virtually unrestricted behind-the-scenes access and more than three dozen personal interviews with cast and crew members—will provide

unprecedented detail in examining the making of a single *X-Files* episode, the year's cliff-hanging finale "Talitha Cumi." Over the course of more than two months, I followed that episode from "pitch to post"—in other words, from the conception of the plot through the arduous process of postproduction.

No stage of the creative process was overlooked. I was there, whether it meant sitting in with an exhausted Chris Carter as he worked on blocking out the story (known as "boarding"), or spending more than a week on the set, including an entire day of torrential rain and long hours trying to capture a single shot that would provide the basis for a brief computer-generated graphic.

Once the cameras stopped rolling, the postproduction wizards took over, and visual effects coordinator Mat Beck, composer Snow, and postproduction maven Paul Rabwin were equally generous in opening up their shadowy worlds, sharing with me the late nights, last-minute changes, crazed deadlines, and reluctant sacrifices that go into producing every episode.

Although considerable focus will thus be placed on this one episode, any of the 24 episodes produced last season—or for that matter, the 49 (including the pilot) created during the first two—could tell a similar story about the inspiration and perspiration that goes into turning out a single installment of *The X-Files*. In this book I will endeavor to provide a sense of how each show begins as no more than a concept and, weeks later, emerges as a unique hour of television capable of keeping viewers glued not only to their sets and their chairs, but sometimes to each other.

Having spent so much time observing the team that ultimately makes *The X-Files* happen, I have developed an appreciation for their work that extends from the stars and storytellers to the folks who operate the catering truck and transport visitors from place to place—people who don't get their pictures on magazines covers yet contribute, each in their own way, to every hour.

Hopefully, the result will be both entertaining and informative for anyone with an interest in the show—from those who trust no one to those who prefer to trust everyone, those who want to believe to those who simply want a good heart-pumping jolt each week. Wherever one falls within that spectrum, rest assured that the truth is still out there, and in here as well.

That much, those with a mind to, can trust.

The digital effects crew also begins on their tasks, which, in this case, include the three morphing sequences, with a man morphing into the bounty hunter and the Healing Man changing into both Deep Throat and Mr. Mulder. "We have the ability to take a green suit and make it blue if we want," notes Rabwin. The day begins early again on Monday, May 13, as Rabwin and Carter convene 8:30 a.m. at Snow's house to listen to the score. The weather is expected to rise into

THE MAKING OF "TALITHA CUMI"

PART I
BOARDING & WRITING

I t's March 16, a warm Saturday afternoon in Southern California, and Chris Carter is clearly tired, if not flat-out exhausted. He's just returned from Vancouver, where not only is the 21st episode of *The X-Files* filming but the pilot for Carter's new series, *Millennium*, is in its fourth day of production. In addition, preparations are underway to begin shooting Episode 22 of *The X-Files*, and the script for the season's penultimate episode has just come in but needs some revision and is currently being rewritten. There's more than a little pressure associated with the results on *Millennium*, since Fox Broadcasting will announce its prime-time schedule for the 1996–97 television season in May—about two months off—and although the network has committed to ordering 13 episodes of the show, the perceived quality of the prototype will go a long way toward determining where and when the show is scheduled and thus its chances for success.

Chris Carter
at his desk.

A fairly brisk breeze wafts through Carter's office on the Twentieth Century Fox lot. This isn't an accident, since the room has recently been painted and all the windows and doors have been left open to forestall the likelihood of someone passing out from the fumes. Workmen continue to file in and out, finishing up the task of remodeling another part of the office. With the success *The X-Files* has enjoyed, Fox can afford to spring for a new coat of paint and certain other amenities.

Wearing jeans and struggling at times to keep his eyes open, Carter sits in a chair while story editor Frank Spotnitz leans back on the couch with his feet on the coffee table, which features an array of *X-Files*–related books and magazines under the glass top. The two stare intently at a 4-by-5-foot board as they engage in the process of "boarding"—blocking out the various scenes that will become an episode of *The X-Files*.

The office is virtually empty now, but one seldom finds it that way; rather, there is usually a buzz of frenetic activity, with a cadre of dedicated people working long hours to produce the best program they possibly can. Carter's spacious office remains the show's nerve center, his own plush chair its cerebral cortex. The office includes considerable memorabilia from the show—including alien dolls, drawings, and other gifts grateful fans have sent him—as well as newspaper and magazine clips that will often provide the seed for future episodes. Because most of the production personnel are in Vancouver, a small staff of assistants work within his shaded bungalow, stopping to chat with each other and share a laugh as they go about their tasks, deadlines always at their shoulders. The staff is for the most part young, casually attired, and in remarkably good spirits given the pressures they regularly face. The rest of the writing staff, producers, and technical people (such as the sound, editing, and post-production departments) are scattered in their own one-story bungalows and work spaces on the vast Twentieth Century Fox lot in the heart of Los Angeles's swank west side. Because of its size, golf carts are used to shuttle about the place, with *The Simpsons* writers across the way, the production company responsible for *NYPD Blue* down the street, and the usual assortment of Mercedes and BMWs one would expect at a major movie studio filling the parking lot.

Carter can usually be found behind his desk (virtually never wearing anything more elaborate than jeans and a work shirt or T-shirt), either on the phone or tapping away at his laptop. The room includes a TV and conference table, with a shower and bathroom adjacent in the back. A toothbrush sits on the sink, indicative of the sort of hours the producer works, turning his office into a second home. Across the way are trailers that house co-executive producer Howard Gordon and producer/directors Kim Manners and Rob Bowman, while writers like Frank Spotnitz, John Shiban, and Vince Gilligan are a short walk away, though they frequently pop into the office.

While some staffers have been thrown together by their work on the show—forming a collegial and tightly knit unit—others have longstanding ties. Spotnitz, for example, was a friend of Carter's who has known the producer's executive assistant, Mary Astadourian, since the two attended college together at UCLA in the early 1980s. Despite joining the show during its second season, he also possesses an unerring ability, shared by many of the writers, (nowhere more formidable than in Carter himself) to cite episodes from two and three years earlier with meticulous detail.

Every *X-Files* episode begins this way, with the process of conquering an empty page—or more precisely, an empty board and box of blank index cards. Carter has already tacked a few 3-by-5-inch cards on the board, with 6 to 8 cards usually comprising the teaser sequence and anywhere from 9 to 11 for each of the show's four acts. Production on the season finale is to begin

in late April—at this point, roughly six weeks away. Carter hopes to finish the boarding in a few days and plans to write the episode the following weekend.

Carter has blocked out aspects of the story with *X-Files* star David Duchovny, and the two have a number of main themes they want to hit upon—perhaps the most significant being a sequence inspired by the Grand Inquisitor in *The Brothers Karamozov*, where God returns to Earth during the Spanish Inquisition. As conceived by Carter and Duchovny, the Cigarette-Smoking Man will interrogate an alien visitor with strange healing powers, creating a Christ-like biblical analogy. The original story has Christ returning and healing a young girl, only to be told by the aged Inquisitor that he's no longer welcome on Earth. In similar fashion, the Cigarette-Smoking Man will tell the Healing Man that people want authority, not faith, and, in his own skewed view of the world, need to be safeguarded from freedom.

"I suggested the Grand Inquisitor for the first episode Chris and I worked on together, which was 'Colony,'" Duchovny explains. "It got away from me and it turned into something else—'Colony'/'End Game'—which I thought was really good, but it wasn't the idea."

According to Duchovny, who came close to completing his Ph.D. in literature before chucking that career to pursue acting full time, the Cigarette-Smoking Man, as the character developed, naturally began to fit the profile for such an endeavor. "It made sense for him to become the Grand Inquisitor—this kind of cynically heroic character. He's like Nietszche's Socrates—he's the rational man, saving the masses from their own imagination."

The actor pauses, as if pondering the analogy. "I can't take credit for Dostoevsky, I can just take credit for having been educated well. If it drives people to read that, that'd be great," he says, adding wryly, "but just read that part. It's short. Don't read the whole *Brothers K.*"

Participating in the show's creative direction has helped keep Duchovny engaged in the process, but he rejects the notion that *The X-Files'* popularity and his own burgeoning celebrity have contributed to his ability to influence such matters. "I don't think the success of the show has anything to do with that," he says. "Right from the beginning, Chris and I have had a very reciprocal

dialogue about where the character should go and what the show's about. Either he listens to me," the actor says with a slightly imp-ish grin, "or he's very smart and makes me *think* that he listens to me."

"We had talked about a Grand Inquisitor episode a long time ago, and I realized that Cigarette-Smoking Man was the perfect Inquisitor as it fits my mythology," says Carter, who freely admits that the show has evolved and gone in directions he scarcely antici-pated when he wrote the pilot. Some of that pertains to the intricate web that has grown around the Cigarette-Smoking Man, whom Carter never anticipated would be speaking this much in the show, if at all.

Indeed, although each episode of *The X-Files* represents a group effort, everything begins and ends with Chris Carter, whose energy in pursuing his vision of the show can be seen in the smallest details—a commitment to quality that is passed from him to every member of the crew. Carter's goal is nothing less than perfection, a determination even under the rigors of television deadlines and limitations that informs every choice made in producing the series. Those writing the show frequently marvel over his grasp of even the most subtle nuances, which almost inevitably serve to improve a scene, and each story must ultimately pass through his typewriter. As a result, his imprint can be found upon each episode, whether the script bears his name or not.

The blueprint of the Grand Inquisitor, however, is only a small part of the handful of central elements that will make up the skeleton of this episode, over which various strata of events will then be laid. Other key aspects of the story, as blocked out in the earliest stages, include the Cigarette-Smoking Man learning that he has cancer, thus facing the dilemma of whether to use the Healing Man's powers to heal himself; the existence of an alien stiletto like the one featured in "Colony"/"End Game," the second season two-parter where an alien bounty hunter tracked a replica of Mulder's sister; Mrs. Mulder suffering a stroke after an encounter with the Cigarette-Smoking Man, scribbling the word "palm" and transposing the letters when she really means "lamp," where the stiletto is kept; and the desire to come up with an appropriate ending to keep fans breathless through the summer. Asked whether the episode will be a cliffhanger, Carter says, "It will. I'm not sure how, but it will."

The interrogation sequence, they've decided, belongs in the third act, but that leaves considerable indecision as to what will precede and follow that exchange. The challenge Carter and Spotnitz face, then, requires spreading an entire canvas over those thematic posts—or, perhaps more accurately, assembling a jigsaw puzzle that not only involves figuring out where the existing pieces fit but also coming up with new ones that will fill in the picture.

Much of the riddle initially involves the alien visitor, who, as Spotnitz puts it, has "gone native" and wants to live among humans without revealing himself. "He does something in the teaser that lets

Cigarette-Smoking Man know he's at large," Carter muses, followed by a long silence as the two simply stare at the board, as if waiting for the answer to appear before them.

Eventually, Carter scribbles on the index cards, tacking one of them on the board in the teaser section:

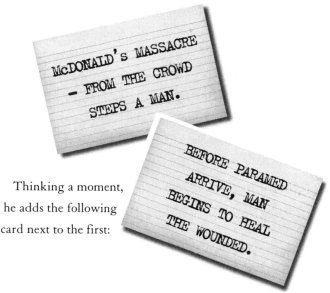

McDONALD's MASSACRE
- FROM THE CROWD
STEPS A MAN.

Thinking a moment, he adds the following card next to the first:

BEFORE PARAMED ARRIVE, MAN BEGINS TO HEAL THE WOUNDED.

"It's got to be a real interesting effect," Carter says, contemplating the board a few moments before writing a third card:

MAN DISAPPEARS
INTO THIN AIR -
POLICE BAFFLED.

Spotnitz expresses concern about the lapse until Mulder and Scully come into the story, and how they'll locate the alien. "Did our guy leave behind any kind of clue to help Mulder and Scully find him?" he asks. At that point visual effects supervisor Mat Beck comes in. "Is that Number 24?" he says, adding with a mock tone of accusation, "Is that *all* you've got done?"

Beck leaves, and Carter and Spotnitz return to wrestling with the episode's time frame. The Cigarette-Smoking Man, they note, has to apprehend the healing man in Act II if the Grand Inquisitor sequence is to occur in Act III. They also discuss how best to involve the character X, played by Steven Williams. Spotnitz, who's been active in writing a number of the show's big-picture mythology episodes (those that advance the histories of Mulder and Scully and their involvement, including that of Mulder's father decades earlier, in the government's UFO conspiracy), wants to use X but notes that he prefers it "when he's *doing* something," not simply providing vague clues before slipping into the shadows. The pair also try to get a handle on the act breaks—coming up with moments that will offer some "oomph" heading into the commercials.

Co-executive producer Howard Gordon pops into the office to check on their progress before heading back to his own space to make some final revisions on Episode 21, "Avatar." Meanwhile, Carter suggests an ending for one of the act breaks. "You buy that?" he asks Spotnitz, suggesting that the low-key approach is "better than doing a flashy one. It's stranger." Getting up, Carter now takes one of the existing cards—"MULDER FINDS ALIEN WEAPON IN HOUSE LAMP"—and places it down farther on the board. "Maybe that's an Act II kind of thing," he says.

Spotnitz suggests Mulder be offered his sister back in exchange for agreeing not to expose the overarching scheme. Such a moment, he notes, would test Mulder's commitment to his crusade. Similarly, the Cigarette-Smoking Man would face his own moral decision regarding the cancer, setting up a dual plot line exploring the theme of loyalty—questioning whether each character's first allegiance is to himself or his cause.

As if seeking a different perspective (or maybe just to keep his eyes open), Carter shifts from sitting on the chair to leaning over it, propping himself up on his elbows as he studies the board. He and Spotnitz have been working for nearly 3 hours now, and they have 13 cards to show for it, with nearly 50 needed in all to flesh out an entire episode. It's a process that can take anywhere from a few days to as long as two weeks, a somewhat dubious record lengthwise established on the previous episode, "Wetwired." Carter's ever-present assistant and head researcher, Mary Astadourian, returns to the office, and her boss ribs her about taking such a long lunch, prompting Astadourian to gently remind him that it is, after all, a Saturday afternoon. Around *The X-Files* offices, weekends and regular hours are a nicety the production crunch seldom recognizes.

Spotnitz keeps trying to hone the plot by questioning Carter about character motivations, such as Mr. Mulder's purpose in stashing away the alien stiletto or why he would leave a device of such potential importance at a house he once shared with his ex-wife. "Why did he keep this thing? Protection?" Spotnitz asks.

"Nostalgia," Carter says, after a beat.

They decide the Healing Man should tell the Cigarette-Smoking Man he has cancer during the inquisitor scene. Looking for a "cool effect," Carter indicates that the alien could "morph" into all the peo-

ple for whose death the Cigarette-Smoking Man is responsible, which would necessitate bringing all those actors—Jerry Hardin as Deep Throat, Peter Donat as Mr. Mulder, Melinda McGraw as Melissa Scully—back for cameo appearances. "The biggest cast ever," notes Spotnitz.

Moving on, Carter studies the board intently. "There's something here that's just not occurring to me," he says. How, for example, does the Cigarette-Smoking Man become involved? Perhaps publicity about the man who disappeared at the crime scene creates the threat of exposing the Cancer Man's activities, he proposes, so the Healing Man must be killed. With that, Carter adds another card:

PICTURE AT CRIME SCENE SPLASHED ON EVERY PAPER.

Carter moves down to the scene at the Mulders' house, and Mulder's eventual discovery of the alien stiletto hidden in a lamp—his mother having provided the clue. The producer scratches down a card and places it on the board:

MULDER PLAYS W/PALM ANAGRAM PALM = LAMP.

At first it's assumed that Mulder will go to his family house alone, but now Carter and Spotnitz raise the idea of having Scully go with him so Mulder can play out a dramatic scene with her, discussing his feelings about growing up in the house. "Mulder, I know you're upset," Carter mumbles, almost to himself, providing potential dialogue for Scully during the scene. There are also biblical aspects to the episode, and since the episode doesn't have a title as yet, Carter mentions that he'll need a biblical reference book to come up with one.

The workmen have finished, so the only sound now—as the two writers stare at the board for several minutes—is that of birds chirping in the background. "So what's this show about?" Spotnitz asks, breaking the silence, again seeking to refocus what's at stake in this particular episode.

"It's about the bigger picture," Carter says. "There's nothing anthemic yet." Mulder's sister, he adds, and that portion of the character's persona haven't been in the third season "mythology" at all. In addition, Carter wonders if they need a scene featuring The Syndicate—the shadowy cabal with whom the Cigarette-Smoking Man is connected that conspires to cover up the existence of extra-terrestrial life.

Spotnitz adds that the episode "needs something to happen at the start of Act II to propel the story forward," perhaps having the audience learn that the Healing Man has the power to morph and assume the likeness of others. By this point, the two have been working nearly five hours, and Carter is a bit punchy. He keeps joking about concocting a way to capitalize on the fact that William B. Davis—who plays the Cigarette-Smoking Man—is a championship-caliber water skier. "Why don't we have him ski up to the house?" Carter says with only a hint of a smile, pondering how Davis would look on water skis in his usual severe dark suit. (The jokes will later manifest themselves in the script, when the Cigarette-Smoking Man reminisces with Mrs. Mulder about water-skiing with her husband on vacation.)

"I think my brain is kind of fried right now," the executive producer concludes, deciding to take a break and have dinner with his wife, whom he hasn't seen in days. "Let's sleep on it," he tells Spotnitz. "We'll come up with something overnight." They agree to reconvene and resume the boarding process at 10:00 A.M. the next morning. If anyone had designs on spending the day watching the NCAA basketball tournament, forget it.

Sure enough, the next day—still sunny and smoggy, characteristic of Los Angeles—finds Carter and Spotnitz back in the office, the only perceptible change being that at this point they're both perched on the couch. The clock is ticking as they work, since Carter has to leave the office by 3:45 P.M. to attend the Writers Guild of America awards in Beverly Hills, where he's a nominee for the season's fifth episode, "The List," which he wrote and directed. Astadourian is again on hand, realizing Carter's singular focus on the episode and therefore reminding him on several occasions of that deadline.

As for the episode, the loyalty theme has now clearly emerged: The Healing Man, having breached a certain loyalty by breaking with his cause; Mulder, offered a chance to get his sister back at the expense of finding out what the big picture is; and the Cigarette-Smoking Man, who must choose between loyalty to his cause and curing himself.

As a story device the writers have also decided to bring back the alien bounty hunter from "Colony"/"End Game," played by actor Brian Thompson, though they're not sure where to include him in the episode or, for that matter, whether he'll even be available. "I like the idea that it's their bureaucracy as well," Carter notes, referring to the alien culture paralleling our own.

"It seems like Skinner belongs in here somewhere," Spotnitz adds. Carter agrees but has started to rethink whether they need a scene featuring the Shadowy Syndicate—unless, he quips, to have the Cigarette-Smoking Man ski up while the Syndicate members lie on the beach in their own dark suits. X indeed has a role to play in this episode, but neither of them are sure as yet exactly what it will be. Several scenes have also moved around in the intervening 24 hours (Mulder finds the alien weapon in the second act, for example, instead of the third), and several new cards have appeared, such as "MULDER FINDS ALIEN WEAPON" and "BOUNTY HUNTER APPEARS WITH MAGIC ALIEN ICEPICK." The second act has taken shape, in fact, with Mulder finding the stiletto and the Bounty Hunter arriving in the last scene, or "act out."

"There's still some problems with Act I," Carter says as he scans the board. "It has some logistical problems."

"But I think we've found our theme here," Spotnitz points out. "It's loyalty." It would be interesting, he adds, to discover that Mulder has to put his commitment to the X-Files unit ahead of everything, including his own quest to locate his sister. That commitment, in turn, could later be tested by seeing if he'll sacrifice Scully.

As always, Carter isn't only writing the episode but also visualizing it, all the while calculating limitations pertaining to time and money. The alien stiletto, for example, will eventually be used to slay the Bounty Hunter, providing the opportunity for a nifty special effect. "You get a nice kill there," Carter says, without a trace of irony. "A melting kill."

True to his word to Astadourian, Carter ends the session at 3:45, motoring home to change for the awards ceremony. By Wednesday, March 20, the board is nearly completed, and aspects of the episode have again changed in the process. The third act now includes a scene where an angry Mulder accosts Skinner, plotted out in two new index cards:

MULDER GOES TO SKINNER - WHERE'S CSM?!! WHO IS HE?!!

SCULLY PULLS MULDER OFF SKINNER - SUSPECT TURNED HIMSELF IN.

In addition, new cards in the fourth act have the Cigarette-Smoking Man come to Mulder, saying, "You've been looking for me?" Mulder responds: "I have what you want. Tell me about your project." Perhaps most significantly, Mulder, and not X, will now defend the Healing Man by using the alien weapon against the Bounty Hunter.

Fortunately, Thompson, Hardin, and Donat are available, but McGraw ultimately won't be. Hurdles still exist, however, concerning the fourth act, among them what Scully is off doing while all this occurs, as well as when and where X will appear. The Cigarette-Smoking Man has also gone a less heroic route by letting himself be healed, choosing selfish interest over that of his cause. The Bounty Hunter will confront Mulder, Scully, and the Healing Man at the end, they've decided, as the cliffhanger. Those details are filled in before the week is up, and Carter, as planned, begins writing the episode that weekend.

Three weeks later, on April 12, Carter enters the office looking somewhat weary, having completed the script for Episode 24 only hours earlier. Copies are actually still warm, having just come off the copying machine. The producer's plate remains astoundingly full—*Millennium* is in postproduction, while production for *The X-Files* season finale is scheduled to begin April 22 in time to make a May 17 airdate. Even then, that timetable cuts things closer than the producers would like.

It's a little after 2:00 P.M., and department heads in Los Angeles and Vancouver gather for the "concept meeting" that precedes each episode to go over any unique requirements of the latest installment. Connected by speakerphones in each office, production personnel in Vancouver ask a few specific questions about the nature of surveillance photos that are to be displayed in the episode, the color of prison uniforms needed for wardrobe (orange, they're told, is fine), whether the prison is fictitious (yes), and if the narrative is set in any particular state (as yet, no). The prop folks, thinking ahead, also want to know if the stiletto weapons will have to do anything in the second episode they need to know about now.

"They turn into a helicopter," Carter deadpans.

Vancouver-based assistant director Tom Braidwood, the sometime-actor who plays the Lone Gunmen's lecherous Frohike, also wonders whether a scene written to take place outside the prison could possibly be played inside, since the location managers remain uncertain if they have an appropriate venue for the shot. Carter tells them to do their best, and the meeting wraps up in near-record time, taking all of five minutes.

HOW MANY X-FILES CHARACTERS HAVE COME BACK FROM THE DEAD?

Eleven.

• Murder victim Howard Graves watches over his secretary in "Shadows."

• In "Lazarus," bank robber Warren Dupre returns in the body of FBI agent Jack Willis to reunite with his wife.

• In "Miracle Man," the martyred Samuel Hartley walks out of the morgue.

• A police detective is reborn as a young girl in "Born Again," to seek revenge on his killers.

• In "Roland," the disembodied, frozen head of a dead scientist exerts a powerful psychic control on his retarded twin.

• In "3," a vampire killed by the sun regenerates.

• In "Fresh Bones," a dead corporal rises from the grave.

• In "The Calusari," stillborn Michael Holvey's ghost leads his brother to his death and kills his father.

• In "The Blessing Way," of course, Mulder himself comes back from the spirit world ("They killed my father and then they killed me," he says).

• "Neech" Manley reincarnates as a fly to wreak vengeance on his tormentors in "The List."

• Amy Jacobs is brought back from drowning when Lucy Householder dies in her place in "Oubliette."

Of course, in "Talitha Cumi" itself the Bounty Hunter morphs into both Mulder's father and Deep Throat, but, while it's close, this doesn't qualify as truly coming back from the dead.

Staffers linger and chat awhile, realizing that this will be the last such meeting they'll hold this season. Everyone looks forward to the end of production and having time to themselves to see family and friends, as well as take much-needed vacations. (Hawaii, five hours flying time from Los Angeles, is a particularly popular spot to which some will escape.) Yet there is also a certain amount of nostalgia involved with the conclusion of any season. The show, after all, takes so much of their time that the staff becomes an extended family, with all the ties (and occasional exasperation) that entails. Given the staggering dedication visible from Carter all the way down through the ranks, such respites are consequently viewed less as the end of something than a mere page break in that chapter of their lives which is *The X-Files*.

The call over, those in the Los Angeles office scatter in various directions—the writers retiring to their offices about 50 yards away to watch dailies (the raw unedited footage that comes in, well, daily) from the episode that's currently being shot, "Wetwired." Stepping outside, Carter sees Gordon, taking a respite from his own episode. "You should take a victory lap," Gordon recommends, to mark completion of the season's final script, the 72nd regular episode (excluding the pilot) of *The X-Files*. With several episodes still to finish and work left to do on *Millennium*, however, Carter's mind remains seemingly elsewhere—on any one of the myriad tasks still ahead of him—as he wanders off, if not for a victory lap, at least briefly savoring the Friday afternoon sunshine with a stroll around the lot.

PART II
PREPRODUCTION

I t's April 18, and a rainy morning in Vancouver. By 9:30 A.M. the *X Files* production staff is just starting to bustle with activity in the North Shore Studios. Inside the main office, a board announces comings and goings of cast and crew based in Los Angeles. Chris Carter arrived the previous night, for example, and will depart that Saturday. Steven Williams, who plays the mysterious X, gets to town the next day and is scheduled to leave April 24. The only slightly disquieting entry pertains to director Rob Bowman, listed as "IN – NOW" and "OUT – NEVER."

Like Carter, Bowman is based in Los Angeles but spends considerable time in Vancouver, directing eight—or one-third—of the most recent season's two dozen episodes (another seven were helmed by Kim Manners). Bowman, whom co–executive producer Robert (Bob) Goodwin credits with having "boundless energy," is currently on location directing the 23rd episode, "Wetwired." As a result, the office situated next to Chris Carter's digs—which goes to whoever's directing that particular episode—has a water dish and bowl of food left in the corner for Bowman's golden retriever, Bear, who sometimes accompanies him to work. Duchovny's dog, Blue, a near-constant companion when the actor is working, today is trotting around the office while her master films on location at an apartment complex in East Vancouver. Anderson has also added to the *X-Files'* canine population in a big way with a huge mastiff puppy named Cleo, who's actually with her on the set.

A brief tour of the office features the usual assortment of gags, such as a photo tacked on the door of the assistant directors' office featuring A.D. Tom Braidwood, with the caption "Frohike on Location." Beyond that, someone has affixed a sign over his crotch that reads, "Sterile – Do Not Tamper." *The X-Files* commands the entire ground

David Duchovny and Blue on the set.

floor of the building it inhabits, on a lot where several other television shows and movies get produced in the heart of lush, tree-lined Vancouver. The central lobby area is constantly abuzz, leading down a long hallway past the offices of producer Joseph Patrick Finn, executive producer Bob Goodwin, and the director-of-the-week to that of Chris Carter, a modestly appointed room somewhat smaller than his space in Los Angeles, decorated with several framed articles about the show.

A small lunchroom connects that side of the building with the other, where the assistant directors share their office, adjacent to the production coordinator and other staffers who work in such areas as accounting. Moving to the other side of the entrance to the maze-like building, meanwhile, many of the technical crew can be found, including the half-dozen members of the art department who, not surprisingly, occupy the best-decorated room, with large drafting tables and sketches from shows past and present dotting the walls. The prop department and wardrobe are situated nearby, the former housed next to the location managers' office, where desks are stacked with pictures of potential settings. The props area includes everything from a hockey game (this is, after all, Canada) to various mock newspapers featured on the show, many of which incorporate pictures of different staff members under embarrassing screaming headlines, like "Man Marries Gorilla." In wardrobe, photos are prominently displayed of department members with various stars and other performers, including several actors and extras made up as the unfortunate, ill-fated lepers featured in the episode "731"—incongruously shown hugging various crew members, with big smiles through their grotesque makeup. Meanwhile, makeup effects ace Toby Lindala and his staff ply their trade out of a separate location.

The Vancouver set of Mulder's office.

Despite the frenetic pace there is order in the seeming chaos as crew members go about their work, picking costumes, designing sets, crafting props for an upcoming episode, or working the phones setting up where the next location shoot will be. Virtually all U.S. visitors to Vancouver are struck by the warmth of the people who reside there, and *The X-Files* staff fulfills that pleasant stereotype—going out of their way to make newcomers feel welcome, even including them in the seemingly hourly runs that production assistants make to the nearby Starbucks coffee bar. Other than the technical survey prior to shooting an episode, most of these personnel work almost exclusively in the office, while those on the shooting crew travel around Vancouver (that is, when they're not working out of the soundstages about 50 yards away across the parking lot). Yet all these interrelated functions are equally vital to making an episode of *The X-Files* a reality.

With the second-to-last episode being shot, final preparations are underway before production can begin the following Monday—just four days away—on "Talitha Cumi," the obscure name chosen for the season finale. Carter's title means "Arise maiden" in Aramaic— the ancient language in which the Bible was written, which was used from roughly 300 B.C. to 650 A.D. At just after 10 A.M. Carter, Goodwin, and Vancouver casting director Lynne Carrow file into a small, spare white room to audition actors for the episode.

Goodwin—a veteran producer who spent several seasons on the ABC series *Life Goes On* before beginning his affiliation with *The X-Files*—will direct this episode, having directed the season-ender each year. As with the second season into the third, he'll also direct the fourth-season opener. Since part of his job is "directing directors," as he puts it, because he's a constant presence in Vancouver while they tend to flit in and out from Los Angeles, Goodwin has found it easiest to get in the chair himself only at the beginning and end of the season, when he can devote more time to an individual episode.

Goodwin learned that lesson the hard way, directing "One Breath"—the acclaimed installment in which Scully lies in a coma— which fell about a third of the way into the second season. "That was very disruptive," Goodwin recalls. "By contrast, I can devote all my attention to the last show, and I like doing the first show to break the crew in and get everybody rolling."

There's a downside, however, to directing the season finale, since cast and crew begin to scatter almost as soon as filming ends, mean- ing they won't have the luxury to go back and reshoot sequences or do second-unit shots if, for example, the episode comes in short time- wise. In addition, there will be only two weeks for postproduction. "It's like being on the high-wire without a net," Goodwin observes, adding that with most shows "you shoot almost up to air."

In addition, crew members are eager to begin their summer breaks after 10 months of production—whatever pangs of nostalgia they feel about the show's third year coming to an end minimized by sheer exhaustion and the tight production schedule of the season finale. Carter and Goodwin are aware of this, delicately balancing those emotions as they seek to keep everyone focused until the task at hand is completed while still maintaining a celebratory mood and letting everyone have some fun in the process.

Tom Braidwood and Bob Goodwin in discussion. Gillian Anderson looking on.

Most of the parts being cast in this session are relatively small, and major roles are frequently set in Los Angeles via Carrow's counterpart there, Rick Millikan. Each of the hopefuls this morning has little more than 30 seconds to do their scene and try to make an impression on the producers. "How are you at crying?" Goodwin, seated on the couch next to Carter, asks two young women, having added a wrinkle to the opening scene. Goodwin's idea (not in the script) is to have a woman begin crying when a man pulls a gun in a fast food restaurant during the teaser sequence, and Carter likes the nuance. Each woman is given time to go outside and compose herself, then "come in and give it a whack."

Several men audition for the pivotal role of the gunman, reading the scene in which he opens fire in the restaurant, getting shot himself and subsequently healed. One actor—Hrothgar Mathews, clearly the producers' choice—is asked to try the scene several times giving a different reading, trying to capture the elusive quality Carter seeks. Mathews, who has appeared on the series previously, initially plays the moment when Mulder questions him about what happened with an almost messianic quality, assuming the gunman has just had a life-altering experience by encountering what he believes to be God. "You're still a lunatic," Carter reminds him as the actor tries the scene again, then acts out the shooting sequence, which calls for him to take a rather hard fall when his character gets shot. The third time's the charm, and when Mathews leaves Carter appears sold, feeling the actor has the hollow-eyed look the producer is after.

There are nevertheless more men to see for the part, and one has brought a plastic gun as a prop, warning the producers sitting across from him that he'll be pulling more than a cocked finger. "Thanks for telling us," Carrow says. "This isn't L.A., but it's still a good idea."

As always, the producers are not only looking to cast that particular episode (especially with a choice for the gunman's role essentially already in tow) but simultaneously keeping an eye out for talent they may want to use later. "He'll be good for something," Goodwin says when one aspirant leaves. Another actor, with a slightly more offbeat look, is deemed as being appropriate for one of writer Darin Morgan's scripts. "We'll save him for Darin," Carrow jokes.

After seeing more than two dozen candidates in roughly an hour, Carter and Goodwin huddle briefly on casting selections, picking actors for each of those smaller roles. Such decisions on even the smallest parts are made with considerable care and deliberation, and despite the short time each actor has, they are treated respectfully and professionally. Indeed, many of them have become familiar faces as part of the pool of talent in Vancouver and will doubtless be back auditioning for parts again in a few weeks time, when the show resumes production.

Following a few quick calls they pack up for the technical survey—a day-long scouting expedition to examine the show's location shots and allow members from the construction, art, effects, and other departments to get a fix on what will be required to pull off various shots. Six locations is about standard for an average episode, with the other half-dozen settings to film in one of three soundstages devoted to *The X-Files* (the third has been added since season two) at the North Shore Studios. With the 18 crew members all having piled aboard the air-conditioned bus, Goodwin announces they've gotten off to a late start already (it's roughly 11:40 A.M., when they were scheduled to leave at 11), and he wants them to move quickly and finish on time so he can see his wife and kids before they take off on vacation. "That means you, Shirley," a voice from the back yells, ribbing set decorator Shirley Inget.

The first stop is an A&W restaurant that will serve as the fast food joint where the shooting occurs. Some patrons barely look up as the crew files in, sketching dimensions and scribbling notes as they study both the restaurant's interior and the parking lot, since unmarked police cars have to be visible through the windows in one scene. The art department must also design a logo for a fictitious restaurant, Brothers K, which will cover the A&W sign. Demonstrating the ability to reuse locations, the same restaurant stood in for the diner featured as part of the teaser sequence in "Oubliette," but once the art department has worked its magic no one would recognize any similarity. Satisfied, Goodwin tries to keep things moving. "Mount up," he yells to his troops.

The next stop, more than 30 minutes away, is a beach house that will serve as the New England cottage owned by the Mulder family, where Mulder's mother encounters the Cigarette-Smoking Man. Again underscoring the painstaking attention to detail, workmen from the show are already there wheeling barrels of weeds into the yard—which is supposed to be in disrepair—to obscure a neatly manicured lawn. "You're early," the owner, a pleasant-looking woman, says as crew members pass into the house, having put on shoe covers so as not to track mud inside. "It feels East Coast-y," Carter muses, surveying the yard as rain begins to fall again. The most conspicuously un–East Coast-y element—a bald eagle's nest in one of the trees, since the majestic birds are prevalent in the region—is pointed out by a crew member but will otherwise go unseen.

All's well at the house, but a call to Goodwin's cell phone presents the producers with the day's first mini-crisis: They may need another gunman because the actor cast, Hrothgar Mathews, has a scheduling conflict, having taken a part in an independent film that's supposed to shoot the same day. The X-Files staff, meanwhile, has little flexibility, since Duchovny will leave to begin filming his latest feature, Playing God, almost as soon as production concludes. Goodwin says to try and work out schedules with the actor's agent, but as a fallback the casting folk are alerted to begin contemplating replacements.

With that it's back on the bus, but even on the open road—with one episode in production and one being prepared—Carter's mind is still spinning, always seeking new places to film in the future. "Hey

Louisa!" he yells to locations manager Louisa Gradnitzer, who has been with the series since the pilot. Carter has spotted a strange-looking home in the distance, sitting alone in the center of a vast, empty field. "Look at that house out there, all by itself. Can you find out about it?"

Having phoned their orders ahead to save time, the group stops for lunch at Queen Elizabeth Park's Seasons Restaurant, which offers a dazzling panoramic view of Vancouver. There's also a nostalgic aspect to the location, given that the graveyard scene in the pilot was shot in the park, as Carter and Gradnitzer reminisce about how difficult the nighttime shoot was, with several people walking head-first into open graves in the pitched darkness.

An almost comical dynamic takes place inside, since so many crew members tote cellular phones around with them, when one rings nearly everybody reaches for a phone—a sort of modern-day version of a Western shootout. Celebrating the last location scout trip of the season, Carter rises to toast Goodwin: "For his leadership . . . and his jokes," he adds dryly.

Lunch ends around 3:30 P.M. and the bus heads for downtown, where the *X-Files* crew proves that you may not be able to fight City Hall, but you can at least redecorate it. Making its first appearance in the show, Vancouver's City Hall will stand in for the Social Security building lobby in Washington, D.C. Goodwin uses a portable video camera to visualize the scene, with producer Joseph Patrick Finn drafted to play the Cigarette-Smoking Man, popping a cigarette into his mouth for effect. Thirty extras have been lined up for the scene, but Carter thinks they need more—at least 50, in order to fill both elevators and the lobby area. "You need the confusion," he says, examining the space, where the alien visitor eludes capture by

Director Bob Goodwin.

"morphing" into the likeness of someone else. "It's got to be like he grabbed the wrong guy." Set decorator Inget, meanwhile, surveys the walls, planning to remove what's there and put up new signage.

Carter's observation about the need for more extras underscores both the producer's perfectionism and the advantage of having the writer of that particular episode accompany the crew on each technical survey—a practice Carter implemented in keeping with his own concerns about protecting a writer's vision. Who better, after all, to know how a scene should look than the person who first conceived it? The producer also seldom hesitates to take whatever steps he deems necessary to make the show the best it can be—negotiating later, always reluctantly, what sort of compromises and sacrifices he might have to make on the altar of time and monetary constraints. Cell phones continue to ring, meanwhile (including a call to revise the number of extras), as the group hits the road again.

"Okay, wake up!" Tom Braidwood shouts to the dragging crew as the bus reaches its next destination, an empty department store where Carter has just spent four days filming part of his pilot for *Millennium*. In unison the group follows Goodwin as he walks through a dolly shot that will lead past rows of white-collar workers to Jeremiah Smith's desk. Workmen drill and pound away in the background, as Inget is told she'll need 60 desks to create the office setting. "Piece of cake," she says.

Across the street sits a vacant parking garage where another shot must be set up. Carter estimates they'll need 20 cars brought in to capture the sense of a sparsely populated office parking lot at night. Entering a dank stairwell to leave, crew members are somewhat mortified to stumble across a teenager smoking what appears to be an illicit substance. "He thinks he's got the perfect spot, and all of a sudden twenty people come in," marvels construction coordinator Rob Maier, who says he's "seen everything" on technical surveys— including more than a half-dozen people openly shooting heroin in broad daylight as the crew scoured back alleys scanning locations for the episode "Hell Money."

The day's final stop is at a massive lumberyard, requiring the crew to don hard hats. "The forklifts have the right of way, just so everybody knows," Gradnitzer announces. As the group looks over the spot, the sun makes it's first appearance of the day and just as quickly disappears, as raindrops begin to fall again. Welcome to Vancouver.

Goodwin and Carter, at least, have some good news with which to end the day: The actor they want for the gunman will likely be available after all. Goodwin, it turns out, even knows the producer of the film he's doing, which may help in the process of reaching some sort of mutual accommodation in which *The X-Files* will be through with him by early evening and the movie can shoot his scenes that night.

The survey bus pulls back into North Shore Studios at 6 P.M.—as Goodwin hoped, a bit ahead of schedule. Yet most crew members are still there for several hours, racing through the work necessary to adapt those locations in time to begin production.

It's merely overcast, not raining, the next morning as department heads cram into the conference room for the production meeting, which always precedes filming. An elaborate mural of the galaxy decorates the wood-paneled room's far wall, while the other end is graced by a stylized poster with a caveman on it that reads, in part, "WASTE IS YOUR ENEMY! . . . YOUR WORK MAKES A DIFFERENCE"—a gentle reminder, perhaps, of the ever-present need to keep costs in mind. Yet despite the obvious limitations presented by television (the show's budget has climbed to roughly $1.6 million per hour, still a pittance compared to feature films), that's not the biggest enemy. "Money has never been the problem," says special effects supervisor David Gauthier. "It's just time."

The department heads banter playfully while waiting for Carter and Goodwin, both tied up on phone calls, to join them. "All the kids are here," quips construction chief Maier. Goodwin, as the episode's director, sits at the head of the table, as Braidwood—who alternates on episodes with fellow First A.D. Vladimir "Val" Stefoff—rifles one by one through the 48 scenes (some of them merely stock exterior or second-unit shots) in Carter's 51-page script.

"Plunging ahead then," Braidwood says loudly. "Scene one. Any questions?" There are relatively few, with props master Ken Hawryliw reminding them that as a safety precaution the shooter "shouldn't be closer than eight feet" to anyone during the shooting sequence in the restaurant. Goodwin is also concerned that having trays splattering as the mayhem begins will require considerable clean-up time between each take, so they agree to forestall any delays along those lines by using fake hamburgers and no drinks.

Three plate-glass windows are available, meaning there will be that many chances, if necessary, to get the shot right when the window shatters. In similar fashion, the props department has rigged five breakaway lamps for the shot when Mulder discovers the alien weapon. Several identical shirts will be needed to outfit the gunman, who is covered with blood before the Healing Man lays hands upon him. Art director Graeme Murray also assures Goodwin that old, beat-up lawn furniture is being assembled to stack outside the beach house, reinforcing the notion that the residence has gone unused for several years.

Other small points are dispatched easily. A photo double must be brought in for Jerry Hardin, who makes another from-beyond-the-grave cameo as Deep Throat, because the actor is available Monday only and additional shooting may be done Wednesday. Carter, whose directing credits include "The List" and "Duane Barry," intends to oversee the sequence involving Hardin himself, which is not unusual, since other directors frequently help out with selected shots within another's episode. Hawryliw also rattles off a list of props for the interrogation scene in the prison cell where the Healing Man is held. Carter jokes that the roster has overlooked a bedpan, then adds wryly, "Actually, I think it would be an oil pan."

The increase from 30 to 50 extras in the lobby sequence means wardrobe will have to account for that disparity, and costume designer

Jenni Gullett needs to know how many gray suits she'll have to provide. They agree to do without extras, however, during the Inquisitor sequence. "It was a quiet day at the prison," cracks Braidwood.

On the flip side, a technician will be on hand to make sure all the machines in the hospital sequence are used properly—part of a conscious effort to keep the show grounded in reality in order to make its forays into the fantastic seem more believable. "We have a lot of technical advisers, because I try not to fake everything," says Hawryliw. "I try to make everything as realistic as possible." Makeup artist Fern Levin echoes those sentiments, frequently consulting pathologists when researching bruises and burns, she says, to maximize their authenticity.

Braidwood nears the end of the meeting, reaching scene 45, when Mulder fights with X over the alien weapon. "We meet X, we talk, we slap each other around, we fall down. It's going to be fabulous," he says. The last few scenes fly by, and Goodwin announces—to smatters of applause—that they've just concluded the last production meeting until they embark on the fourth season, with most crew members getting a two-month hiatus period before they begin another exhausting 10 months of production. "Can't wait to get back and get started in July," Goodwin says.

Not everyone, of course, will be back in July. Some crew members will be moving on, among them award-nominated cinematographer John Bartley, who admits to being exhausted by the 13-hour days, having been with the series since its first regular episode. "He's burned himself out," Goodwin confides, noting that he makes an effort to give people rest to prevent that from happening but Bartley's own work ethic made such respites rare. Others, such as visual effects supervisor Mat Beck, will pursue outside opportunities—the success of *The X-Files* having added to the cachet of its staff within the entertainment industry. Bartley, conceding that Goodwin's appraisal is "probably true," says he'll take a break, travel a bit, and reacquaint himself with his family before getting back to work.

For now, though, department heads apply themselves to more immediate tasks, retiring to their respective offices. And while most of the attention is on the season finale, some are already working on the fourth season, with locations manager Todd Pittson planning an airplane ride with Carter to survey the interior of British Columbia—an arid region that could be used in place of California's desert, though Carter has also flirted with the idea of taking the show out of Vancouver for the first time to shoot part of an episode in Southern California.

The production meeting is followed by the tone meeting, where the writer, director, and executive producers (in the case of this episode, a foursome made up solely by Carter and Goodwin, who are each wearing two hats) go over how scenes in the script should be played, again down to the most minute details. Carter has agreed to write a few more lines to flesh out the gunman, "a gentle man pushed to the brink," he tells Goodwin. The scene where he recounts to Mulder his salvation by the Healing Man, he adds, "is less his moment than it is ours. . . . The 'moment' is the paranormal one—the *X-Files* moment."

Moving shot by shot, Goodwin seeks clarification about such matters as people's demeanors in the aftermath of the shooting ("Completely confused," Carter explains), as well as how the principals react when visiting Mulder's mother in the hospital (Mulder: totally focused; Scully: gentle and caring). Since neither of them are precisely sure how to pronounce Quonochontaug, where the beach house is situated, a note is made to call Rhode Island in order to double-check.

Carter munches on his lunch through the meeting, deftly snagging pieces of sushi with chopsticks while explaining that as the Healing Man "morphs" into different characters during the "Grand Inquisitor" encounter with the Cigarette-Smoking Man, his persona should remain consistently benign throughout: "There's no anger.

No bile. The power of the image should be enough," he suggests. "He doesn't change personalities. He just changes shapes." This is significant, since various actors—including Hardin and Peter Donat (who plays Mulder's father)—will have to capture that persona playing the different images the character assumes. The Cigarette-Smoking Man, meanwhile, should be standing, "trying not to show his fear, but he's afraid of this guy," Carter says.

Goodwin periodically types notes into his computer as they go along. "Do you want David to cry?" he asks, referring to the scene where Mulder visits his mother in the hospital.

"Definitely, but I want to see him stifle it," Carter responds. They also agree that Duchovny will "have to be messed up a bit" after the fight with X—given a bloody lip and bruises that will linger in subsequent scenes. Most of the changes discussed are minor, though Carter indicates that he has decided to remove the word "colonization" from the script, deeming it to be too  revealing. The producer later reverses himself on that point.

Indeed, most of the time Carter is still toying with aspects of an episode up to and even during production, constantly looking for ways to make improvements and ensure that the episode itself fits within and doesn't violate the canon of *The X-Files*. In that respect, producing the show encompasses far more of a challenge than one might imagine, since each episode must also conform with what has gone before in each preceding installment. Carter frequently speaks of his own world, his own mythology, and every hour of *The X-Files* must provide not just the requisite thrills but adhere to those established principles. Carter, then, can maintain a wry sense of humor about the almost clinical dissection that follows each episode, since the standards to which those fans hold the show could seldom be as rigorous as those he applies himself.

Carter assures Goodwin he'll have the revisions done by day's end. The meeting over, Carter retires to his office, while Goodwin begins working on his "shot list"—a scene-by-scene breakdown of where he wants to put the camera as well as the attitude of the characters. The director also frets about a new problem: The tide at Crescent Beach, the beach house location, goes out—way out—in the afternoon, so any shots with the water behind the actors will have to be accomplished during the morning.

Down the hall, an actress arrives to pick up the portion of the script she needs. "Tell them 'the Smirking Woman' is here," she says, underscoring the show's penchant for colorful names. William B. Davis, the disarmingly genial actor who plays the Cigarette-Smoking Man, also shows up to rehearse his scenes with Rebecca Toolan, who plays Mrs. Mulder. Davis notes happily that his schedule—perhaps appropriately so for a Vancouver resident—is suddenly not only raining but pouring: In addition to perhaps the year's meatiest part for him on *The X-Files*, he'll play a role later that week on *The Outer Limits*, and he's still running an acting school. *The X-Files* gave him relatively short notice, as usual, that he'd be needed in "Talitha Cumi," and little indi-

cation about how significant the part would be. The show's nucleus of supporting players frequently joke about how in the dark they're kept as to what the producers have in mind for their characters, in part—as the scripting phase on the season finale demonstrates—because those ideas are constantly evolving.

As a result of this spurt of activity, Davis has had to have somebody take over his teaching duties. "It actually feels like a holiday, getting to be an actor full time for a couple of weeks. It's great," he says. Davis wasn't even disconcerted to learn that the Cigarette-Smoking Man had cancer, despite the fact that the character's demise would certainly hamper (if not necessarily end, as has been proven with other characters) his fortuitous and unexpected role as a semi-regular on *The X-Files*. "It's okay," he says of his future, mustering a sly smile as he heads down the hall to chat with Goodwin about his scenes. "David says I'm going to recover."

PART III
PRODUCTION

ilming of "Talitha Cumi" begins at the beach house in Crescent Beach, British Columbia, at nine o'clock in the morning. After a dazzling sunny weekend, rain clouds have moved in overnight, and the downpour becomes torrential at times as the day wears on.

Director Bob Goodwin has already survived one scare over the weekend by temporarily losing several hours of work assembling his shot list—all told a 53-page document, longer than the original script itself—when he inadvertently hit the wrong key on his computer. Goodwin tried unsuccessfully to locate the material with the help of a computer expert before finally calling Microsoft, where someone talked him through the process of salvaging his work, which he recovered in its entirety minus "a couple of sentences of hieroglyphics."

The opening shot proves relatively simple as Rebecca Toolan, playing Mrs. Mulder, arrives at the beach house, which has been remarkably transformed from just a few days earlier: The yard work has achieved the desired effect, and what once was a neatly manicured lawn is now an unkempt mess, covered with unraked leaves. Even the windows have been dirtied, as if no one has washed them in years. A sign tacked near the door reminds crew members not to track dirt into the house, saying, "Wear booties or remove shoes, please." Indeed, the producers are always mindful to do as little damage as possible, as well as to clean up whatever mess they make.

Television shows, and for that matter feature films, are invariably shot out of sequence. As a result, production opens this week with various scenes from the first act, while both David Duchovny and Gillian Anderson will shoot their final scenes the following Monday, even though production won't actually conclude until Wednesday, May 1. The opening teaser sequence will be shot on the second-to-last day and filming will conclude with the Grand Inquisitor–inspired scenes.

Production has been broken down over an eight-day period. The objective is to shoot roughly five pages of script on the first day, with anywhere from seven to nine pages completed on average. "The crew's tired," notes one staffer, explaining the relatively light load at the outset.

While David Duchovny shoots his scenes here, Gillian Anderson labors elsewhere with the second-unit team, doing some shots for the previous episode. The actress has gradually garnered more media attention during the third season, as Carter predicted she would after a period in which magazine covers and the like skewed somewhat toward Duchovny. Eschewing the opportunity to shoot a movie during her two-month hiatus from production, Anderson will travel across Europe and Asia, promoting the show abroad.

During a break on the set, Anderson—her dog Cleo not far off and her daughter Piper, now walking, playing nearby under her nanny's supervision—is in good spirits regarding the show's third season. Then again, the actress did add a significant degree of difficulty to season two by becoming pregnant, continuing to work up to a few days before and after she gave birth. "It's been easier, I think, because we're all kind of used to the routine now, so it seems to go by quite a bit quicker," she says, sitting on a curb near the set.

Gillian Anderson in Vancouver.

The stars have signed contracts through at least a fifth season of *The X-Files*—which will end in mid 1998—with options on two additional years. While the production grind makes seeing past that window difficult, Anderson's experience during the third season has made the prospect of continuing beyond that point seem more reasonable. "Because this year has gone by so quickly, in retrospect, it doesn't seem that daunting," Anderson indicates. Even in the midst of production, in fact, the actress—who still remains seemingly unaffected by her sudden notoriety—can feel a sense of nostalgia. "The closer we get to the supposed end," she says, "the more I realize that I'm going to miss it when it's over and enjoy that I'm in it."

By contrast, Duchovny has consistently been outspoken about his periodic discomfort at the strictures of TV production, having never anticipated that the series would achieve such popularity or that his involvement with it would extend for years on end. No less the perfectionist than Carter, Duchovny—wearing a long black coat and sheltered from the pelting rain under a tarp in the final days of shooting—therefore sounds a bit less enthusiastic when discussing the program.

Part of that may have to do as well with the actor's own grueling schedule, which includes beginning production on a movie, *Playing God*, a mere day or two after filming his final scenes on *The X-Files*. For that reason and others, Duchovny has publicly lobbied to reduce the show's annual production order from 24 to 22 episodes—the latter having traditionally been the conventional number for a prime-time drama series. "That's why I wanted twenty-two," he notes, referring to the virtual lack of downtime between concluding the season and beginning the movie. "I'll have no break." With *The X-Files* its highest-rated show and viewers already complaining about prime-time repeats, Fox, not surprisingly, wants as many original episodes as the series can generate, especially in an age when viewers with cable and VCRs have no shortage of options when presented with reruns.

Duchovny's bluntness in appraising the show or frankly discussing such business considerations seldom seems malicious; rather, his comments reflect playfulness (leveling many of his complaints with an arch grin) as well as a performer who seems to pride himself in speaking his mind, even if that occasionally means stepping on a toe here and there. In discussing matters like some of *The X-Files'* most vocal fans, then—those who hop on the Internet to nitpick episode foibles or lobby against Mulder having an outside love inter-est—Duchovny stresses that his priorities entail whatever he feels to be best for the show and his own peace of mind, letting the chips fall where they may. While that cynical edge may be perceived as aloof-ness, there is something refreshing about Duchovny's willingness to convey exactly what he thinks and vent periodic frustrations, espe-cially in an age when celebrities so carefully seek to monitor what they say and control their public images.

In discussing the show, Duchovny focuses on certain themes: First, what the series can and does offer him as an actor; and second, the fact that starring in a dramatic TV series—however alluring such a life may appear—is very, very hard work.

Stories have alternated during the third season between epic two-parters and stand-alone monster episodes, between flights into black comedy and the usual assortment of brooding dramas. "The smaller ones give us time to breathe a bit," Anderson says. "You need the break from the two-parters because they're so dramatic."

One would probably assume that the comedies, which have prompted a mixed reaction among some die-hard fans, would also help provide a respite from the more emotionally taxing episodes; however, Duchovny at least hasn't found that to be the case. "Not really, 'cause comedy's hard—comedy's harder to do than the space stuff," he contends. "You read there's a dead body in front of you, it's not very hard to figure out what's going on. The funny stuff—because so much of it is timing and reaction—can be more nerve-wracking than you'd think."

Duchovny also constantly examines other aspects of the show, among them the nature and tone of the bantering between Mulder and Scully. "To me, it's okay," he says with a shrug. "I don't like play-ing the relationship, and I don't like playing *against* it either."

Similarly, the actor wants to curb some of the self-referential moments that periodically find their way into the series, which he fears can feel stilted. The real aim, from his perspective, rather

involves developing Mulder as a character. "I like having a history, having created a history for the character. I like the fact that people know who these people are."

Duchovny prefers lightening up the show through smaller moments, such as Mulder's dry one-liners, sometimes ad-libbing or expanding on jokes. In the episode "Pusher," for example, in a tense moment when Mulder gets wired with a portable camera, he asks if the device picks up the Playboy Channel (Scully has frequently ribbed Mulder about his taste in magazines), as opposed to a script reference to the Discovery Channel. "I feel like those moments have always been there for the character," Duchovny says. "Eventually, people are going to pick up on the fact that they're there. To me it's always been part of the character. I just didn't telegraph it, so it took a while for people to listen."

Anderson remains more reserved in discussing such matters, and perhaps slightly more forgiving of some elements to which her cohort takes exception. When it comes to exploring the Mulder-Scully relationship, for example, through playful banter, she offers, "I think once in a while it's okay—it gives some insight into what we think of each other underneath the work."

Still, Anderson also aspires to explore aspects of her character that would broaden Scully, while realizing that the show's core will inevitably focus on the duo's investigations of the paranormal. "I think it would be an interesting challenge as an actor to see how they react in certain situations—how they act on a personal level ... maybe have her go on a date, or someone she's attracted to just to see how it affects her relationship with Mulder," Anderson concurs, while adding that she understands the show's parameters dictate that they "not take it to any great detail, or take it any further. Just that sideline would be interesting. It can't *just* be about extracurricular relationships," she continues. "The show's not about that. That would ruin it."

Duchovny has generally shunned much of the cultish adulation

surrounding *The X-Files*, while Anderson—though understandably cautious— has proven more willing to test those waters. The actress attended her first *X-Files* Convention in Burbank, California, in January 1996. "I was nervous going in," she concedes, "but everyone was so wonderful and warm, it was just a really pleasant experience." After a raucous welcome, Anderson sat patiently signing autographs for more than two hours, and while she doesn't intend to make a habit of it, Anderson wouldn't rule out additional appearances along those lines.

Anderson also discovered that growing celebrity has its occasional drawbacks, and she admits she's still scratching her head over a rather befuddling guest shot on *Late Show With David Letterman*. It was Anderson's first appearance on the show (which has featured Duchovny several times), but she found the host—whose familiarity with *The X-Files* seems decidedly limited—in rare and somewhat peculiar form, as Letterman kept grilling her as to what the program's about and yammering on about aliens with green hair. "It was strange, wasn't it?" she says quizzically. "I got to a point where I just couldn't get him off it. In retrospect, you think of a thousand things that you could have said, but at the time it was just really odd. I thought I was in *The Twilight Zone*."

The quiet neighborhood in Crescent Beach probably feels as if it's having its own run-in with Rod Serling on this quiet morning, dealing with an army of strangers—though this invading force arrives in trailers and vans rather than spaceships. Four large trailers line the street, with tags like "Mr. X" and "Mulder" stuck on the doors where the stars will get their makeup done.

Steven Williams, X himself, arrived late the night before, and due to separate production commitments—a cop show in which he's starring entitled *L.A. Heat*—the actor will have to fly back to Los Angeles Tuesday to work on that series before returning again Friday to shoot his character's brutal encounter with Mulder. Although the script seems to indicate that X will get the better of that match, Williams says not really. "We fight to a standstill," he says, adding with a chuckle, "or rather, our stuntmen do." In fact, Williams will bring his own stunt-man from Los Angeles

IN WHAT EPISODE DID THE CIGARETTE-SMOKING MAN FIRST SPEAK?

"Tooms."

with him to shoot the scene, since the producers are having difficulty finding an appropriate double for him in Vancouver.

Williams is amused by the fact that head-butting will again be employed in this fight, since he essentially initiated the practice by suggesting that X head-butt Skinner during their tussle in "End Game." Skinner retaliated, and Mulder subsequently used his noggin to bloody Krycek in "Piper Maru." "I can't imagine doing it myself," Williams says en route to the set. "I'd have a headache for a week."

Goodwin and the crew, meanwhile, grapple with their own headaches. One shot, as a camera pans through the abandoned house, is accomplished with relative ease, as Goodwin and cinematographer John Bartley monitor the look through two monitors several feet away. The images will be edited together into a montage providing Mrs. Mulder's point of view. "This montage we're doing is a killer," says Goodwin. "It's going to take a thousand cuts to make it work."

Williams and Duchovny are called to the set, carrying large umbrellas so as not to spoil their makeup. The crew members, however, simply stagger around in rain ponchos, with the downpour now so heavy that the staff places plywood boards down so people can walk on them rather than risk sinking ankle-deep into the grass. The widely held perception that producing a television show is glamorous seems rather funny at such a time to some crew members, as they slosh through the process of setting up shots. "People have no idea," says assistant director and part-time actor Tom Braidwood as the rain pelts down on him. "I tell them I work for *The X-Files* and they say, 'Wow!'"

One of the few dry spots lies under a canopy with a table of munchies, including lox and bagels, coffee, fruit, and an assortment of pastries. A scheduled lunch break won't come until 3:00 P.M., with production scheduled to wrap up by eight or nine o'clock that evening.

Not surprisingly, the rain itself presents only one of the logistical considerations to be overcome. Goodwin frets about completing shots before other elements turn on him. "I have a problem with the tide," he says. "I have to finish shooting behind the house by three P.M., before it turns into a mud flat."

Rain continues to fall steadily, so a tarp has to be assembled and mounted on the edge of the roof. The clear awning is about 10 feet square, standing on posts. As a result, viewers would never suspect it's raining as the scene is shot, and a spotlight even establishes the illusion of sunlight glinting off the window. Crew members quickly erect a blue tent nearby as well, where Goodwin and Bartley can sit watching the monitors. Duchovny's dog, Blue, takes refuge under the awning.

Despite his trademark reserve, Duchovny does seem enthusiastic about the episode's guest star, who'll play the Healing Man. "You know Roy Thinnes?" he asks Goodwin during a lull regarding the accomplished actor, whose credits include the sixties TV series *The Invaders*. "I met him on the plane and told Chris he'd be very good. Next thing you know . . ."

By now they're almost ready to begin filming, but first Williams and Duchovny rehearse the scene, with X handing over photos of Mrs. Mulder with the Cigarette-Smoking Man. "*She's* not my mother," Duchovny quips, lightening the mood.

The actor turns more serious, though, conferring with Goodwin as to how the scene should be played as X comes out of the house, surprising Mulder. "Bob, you really have to sell my shock," he indicates, suggesting that X deliver his first line as he's exiting the house, "maybe even before I see him."

As the crew positions the camera the two actors wait with their umbrellas in hand. "We can fight with the umbrellas," Duchovny says with a smile, brandishing his toward Williams. "It'll be like *The Avengers*." Because setting up the shot will require about 20 minutes, the performers leave the set, with Duchovny returning in wardrobe (a suit and trenchcoat) after rehearsing in a pair of jeans.

While preparing to shoot, a plane loudly flies over. Goodwin confers with Williams as various folks fuss over Duchovny, from fixing his hair to brushing lint off his raincoat. The pelting rain proves so loud that the actors must wear wireless microphones, since the overhead boom mike usually employed keeps picking up the ambient sound. Goodwin and Bartley wear headphones to hear the dialogue, which thanks to the rain caroming off the awning isn't audible from more than a few feet away. Crew members crowd under the tent, around the director and cinematographer, seeking to keep dry. "Only seven more days," one mutters.

Another plane flies by, a hazard given the location's proximity to the airport. "Let's cut. Sorry, airplane," Goodwin says, with the roar of aircraft interrupting the process on more than one occasion. After shooting the scene once they prepare quickly for a second attempt while the skies remain friendly, as Duchovny and Williams chat on the steps. Much of the communication around the set gets done with the use of headsets, with the range to contact a fellow crew member from the North Shore Studios at the nearby shopping center. In this case Braidwood uses a walkie-talkie to cue the actors when to come out of the house, and Duchovny decides he wants a few seconds more to establish Mulder's torn feelings as he exits his old family house in the wake of his mother's stroke. "Bob, give me just a little longer out at this mark, will you?" he says, indicating where Mulder will stand.

The producers do have some leeway in such matters but not much, and an episode's length always remains a concern. Prior to shooting the script is timed, with the duration in this case estimated at 44 minutes, just about how long the average episode runs minus the commercials, credits, and promotional spots that fill out each hour. There is some wiggle room on the length of the fight between X and Mulder, notes script supervisor Helga Ungurait, who literally takes the script and times every beat of an episode—down to slowly puffing a cigarette, she says, as she acts out the Cigarette-Smoking Man's role. During production Ungurait then uses a stopwatch to time each scene, keeping track of whether the episode is running long or short based on her initial estimates.

A plane interrupts shooting again, and birds crow loudly in the distance. The camera crew has set up a horizontal track on which the camera can roll in order to shoot Williams's close-up, and they do the scene again. Williams inadvertently omits (or drops) a line the first time but delivers his lines flawlessly the second time around. "Cut. Good. Steve, happy?" Goodwin asks economically. Williams would like to do the scene one more time, and they do—with near-identical results—before turning the camera around to film Duchovny's close-ups. Again, they run through the scene twice. "Print both of those," says Goodwin. "David, are you happy?"

"Once more," the actor says, whose third take is met with an approving "Cut. Beauty." Duchovny retires to his trailer, while Williams tries to warm up with a cup of soup as reinforcements arrive for the rain-soaked crew, bearing boxes of hot Starbucks coffee. Williams has appeared four times during the season as X, and he's not above lobbying for more exposure, while noting happily that the character has shifted from a man of words to a man of action. "Every time you see him you know someone's going to get blown away," he laughs.

Like Duchovny, Wil-liams also yearns for his character to eventually open up at some point, though he jokes that the payoff could underscore the show's "Trust No One" slogan. "I'd like to see what X does when he's not in the shadows. Does he have a family? Then in the next episode, they could tell you it's all a lie," he says with a grin.

Shooting continues into that evening at the beach house, shift-ing the next day to FBI Assistant Director Skinner's office. Each scene is identified in the shot breakdown by brief descriptions like "Serious Condition," "Cool Off," or "Looking for Mom." Action during Day Three occurs at the hospital, where Mulder and Scully visit his mother and he later encounters the Cigarette-Smoking Man. According to Goodwin, based on initial dailies Duchovny's scenes in the hospital are in his view "some of the best work David has done" on the series.

The climactic sequence where Mulder and Scully confront the alien bounty hunter, set at a lumberyard in North Vancouver that's standing in for the sawmill, actually films during the midst of production. The crew spends the next day at the Social Security building (or more accurately, Vancouver City Hall), capturing the Cigarette-Smoking Man's search for the Healing Man, later shooting at the makeshift office building, which also entails the elaborate dolly shot craning past dozens of desks.

The week concludes across the street from that location in the parking garage, where the brief but bruising fracas between Mulder and X is staged. Although stuntmen handled most of the action, the brawl still took its toll on Williams, who injured his shoulder and needed a massage after shooting. Goodwin points out that Nicholas Lea also wound up a bit roughed up and in need of a session with a masseuse following his first battle with Duchovny in "Anasazi." "David never gets hurt," chuckles Goodwin, who told the star that if he wants such treatment he should at least *pretend* to have some aches and pains.

Some crew members look bleary-eyed when production resumes early on April 29, the sixth day of filming. Shooting will occur entirely at the A&W fast-food restaurant in Burnaby, though that sign remains visible only from the street, as logos on the left side of the building have been replaced by the logo "Brothers K"—the name of the fictitious fast-food outlet, and a joke Chris Carter dreamed up due to the episode's thematic ties to Dostoevsky's *The Brothers Karamozov*. Passersby on busy Kingsway Street crane their necks to see what's happening at a parking lot filled with police cars and an ambulance, though if they look closely they'll be relieved to see all those cars bear tacked-on Virginia license plates.

Similarly, the police and paramedics standing around are really extras, most of whom reported to the set at 7:00 A.M. Though they'll at best be glimpsed fleetingly in the background, one marvels at the show's attention to minutiae, pointing to his badge, which includes his actual picture, as do those worn by all the other extras—the photos having been taken that morning and affixed to the badges. Although it's virtually impossible that any TV viewer would see the one-inch-square picture (unless they have a 70-millimeter movie screen in their living room), the show seldom wavers in its commitment to such precision.

Exercising such rigor is difficult enough, but perhaps more so for some crew members this morning given that they're still recovering from the show's "wrap party" to celebrate the season's end. The party itself was held before production concluded on Saturday night, since the series stars will be gone by the time actual production concludes. Most of the show's principals characterize the affair as being reasonably sedate, with celebrities affiliated with other shows and movies who happened to be in Vancouver—among them Leslie Nielsen and Harry Anderson—having attended the party. Still, some participants joke about nursing hangovers, and there's even some talk (unconfirmed, of course) about a few of the heartier souls engaging in a seemingly unfathomable post-midnight swim in Vancouver's frigid English Bay, though no one—in true *X-Files* fashion—seems to be able to ascertain if that strange and death-defying feat is really fact or fiction. In any event, crew members clearly exhibit a sense of relief to be heading down the homestretch after roughly 10 months of near nonstop production.

Inside the restaurant, producers set up a shot with Scully's stand-in, Bonnie Hay, while makeup artists—who carry small plastic bags with labels earmarking them for each of the main actors—dab gently at Gillian Anderson's cheeks. Duchovny mutters something that makes Anderson laugh right before shooting begins, but she quickly composes herself. "When do I look for the van, Bob?" Duchovny asks director Bob Goodwin.

"I'll say 'Van,'" Goodwin tells him.

Gillian Anderson and Tom Braidwood on the Brothers K set.

"Just don't say it over my lines," Duchovny quips. They try the scene twice, the continuity person chiming in by saying "Ring" to indicate Mulder's cell phone, a sound effect to be added later. "Cut," Goodwin says approvingly. "Everybody happy?" With nods of satisfaction all around, the crew moves outside to begin setting up shots in the parking lot.

Though some extras wear uniforms with the Brothers K logo, no one is being served in the restaurant, with the only food (other than the half-eaten burgers and fries scattered about in the wake of the gunman's massacre) available from a catering truck in a nearby church parking lot. The weather started out slightly overcast, but as the morning has dragged on the clouds have dissipated, leaving behind a blazingly bright sky.

Angelo Vacco in costume.

Among those waiting for his call to action sits Angelo Vacco, a production assistant in the *X-Files* Los Angeles office as well as an aspiring actor. "It seems to be an inside gag that I have to be hurt or killed," says Vacco, who previously appeared in the plague episode "F. Emasculata" playing a gas station attendant who gets brutally assaulted. Vacco quotes director Rob Bowman as saying, "Angelo can only be in another episode if he dies." Vacco does get shot (there's a small hole with fabricated powder burns around the fringe in his T-shirt), but he's hardly complaining about the abuse, crediting Carter with being "extremely generous" in affording him such exposure.

Feeding the set's sense of extended family, the roster of extras includes cinematographer John Bartley's teenage daughter, and the next day finds the daughters of Braidwood and key grip Al Campbell working in that capacity, as well as stunt coordinator Tony Morelli's three kids, ages four through eight, who are among the children who flee the restaurant. Aside from giving the kids an opportunity to see their parents at work—where they often spend 12–15-hour days—and the parents a chance to spend some on-set time with their children, there's a practical application to using family members as extras, crew members note, because they generally understand the long hours involved and what's required of them.

By 1:00 P.M. the crew breaks for lunch, and a handwritten sign on the catering wagon above the day's bill of fare says "GOOD LUCK DAVID AND GILLIAN," wishing the stars well on their last day of first-unit shooting. Some crew members play stickball in the church parking lot as they feast on ribs and noodles. Duchovny remains in high spirits, while his stand-in, the stupendous Jaap Broeker, walks Blue on a leash. Goodwin has everyone back to work by 2:00 P.M., and because the remaining shots are all set outdoors and in daylight hours he's determined to be done before darkness falls. The sun now shines brilliantly, but Bartley anticipated that, he says, by lighting the morning shots very brightly as well. He must nevertheless compensate for the glare, with a crew member carrying a large screen next to the camera to blunt the sun's rays.

The scene calls for Mulder and Scully to pull up in front of the fast-food restaurant exiting the car. "Where are the wounded?" Anderson asks, approaching the bogus paramedics intently but making a funny face at those behind the cameras as she passes by them and out of the frame. "Let's do it one more time," Goodwin says, after a second take. "That was almost perfect." Turning the camera around, A.D. Tom Braidwood reminds crew and extras to move out of the picture. "We're all hot here, guys," he says—"hot," in this context, meaning within the camera's view. After quieting the set, a cry of "Background!" sets the extras in motion, followed by a signal of "Action" to the leads.

With a momentary respite between scenes as the camera is moved again, Duchovny leans against a car, while Blue squeezes in behind her master's legs. A small crowd of onlookers has amassed on the set's fringe watching the shoot, and the dog sits quietly while Duchovny patiently signs autographs for a number of fans, mostly teenagers and children. At that point Chris Carter arrives at the set, having just come from the studio, where he directed Jerry Hardin—aka Deep Throat—in scenes to be utilized in the jail cell morphing sequence involving the Healing Man. Anderson does three takes of the current scene, exiting the restaurant, then walking across the parking lot to talk with Mulder. She briefly confers with Goodwin, then acts out the sequence one more time, to their mutual satisfaction.

With that, Goodwin calls attention to inform everyone that Gillian (who's still scheduled to do some second-unit shooting the next day) has just completed her first-unit work for the season, an announcement met with a round of applause. Realizing that he won't be coming back the next season, Anderson hugs cinematographer Bartley for a long time before gradually making her way around the set, individually bidding the crew goodbye—some for good, others only until they all return to begin the fourth season. Even so, in light of the long hours a two-month hiatus may well feel like a long time, though Anderson's daughter Piper remains oblivious to that concept, toddling around not far away in her own little FBI jacket.

David Duchovny and
Rob Bowman on the set.

Duchovny now shoots his final scenes, a lengthy exchange in the car with the gunman following his salvation by the Healing Man. The camera zooms in tight, and Goodwin eschews the monitor, moving up to watch the scene from just a few feet away as the camera trains in on the actors through the car window. After several takes from different angles Duchovny finishes the scene around 6:30 P.M., quietly bidding his own farewells to the crew before hopping in a minivan and almost literally riding off into the sunset, having to segue with only a day or two's rest from playing Mulder to *Playing God*.

Crew call is for 7:00 A.M. on April 30, returning to the A&W restaurant to film the teaser sequence, in which a gunman opens fire in a fast food restaurant and a mysterious man steps from the crowd to heal him as well as the other wounded. The call sheet not only lists the location and who'll be needed but also the time of sunrise and sunset, which is significant today for two reasons: Goodwin needs to finish shooting by dark and must be done with his gunman, actor Hrothgar Mathews, by 7:30 P.M. so he can fulfill his other commitment. After the brilliant sunlight of the day before this morning remains overcast, and Bartley hopes that it will stay that way. "Please make the sun go away," he groans at a glint of light through the window.

David Duchovny
signing autographs.

Some minor complications have arisen, as usual. Carter wants to do a couple of reshoots at Vancouver's City Hall, changing the expression on the face of the Pleasant Man, whom the Healing Man (actually the alien bounty hunter disguised as the Healing Man) morphs into to make his escape. Because Duchovny and Anderson have left, that will require using their photo doubles, though the likeness in each case is close enough to the star that it shouldn't present a major problem.

Goodwin takes special pride in the day's opening shot, which pans slowly back using a Steadi-cam as Mathews rants about how unappreciated he is before the camera swivels 360 degrees around the gunman after he jumps up and pulls the pistol. "Nobody leaves! Everybody

stays!" the actor shouts. The action then shifts to a hand-held camera, reflecting the sense of chaos that ensues. "I want it to be really bumpy and frenetic," notes Goodwin, who returns to the Steadi-cam when the Healing Man (Roy Thinnes) steps into the scene, providing a soothing influence that will thus also be subtly conveyed by the shooting method.

Prior to the next shot, Braidwood announces that there will be one live round of ammunition used in filming the sequence. Mathews performs the scene in which the gunman rises from his private rambling several times, spinning in choreographed fashion with the gun, firing once, then turning to fire again, as Braidwood yells "Bang!" to indicate each shot. A loud crack emanates from the gun as Mathews turns in the direction of the camera lens, shooting off the live round.

Reloading the camera, the crew sets up the shot from another angle while stunt coordinator Morelli places a thin pad under the doormat to cushion where Angelo Vacco will have to fall after being shot by the gunman. Elsewhere, the special effects gang installs a special window that will crack in spiderweb fashion when a marksman fires through the glass, wounding the gunman. Not far away, the script's Crying Woman and Smirking Woman have time to chat as they await their moments—not to be confused, of course, with the Cigarette-Smoking Man, Healing Man, Well-Manicured Man, Plain-Clothes Man, or any of the show's other uniquely named characters.

Rehearsing another angle on the shooting, in which the children can be seen streaming out of the restaurant, one of the kids trips and falls heading out the door but fortunately isn't hurt. The children are gently reminded again to be careful as they leave as well as quiet and serious once they've gone outside, having burst into laughter earlier. With the long lapses between action, the tots face a strong temptation to laugh and horse around—not exactly the reaction most kids would have in a hostage situation. Braidwood, watching Morelli's brood get into the act, wonders if they'll follow in their dad's footsteps and perform stunts as well. "I'm surprised you don't have all your kids taking [bullet] hits at the door," he teases.

Thinnes now does his scene in which he seeks to calm the gunman, as Braidwood quietly cues the police cars—caught only peripherally in the camera—to drive past the restaurant by whispering "Cars, cars" into his walkie-talkie. Getting the timing just right requires several takes, as the gunman fires and Vacco crashes to the floor. Finally Goodwin has the shot he wants and decides it's time for a break. "Shall we have lunch?" he declares.

"I love lunch after a good killing," Morelli says pleasantly.

Lunch passes quickly, and the afternoon promises to be busy. Considerable planning goes into the scene in which the gunman gets shot through the window by a police marksman, since the crew will only have a few passes at the shot. The black-suited marksman lines up across the parking lot, and a small circle is drawn on the glass where the shot is supposed to connect. A glass ball will be rocketed into the window, which doesn't cause any danger since the projectile gets destroyed by the impact. "It disintegrates," special effects chief David Gauthier explains, surveying the window. "That's why you use glass."

Braidwood warns that the sound will be "somewhat loud," and earplugs are passed out to everyone who wants them inside the restaurant. After two rehearsals, the shot gets fired off and the window splinters perfectly as the gunman collapses to the ground—just as hoped, capturing the effect in one take, leaving behind only a faint smokelike odor from the powder used to propel the glass ball.

Mathews now lays on the ground for some time ("I'm getting cold," he says at one point) as they film his healing scene, with Thinnes kneeling over him. The actor must "start looking blissful and end up looking dying," as Braidwood puts it, since part of the plan involves running the footage backward to create the effect of the Healing Man's touch drying up the blood, which will be pumped onto the wounded man's shirt through a small tube. "Blood," Goodwin cues. "A little more fear in there, Hrothgar," he also counsels after one take. By now it's 6:30 P.M., and Goodwin tries to hurry things along to make sure he meets the actor's deadline. In addition to having Mathews for only another hour, just two hours remain before sunset.

The Lone Gunmen's Dean Haglund pops onto the set simply to say hello, while a second camera outside is being used to film scenes of the marksman setting up in the parking lot. With a few more takes completed, Mathews, after nearly 12 hours' work, leaves to his own round of applause just after 7:00 P.M., as promised. Meanwhile, Thinnes moves outside to do a brief shot in which the Healing Man absconds from the crime scene. Second assistant director Collin Leadlay continues to shoot within the restaurant, staging stunned reaction shots of the extras to be used, if necessary, in the sequence in which the gunman gets healed. Shooting ends not long after 8:00 P.M., though the work crew will labor late into the evening restoring the restaurant, which will reopen for business at 6:00 A.M. the following morning with no evidence the crew had been there.

Production begins not long after 9:00 A.M. on May 1, the final day of shooting, and Goodwin hopes to conclude before midnight—a welcome contrast from the two previous years, when the last day dragged on until roughly four o'clock in the morning. The first season's final installment, "The Erlenmeyer Flask," caused a few hearts to flutter, in fact, as dawn gradually approached because the sequence (Deep Throat's death scene) called for darkness and would have become near-impossible once the sun rose.

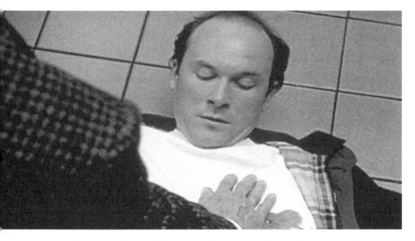

The entire day of filming will occur on Soundstage 1 at the North Shore Studios on the vast and elaborate two-story prison set constructed originally for "The List." The art department has made modifications to alter the look, but the venue still conveys a dank, claustrophobic sense of menace. Both inside and outside the soundstage a red light flashes when shooting begins to prevent someone from interrupting, over a sign that reads "Please Do Not Enter When Red Light Flashing."

Brian Thompson, the imposing presence who plays the alien bounty hunter, repeatedly enters a doorway as elevated spotlights create the illusion of sunlight filtering through the prison bars behind him. The back wall has been removed, creating room for the camera to operate, and after several passes trying to get just the right backlit effect Thompson is dismissed. Because he'll be back for the season opener, Thompson says he'll see everyone in July, then, realizing that some will be moving on, adds that he'll see "those of you who aren't abandoning ship."

Now it's Thinnes's turn, and the actor—today clad in a bright orange prison jumpsuit—rehearses with William B. Davis, speaking in hushed whispers within the 10-by-10-foot cell. Though his schedule remains crazed, Chris Carter—who'll deliver *Millennium* to Fox Broadcasting officials that weekend—pops in to observe the key interrogation scene. The crew, however, must first reset the shot, erecting a platform behind the cell and black tent over the camera, since the cubicle is actually elevated about 18 inches off the ground.

Over and over, Davis steps methodically into the cell, where he's bathed in darkness before slowly emerging from the shadows. Both the look and Davis's performance please Carter, and they break to move the camera in order to shoot the scene from another angle. Davis plops into a director's chair during the downtime, donning glasses and reading over his lines.

There's considerable tedium associated with these lulls, and on-set amusements include a bubble-blower near the snack table. "Well, it *is* the last day," Carter notes. Ample activity goes on, meanwhile, across the lot in the show's main office, where the realization that today marks the last day of production results in a festive if typically frenetic atmosphere. Carter, Goodwin, and Howard Gordon have presented the crew with plush *X-Files* third-year sweatshirts, and the costume department also sells off first-season wardrobe at bargain-basement prices. Gillian Anderson—almost unrecognizable in a baseball cap and glasses, with her hair up—also comes in to do some additional dialogue recording (or ADR), as Piper immediately commands center stage with the office staff.

Shortly thereafter Carter returns to the set, addressing the crew and thanking them for their hard work during the season. He wishes those who are leaving well, adding wryly that the door will stay open when (not if) they come back after discovering the cruel world that awaits them. The producer also marvels at how three years could have passed so quickly, and the group breaks—at 3:00 P.M.—for a special lunch he's provided at the catering truck in the parking lot.

One might think staying on one set all day would speed produc-

tion, but that's not necessarily the case. Shooting in the prison's confined space presents certain logistical challenges, and though things moved briskly when the day began, the pace has slowed considerably by late afternoon. Displeased by the lack of progress, Goodwin seeks to focus his troops, asking them to bear down despite the last-day distractions "or we won't be out of here till after midnight."

Peter Donat, who plays Mulder's father, arrives and stands by in an orange jumpsuit identical to that worn by Thinnes. From a distance they might even pass for a pair of auto mechanics. Donat will lens scenes in which Thinnes's Healing Man morphs into Mr. Mulder, reminding the Cigarette-Smoking Man of all the blood on his hands. A picture of Jerry Hardin—who shot his scene the prior day—graces a nearby monitor so it can be matched precisely with shots of Thinnes in order to create the morphing effect, with computer-imaging turning one face into the other. As a result every other element must match up exactly, down to the positioning of the actor's head or the shape of his collar.

By now the evening has come, and the crew members clearly fight exhaustion. The giddy notion of completing the season's final shot—cause for celebration early in the day—at times seems to feel anticlimactic, given that they've been staring at the same cell (albeit from innumerable angles) for the last 10 hours or so. Goodwin uses the monitor to demonstrate for Thinnes how the morphing sequence will work, as the actor patiently looks on, seemingly intrigued by the technology. "This morphing thing, it's all new to me," he says. "I've never morphed before."

Rain falls heavily outside while a visual effects technician seeks to match the scene Thinnes performs with an earlier shot of Hardin, down to a small tilt of the head. After several tries they finally accomplish the desired effect, and as the camera is repositioned yet again several large trays of sushi arrive—a parting gift from Gillian Anderson. "Thank you, Gillian," someone says as the crew descends on the table, quickly devouring the contents of both platters like a pack of hungry wolves.

Donat, after spending roughly five hours on the set to stage his brief appearance, leaves around 9:30 P.M. "Nice of you to drop by, Peter," says Goodwin, who also informs the crew that "we only have a few more shots, then we can all take a nice rest"—a misstatement in his own case, since he'll journey to Los Angeles that Friday to begin editing the episode, a process that's already underway as the daily footage comes in.

Davis and Thinnes return to the cell to capture their scene yet again, this time to service the morphing composition. The process proves extremely time-consuming, as the monitors try to perfectly align Thinnes's face over that of Hardin. At 11:15 P.M., Davis's day finally ends more than 12 hours after it began. "I guess I'm wrapped," he says, making his way past various crew members. "See you in July."

The few extras needed—who have sought to kill time by doing crossword puzzles or listening to a Walkman—finally get their call for the night's final shot. In it, a crane will glide down the prison hallway, moving from the second level more than 10 feet up down to the ground. A camera operator uses a Steadi-cam and seamlessly steps off the crane, backing up to capture the Healing Man as he's wheeled into his cell on a vertical stretcher the props department rigged up that resembles something out of *The Silence of the Lambs*. A last-minute adjustment is needed, however, because the scene takes place at night, which in the production crush was initially overlooked. Crewmen shimmy up ladders to place green screens over the spotlights, quickly turning the sunlight filtering through into a bluish midnight glow. "It didn't take us long to turn it to night, did it?" says Bartley.

After some time to achieve the setup, Goodwin calls action and shoots the sequence twice, and both shots are executed flawlessly. At 12:11 A.M., more than 15 hours after the day started for most of the crew, he announces, "Let's print those two, and let's have a drink!" Goodwin thanks Thinnes, who joins the understated celebration, as beers—kept cold in two large trash cans—are grabbed while hugs and handshakes are exchanged all around.

The cameras may have stopped rolling, but actual filming related to "Talitha Cumi" won't conclude for several days. Despite completion of the main-unit work, the second-unit crew will continue to assemble material as late as May 7 and is in fact still garnering footage for "Wetwired," which airs only nine days away on May 10. The sort of brief second-unit shots needed to be inserted into the season finale include Scully's POV (point of view) in various scenes that don't require the actress's presence or an angle on Mulder's hand grasping the alien stiletto. The most elaborate chore that remains involves shooting inserts for the Social Security lobby scene, again, using photo doubles to work around the principals' absence.

For the first team, however, the season has come to a close, and a breather from 15-hour days looms before them. Outside, the rain has perhaps appropriately ceased, and a full moon shines over the quiet and—for the first time in perhaps a long time—seemingly sedate North Shore Studios lot.

PART IV
POSTPRODUCTION

ob Goodwin travels to Los Angeles almost as soon as principal photography ends, working over the weekend to help finalize the initial cut of the episode. The show's film editors actually began putting together the footage from the first day of shooting, so some semblance of an episode is already in place by the time the producer-director arrives. There's no time to waste in the postproduction process, with the airdate only two weeks away.

"This is one of the closest ones of the year," says co-producer Paul Rabwin, who's in charge of postproduction, which incorporates such areas as all aspects of sound (including music), dialogue, and visual effects. "We try to deliver on Thursday morning when we can, but this show will deliver Friday morning [for telecast later that night], so there's no room for error."

In the editing, several scenes—all slaved and agonized over in the production phase—are invariably lost, with tough choices to be made to keep the running time at 44 minutes. Gone, for example, is the crying woman during the teaser sequence in the fast-food restaurant, as well as the elaborate shot in which the Cigarette-Smoking Man's henchmen enter the Social Security building and secure the lobby. "We were long, and we had to find ways to cut to [the requisite] length," Carter explains, adding that the Social Security sequence ran nearly a full minute. "You couldn't use part of it," he says. "You could only use all of it."

Once the episode has been put into that shape, the producers begin the task of dissecting every aspect of the show, starting with a procedure called spotting. As Rabwin explains it, they'll spend three hours or more talking about every possible effect within the show, adding dialogue where necessary and deciding what sort of sound effects and music are needed to augment each scene, working off a list of preliminary notes assembled by Carter, Goodwin, and co–executive producer Howard Gordon.

Gordon serves as the point man in terms of spotting, and it's rare for the directors to be involved because they're usually either working on a subsequent episode or preparing for one. The session is scheduled for 9:00 A.M. on May 9, a Thursday morning. Gordon acts somewhat distracted, since there's a content question pertaining to Fox Broadcasting, whose broadcast standards and practices department has expressed misgivings about Mulder's fight with X—questioning both its length (at this point 37 seconds, to be precise) and brutality.

Rabwin, supervising sound editor Thierry Couturier, editor Jim Gross, and postproduction supervisor Lori Jo Nemhauser (who comes in a few minutes late, having been up till after 3:00 A.M. the night before working on "Wetwired," which airs the next day) crowd into Gordon's office. The space sits only a few yards from the main office on the Twentieth Century Fox lot and features an imposing gargoyle sculpture from the episode "Grotesque"—which Gordon wrote—tastefully situated on a corner table right behind a picture of his young son. (Couturier's son, many will remember, provided the "I made this" voice heard over the closing credits and was compensated for his services, his father confesses, with a new Nintendo set.)

The process begins with the teaser sequence, in which the gunman rises and pulls his weapon. There's discussion about what sort of muted conversations might be necessary in the background, and talk of filling a lapse between when Galen stands with the weapon and the next scene. A counter runs in the lower corner so the editors can know the precise second when sound must be added and how long it should run. They run the first scene several times, as Gordon—getting into the character—says lines aloud as possible dialogue. "Now you're going to listen to me. Everybody's gonna listen to me!" he shouts. Later, the producer fills in with "Shut up! I said, Shut up!" as the gunman points his weapon toward a mother clutching her child. "Can we get a kid's squeal?" Gordon asks, while Rabwin suggests the mother say something like, "It's okay, sweetie."

Mark Snow.

Hrothgar Mathews will record these lines—a process known as looping—in Vancouver, though most of the background voices will fall to a group of actors in Los Angeles whose muttering and asides can be dubbed in. That recording session will be held Monday, four days off, while composer Mark Snow will get the episode to begin adding his dramatic underscore later in the day. Because Duchovny and Anderson have both left to fulfill other commitments, it's hoped that the episode can be completed and still spare them from any additional looping sessions.

Angelo Vacco, back in his role as production assistant, swings by to take orders, since he's making a run for juice and Smoothies, fruit shakes that are popular in Southern California. The group is briefly interrupted again when the phone rings, with a call Gordon has to take: It's Fox's broadcast standards executive, calling to talk about cutting parts of the fight. "How is this different from *Gunsmoke?*" Gordon asks, while eluding to the earlier tussle on the show between X and Skinner. "That was a much more brutal fight. Those guys were *killing* each other," he says calmly, adding that concern about length "feels like an arbitrary argument to me." Gordon pauses, listening for a moment. "There's precedent all over network television," he responds.

The rest of the group forges ahead with the spotting while Gordon continues the debate, which principally centers on a moment when X throws Mulder to the ground and kicks him twice. Fox—concerned about charges of excessive violence, as all broadcasters have become given the debate in Washington—wants to lose

Editor Jim Gross.

those kicks. "It's so dark. It's so fast. It's not that violent," observes Couturier, who indicates that the scene might be technically obscured in a way sufficient to mitigate whatever problem the network perceives.

The tape rolls forward to the shot where the Healing Man/Jeremiah Smith mends the wounded gunman, as the blood runs backward at his touch. "Should we have the sound of the blood being sucked into his hand?" Couturier jokes.

Some dialogue sounds garbled in the first act and will have to be relooped. When action shifts to the beach house, there's immediately discussion about where the scene is situated (East or West Coast) and adding sound effects of appropriate sea birds. As Mrs. Mulder and the Cigarette-Smoking Man talk, one of the airplanes that kept passing by during the filming can be heard on the soundtrack. "Uh-oh, incoming," murmurs Couturier, noting that the sound will have to be removed.

Gordon also has to add lines when Mulder and Scully interview the detective, since there's "a big ol' hole there," as Gross puts it, in the way the scene has been edited together because Mulder has to notice a TV truck in the background. "I look around, I can't see him. He's gone. It was like he just disappeared," Gordon murmurs, trying to time the line to bridge that gap.

Switching to the hospital where Mrs. Mulder has been taken, they go over sound effects for the machines, and whether they should hear slight grunts or breathing sounds from the stricken Mrs. Mulder in the wake of her stroke. "They add a great deal to the scene," says Rabwin of such little details. "We spot longer than almost any other show, but it pays off."

The quartet gets through the teaser and first act in roughly an hour, putting them about on schedule for a three- to four-hour session. In Act II, they turn their attention to adding electric buzzes within the prison scene as well as metal grating sounds as the Healing Man is wheeled into the cell. "Hannibal," Gross mutters, watching the video. Demonstrating the manner in which scenes are shot out of sequence, that moment—the final shot executed during principal production with the main unit a mere eight days earlier—comes roughly 16 minutes into the episode.

Foley, the process in which sound effects are augmented or "sweetened" by artists who create those noises, will be used in various other scenes—particularly when Mulder ransacks the beach house, from pulling off the plastic tarp to shattering lamps. As they close Act II, Mulder finds and activates the alien stiletto. "*This* we have," Gordon jokes, referring to the sound effect created the first time the weapon was seen, in "Colony"/"End Game." After a technician wrestled for hours with trying to create something that "sounds like alien technology," as the producers requested in the script, Rabwin simply leaned into the microphone and made a *phffft* sound, which was ultimately used.

Sound effects will work through the weekend while others begin processes like color correction, ADR (additional dialogue recording), and adding the music. Snow normally calls to ask a few general ques-  tions about what the music should sound like and—having the process down to a virtual science by now—turns out the score over the weekend. Voices are continually examined to see if they need to be rerecorded, or in some instances changed altogether. "Sometimes there's an actor from Vancouver who just doesn't sound right," Rabwin notes, in which case a new voice has to be looped in its place. The digital effects crew also begins on their tasks, which, in this case, include the three morphing sequences, with a man morphing into the bounty hunter and the Healing Man changing into both Deep Throat and Mr. Mulder.

"We have the ability to take a green suit and make it blue if we want," notes Rabwin.

The day begins early again on Monday, May 13, as Rabwin and Carter convene 8:30 A.M. at Snow's house to listen to the score. The weather is expected to rise into the high 80s by afternoon, and Carter shows up wearing shorts and a T-shirt, bringing to mind his surfing days of more carefree times. Snow sips coffee as he leads his guests into the separate office behind his house.

Carter looks relaxed, but the heat is on all over Los Angeles at this time of year in television circles, as producers and studio executives sweat out what shows the networks will put on their fall prime-time schedules. Rumors circulate about various scheduling moves at all the networks, among them reports that Fox might consider moving *The X-Files* to Sundays, when viewing levels are higher. Why not take the network's top-rated show, the theory goes, and put it on the night of highest TV viewing each week, when Fox also benefits from airing NFL football during the afternoon as a promotional base?

Carter has heard the rumors but dismisses them as just that, saying he doesn't think the network would be foolish enough to tamper
with success. He's lobbying for the series to remain on Fridays, with
his new show, *Millennium*, to air Saturdays at nine o'clock—seeing if
the producer can essentially create an audience that night, just as

he did with *The X-Files*. To make his point about the prospect of
moving the show, Carter has not-so-jokingly told Fox executives that
he plans on titling his autobiography *Fridays at 9*.

As is, the producer focuses on matters at hand. One finds Snow's
impressive array of musical hardware in the office, where the composer
plays every note heard on the series on his Synclavier keyboard. Snow
(who's also done the score for *Millennium*) has become so proficient at
anticipating Carter's tastes and sensing the show's rhythms that there's
seldom much to discuss at these sessions. "It seems to get easier all the
time," Snow admits. "I've sort of got my arsenal of stuff—what I call
'the Mark Snow cliches.'"

Although people often feel his working conditions sound ideal—
given that he really never has to leave the house—Snow indicates
that's not always the case. "People think, 'Oh man, are you lucky,'"
he says. "But sometimes, it's like, 'Help! Let me out of here!'"

Snow pops in a tape, manipulating sound levels on a large
Soundcraft console as the music plays and dials quiver. The teaser
begins, and the gunman fires soundlessly, since the gunshot effects
have yet to be added. Carter watches silently, occasionally nodding in
agreement as the music rises in intensity. When the teaser ends,
Carter simply turns to Snow and says, "It sure helps."

During Act I, Carter mentions a cut he doesn't like, asking if

Snow can alter the music to help smooth the transition. "I'm on my way," Mulder says in the scene when told of his mother's stroke, and the producer wants the musical beat to come in the midst of that sentence instead of at the end. "Shouldn't that come in earlier?" Carter suggests. "It's not a great transition, and it'll help." Snow plays at the Synclavier, adjusting the music accordingly.

Snow has added music to all but 4 minutes of the 44-minute episode, with especially percussive sounds during the scene in which the Healing Man is wheeled into prison and almost religious, church-like strains in some of the other moments involving the Healing Man. The listening session doesn't take much more than an hour, just in time for Snow to do an interview with an entertainment reporter from CNN who's come to discuss the popularity of the *X-Files* compact disc.

Rabwin spends most of the day after that involved with the looping, while various other elements of postproduction— including visual and sound effects—continue in full swing elsewhere, each being done simultaneously. Late that night, for example, visual effects producer Mat Beck and a group of technicians can be found perfecting the digital effects, with the initial morphing sequences—a five-day process using computer-generated graphics—having been delivered over the weekend.

Beck tends to work late at night in one of the many postproduction houses the show employs at various times in Los Angeles and Vancouver. The technician works on the Henry system, a computer editor with a paint box. Using a stylus pen, he taps colors on the pad and literally "paints" directly on the oversized monitor to introduce various changes to the picture—in this case, fine-tuning the morph of a nondescript-looking bearded man into the alien bounty hunter. Brian Thompson, who plays the Bounty Hunter, has "a good face for morphing," Beck observes, citing the actor's chiseled features.

It's shortly after 11:00 P.M., but for Beck the night is still young. For starters, there's been a miscommunication, and they've been sent a color-corrected print when they'd already done a good deal of work on one that wasn't color-corrected. "You make a plan," Beck laughs philosophically, swiveling back in his chair, "then everything goes haywire, then you fix it on the fly."

Beck concedes that observing the process itself is "like watching paint dry"—a tedious, time-consuming procedure. Morphing, he adds, has become "old hat" as an effect, with viewers accustomed to seeing elaborate computer images on TV and particularly in feature films.

Beck has developed a reputation for close calls, a skill that Carter's assistant in Vancouver, Joanne Service, discusses with awed wonder. According to her, Beck never misses a plane, no matter how close he cuts it. Beck seems to operate in similar fashion regarding the effects, often delivering them at the last minute, causing stomachs to flutter elsewhere while he never outwardly appears to break a sweat. "If it went on the air a week from Friday," he says with a smile, since the telecast date is just a few days away, "we wouldn't be working on it."

Lacking the non–color-corrected tape, Beck decides to re-create the short sequence that's involved using the show dailies, which haven't been color-corrected either. A phone call is placed, and after a few minutes visual effects coordinator Scott Shields arrives with the dailies. The morphs themselves will last only a few moments despite the hours that went into them. Although the technician works on a high-tech monitor, Beck watches the scenes simultaneously on a regular TV set "just to make sure," he says, noting that "everything looks pretty good on a $4,000 monitor."

By Thursday, May 16, the postproduction crew has reached crunch time. That afternoon, the picture gets on-lined from a postproduction house in Burbank to the show's offices in Century City. "We literally send the picture and the soundtrack over phone lines to that room," Rabwin explains, where Gordon and possibly Carter or other producers can watch the episode. "They give notes on it, and then we continue working over here."

Again, the procedure may appear tedious, but there's ample creativity involved. Rabwin begins at one postproduction house in Burbank, while supervisor Lori Jo Nemhauser and editor Bob Minshall focus on other aspects of the program in a Hollywood editing facility, sitting in a slightly claustrophobic rectangular space called Edit Bay 5.

In that room they'll handle all the final aspects of the show, which includes double-checking the on-screen credits as well as creating and checking the legends (the script that says things like "QUONO-CHONTAUG, RHODE ISLAND") and titles. The process also involves making any last-minute changes and corrections, including time-consuming little nuances one would never consider, like dirt-cleaning. "We spend hours and hours cleaning dirt out of it," says Rabwin, who refers to the entire process as "QC," for quality control. "A lot of lesser shows don't have such attention to detail," he adds. "We really detail and nitpick this thing."

Legends get typed out on a little machine, with each letter equaling one frame at 30 frames per second. Luckily, the night crew has all the visual effects and opticals required from Beck for this episode, putting them ahead of the game in that respect. On the downside,

Carter had earlier noticed several moments he wanted to fine-tune, calling for slightly more recuts than usual.

Cleaning out dirt and laying the soundtrack down usually takes about eight hours, and since they've begun in the early evening nobody anticipates being home before two o'clock in the morning. Still, no one's complaining, either, since that doesn't even remotely approach some of the close calls of the past—the record-holder being the second season finale, "Anasazi." In that particular case, the episode actually wasn't physically delivered to Fox until nearly 4:00 P.M. Pacific time—a mere two hours before the episode aired on the East Coast.

Nemhauser watches on a monitor with a counter in the corner, detecting things with the naked eye (and ear) that a regular viewer would be hard-pressed to discern. "At 2:20, I'm hearing all this crackling," she says. Continuing to stare at the screen as the tape rolls, Nemhauser spots imperfections and calls them out to Minshall—perched in front of a separate monitor across the room— as she goes. "Something on his forehead . . . something on his temple . . . something on his eyeball . . . something in the bottom right-hand corner . . . something in the upper right-hand corner on her . . . something on the wall right there."

Many of those "somethings" seem virtually imperceptible, but the search for dirt, dust, hair, and any other impurity that may have found its way onto the film is remarkably thorough, down to what's called concealment—cases where digital information gets passed off strangely and thus warrants correction. The dirt-fixing itself is performed by using a digital-effects device—drawing a matte on the screen with a stylus pen, then filling the flawed area to obscure whatever mark has been noticed. "If you did this long enough you would start to see it," Minshall says, realizing that the average lay-man has a hard time seeing where the dirt is as he taps away at a keyboard to make the corrections, marking and matting out areas with a bright pink dot.

Rabwin shows up at 10:00 P.M. with a bottle of champagne to celebrate completing the last show of the season. Deftly popping the cork, he fills and passes around a few paper cups. The meticulous cleaning process, he explains, is preferable to discovering some sort of blemish got through and made it to air. "I'd rather know about it now than get a phone call from Chris on Saturday morning," he says.

The monitor screen reads "SESSION: XFILES/X24," the number referring to the 24th episode. "Ooh, a big hairy hair," Minshall says as the tape rolls, seeing a flicker that's actually noticeable, for once, and quickly matting it out. The process itself proves simple enough, well, even for a journalist to do, manipulating the pen like a crayon to paint the spot out directly on the screen.

The fight scene, meanwhile, has indeed been cut, and X's kicks to the prone Mulder—lasting at best a few seconds—are gone. "Bob Goodwin wasn't pleased, but what can you do?" Rabwin says, adding that the loop group manufactured some breathing sounds leading right into Scully's dialogue when she sees the Healing Man standing at her door. "It gave a really nice texture," he notes, suggesting that even a small refinement like that can heighten the sense of tension.

Such subtle choices aren't made arbitrarily. It took five hours just building the sound levels for the teaser because the sequence is so multilayered and complex, with all the voices and ambient sounds in the background. By contrast, the prison scene is played without any background noise to convey that Jeremiah Smith may be the only inmate being held at this secret facility.

It's past midnight already, and when Minshall notices a small problem he lets out a little "waah" sound. "Hey, if this is the biggest 'waah' of the night, we're okay," says Nemhauser.

In addition to completing the episode, several other peripheral chores have to be done as well. Clips must be pulled, for example, to provide a tape to Fox's Los Angeles morning show, *Good Day L.A.*, which will air a segment promoting the episode early the next day. The final print must also be closed-captioned for the hearing-impaired before being forwarded to Fox. A separate tape has to be available by 7:00 A.M. so the episode can be satellited to Canada, where the show will air the same day and time as in the United States. Three cassettes must ultimately be prepared, with dubs made for the U.S. and Canada as well as a backup, recorded on Beta SP stock (the SP stands for "Special Performance").

"This show is in good shape," Rabwin concludes as they finish going through the episode, adding, quite literally, "It's just a little dirty."

The producers still learn a great deal from listening to viewers and watching the episodes on the air. When the show converted to Surround-Sound, for example, a woman in Texas complained that her sound dropped out at certain points, apparently because of a technical problem involving Fox's Dallas affiliate. Rabwin called the woman, who sent along a tape so he could see the problem himself, receiving a T-shirt from the producer for her trouble. "The afterlife of this show really demands this perfectionism," Rabwin maintains of all the postproduction nitpicking. "It's a break from the big picture. Now we spend time with the little picture."

The fixes are finished at 12:25 A.M. With all the dirt accounted for, Rabwin and Nemhauser begin checking over their work one final time before taking the tape upstairs for dubbing and laying down the final soundtrack as well as having the closed-captioning done. Minshall remains downstairs in the edit bay as a precaution in case any further changes are needed. Within 20 minutes they've begun making the dubs and watching the increasingly familiar episode one more time.

According to Rabwin, the show tries to deliver episodes to Fox on the Wednesday evening or the Thursday morning before that Friday's telecast and manages to do so 85 percent of the time, but "if we're down to the wire" that can be pushed until the wee hours of Friday morning. In some of those instances Nemhauser or Rabwin will actually take the material directly to Fox, but usually a courier brings the tape over.

Rabwin admits that the studio sometimes "goes crazy" with the show's slavish attention to detail, since an extra day of looping can run several thousand dollars and cost is always a consideration. Still, he points out, "In features, that hour show would take four weeks to dub, and we do it in two days."

Because the show generally arrives so late, Fox frequently uses a temporary version in putting together the trailer in order to advertise the program on the air. In fact, Mat Beck at times generates temporary effects specifically for that purpose, subsequently enhancing those opticals or replacing them entirely when the final episode gets delivered.

The X-Files operates on a tightrope by television standards, since networks usually request that producers provide shows a week prior to the day when they're supposed to air, in part so they can be screened for advertisers and run by the broadcast standards department. Fortunately, Fox broadcasts out of Los Angeles rather than New York, which provides a bit more latitude, and the show inevitably gets done somehow. Still, with more than $1 million riding on each installment, network and studio officials are perhaps to be forgiven if they sweat out the process as much as they savor the results.

Finally, after 2:00 A.M. on what's now Friday morning, a courier arrives to pick up and deliver the cassettes to Fox Broadcasting and the Canadian satellite. Rabwin intends to watch the show on the air, as he always does, and then take a few days off before going to Washington, D.C., to shoot more stock footage—including exteriors of the FBI building, prisons, and so on—to keep on hand for use in future episodes.

In less than 16 hours, meanwhile, viewers in the Eastern and Central time zones will get their first glimpse of the season finale. As they get drawn into the story, few will consider what went into producing this hour, or the choices and occasional compromises that had to be made. One thing, however, is clear: On May 17, 1996—more than two months after Chris Carter and David Duchovny first began spinning ideas and toying with possibilities—"Talitha Cumi" has become a reality.

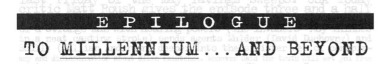

EPILOGUE
TO <u>MILLENNIUM</u>...AND BEYOND

T he *X-Files'* season finale airs on May 17, 1996, the last Friday of the May ratings sweeps. *USA Today* critic Matt Roush gives the episode three and a half out of four stars, saying, "The appearance and disappearance of a strange man with healing powers (*The Invaders'* Roy Thinnes in a neat casting stroke) sends agents Mulder (David Duchovny) and Scully (Gillian Anderson) deeper into the sinister web of conspiracy and disinformation about alien existence. Whoever said the truth will set you free hasn't been watching this deliciously paranoid thriller."

"Talitha Cumi" garners an 11.2 rating, 21 share in the Nielsen ratings, and is watched by nearly 18 million people. The rating is the show's highest since "Grotesque" more than three months earlier, on February 2. Viewers are left to wonder through the long hot summer just what Mulder is going to do with that alien icepick.

The show's fans will also be left to ponder much of the cryptic dialogue, such as references to "colonization," "the project," or "the greater purpose," as well as how all of this affects Mulder's missing sister. Foremost, fan buzz surrounds just what exactly the Cigarette-Smoking Man meant during his conversations with Mulder and Mrs. Mulder in saying that he'd known her since before Fox was born and referring to how he surpassed Mr. Mulder at "so many things." The Internet, not surprisingly, lights up with speculation about a "Luke, I am your father"–type scenario akin to *Star Wars*, but the producers merely seem bemused by the intensity of that response.

A mere four days later, on May 21, Fox Broadcasting announces its prime-time schedule for the 1996–97 broadcast season. In classic Hollywood fashion, the rumors are indeed true: *The X-Files* will move to Sundays, with Carter's newly born series *Millennium* to take over its old Friday time period. Even co–executive producer Howard Gordon, whose wife has just had their second child, and *Millennium* pilot director and co–executive producer David Nutter, vacationing in Hawaii, are surprised to hear the news when it leaks to the trade press.

During a press conference prior to the presentation of Fox's lineup to advertisers, then–Fox Entertainment president John Matoian suggests there is "a humongous upside" in moving the network's top-rated program to a night when more people are home, maintaining that the show will "change the way Americans live" on Sunday nights. "*The X-Files* is the answer the public is clamoring for," he says. "Its loyal fans are going to follow it, I think, wherever we put it." Meanwhile, Matoian calls *Millennium* "the incumbent to *The X-Files'* audience," with his faith in the show tied closely to his convictions about Chris Carter's talents.

Advertising agency media buyers generally praise the gamble, calling it perhaps the boldest scheduling move of the season. Some loyal fans of the show are up in arms, however—especially those on the East Coast, since overruns on Fox's Sunday afternoon football telecasts may push the series later into the evening, making the process of taping episodes more of a chore. Asked by a reporter how Carter feels about the decision, Matoian refers such inquiries to the executive producer himself.

Carter, who had been on vacation in Hawaii, returns shortly after the Memorial Day holiday. By mid-June, as he gears up to begin production on his two series in just a few weeks, he remains less than entirely thrilled about the time period move but philosophical in its aftermath.

"I felt we had carved out this place on Friday night, that we had become an appointment show, to use the network jargon," he says, referring to programs viewers make a point of either taping or being home to see. "It was a good night to be scared, it wasn't a school night, it seemed to be the perfect night for *The X-Files.*"

Yet in regard to Fox, he adds, "I know why they did it. That's the hard part, that's the reasonable part of me. I can't scream and shout. . . . The people who do the programming have their own reasons for doing this. As you have to do with so many things in this business, you have to live with it and have to make the best of it, and that's what we'll do.

"I am happy to have my new show move into that slot," he concludes, noting with only a hint of a smile that he can still rightfully title his autobiography *Fridays at 9*.

Millennium, Carter's latest show, stars Lance Henriksen (*Aliens*) as former FBI investigator Frank Black, a man who possesses a remarkable gift when it comes to profiling killers. Haunted by that grim past, and fearing for the safety of his family, Black moves his wife (a psychological social worker played by Megan Gallagher, of *The Larry Sanders Show* and *Nowhere Man*) and young daughter to Seattle, where he continues to oppose evil functioning as part of a mysterious cadre known as the Millennium Group. (As a sign of his own intensity and commitment to the project, Carter actually slipped a note under Henriksen's door while the actor was in Vancouver, telling him how interested he was in working with him. The show's script then won him and Gallagher over.)

Fox executives, advertisers, and critics were initially struck by both the show's quality and its dark tone, which Carter felt was necessary. "You can only create an interesting and bright hero if you set him against a very dark background," the producer told the nation's

television critics prior to the show's premiere, "and that's what I'm interested in doing with this show." Carter added that there were "certain stories I felt that I couldn't do in *The X-Files*, which had to do with psychological terror, the real world with real criminals and truly human monsters. This was my way of approaching it."

With 2 shows and potentially 47 hours of television to produce over the next 11 months between *The X-Files* and *Millennium*, Carter really doesn't have the luxury, at any rate, of dwelling on the past. His immediate considerations include plans to "start the season off with a bang"—the board for the fourth season opener nearly completed, leaning against a wall across the office, as he sits for this final interview.

Looking ahead, at least as much as he'll allow, Carter concedes that the show's web of intrigue will continue to widen and deepen, but slowly. In short, don't look for any quick answers. "It's a trick, because when you expand a mythology, as I call it, you have to build elements into it and then keep building on top of those, so you have to bring a certain knowledge to it as a viewer," he says. When it's pointed out that the audience has a lot to remember by now, in terms of what's happened in preceding years and where characters' allegiances reside, Carter responds, "It has gotten dense, but necessarily so. I think it appeals to the audience that in fact loves the mythology episodes, but at the same time I know in each one of those episodes there has to be enough of the red-hot element of a thriller in order to sweep the other people along."

During the coming year co-executive producer Howard Gordon will play a more expansive role in overseeing all aspects of *The X-Files*, while the tandem of Glen Morgan and James Wong—who left the fold to produce the now-canceled *Space: Above and Beyond*—are returning on a temporary basis. If all goes according to plan, Morgan and Wong will produce a handful of *The X-Files* episodes as well as a couple hours of *Millennium* for Carter before moving on to develop more programs under their separate production agreement with Twentieth Century Fox Television.

The duo, who helped create such characters as the liver-eating mutant Tooms and the Lone Gunmen, figure to help lighten the load as Carter wrestles with the process of doing two series. "We're happy to have them back," says Carter, adding that he considers their involvement "a personal favor." The producer has enlisted some aid on the executive front as well, bringing Twentieth Century Fox programming executive Ken Horton aboard to oversee the business operations of his company, Ten Thirteen Productions.

Fox has eased the burden a bit by giving *The X-Files* a running start at its new Sunday time period with a number of Friday night airings, the bonus being that the producers have more time to fine-tune *Millennium* prior to its premiere. "This gives us the luxury of that time," Carter explains, noting that extra time in postproduction can often make all the difference in safeguarding a show's quality. Carter cites "Squeeze," the first episode featuring Tooms, as an example, recalling that the initial cut was improved markedly through editing and other postproduction sorcery.

In addition, unlike some character-driven dramas, Carter's shows require enormous attention to all aspects of production, since the look and visual trappings are such a vital part of the storytelling. As the producer puts it, betraying a gift for understatement given his reputation as a perfectionist, "I'm finicky about these things."

Carter does acknowledge a certain sense of loss in some of the people who have left the show, from cinematographer John Bartley to visual effects whiz Mat Beck, who received a feature film offer over the summer that was simply too good to refuse. All one can do in those instances, the producer maintains, is wish the person well and keep moving forward. "You can never hold anybody back," he says.

If there is apprehension associated with the challenge of producing two series simultaneously, Carter doesn't reveal it. Given his involvement with every detail of *The X-Files* for three years, he is certain to face a considerable challenge in stepping back just enough to focus on *Millennium* and still maintain his understandable protectiveness toward his existing franchise. "Doing it on two shows is going to be interesting," he says, in a characteristically calm manner that exhibits just a trace of enthusiasm. "I have to keep a lot in my head."

A witness named Roky comes forward, saying a man in black visited him, telling him he saw Venus, not a UFO, and threatening to kill him if he tells anyone. Roky hands over his manuscript detailing the story, in which he saw two smaller aliens being attacked by a large one named "Lord Kinbote." Mulder acknowledges that Roky is probably delusional but may have seen something, so he has Chrissy hypnotized again, and she seems to support his story. Scully,

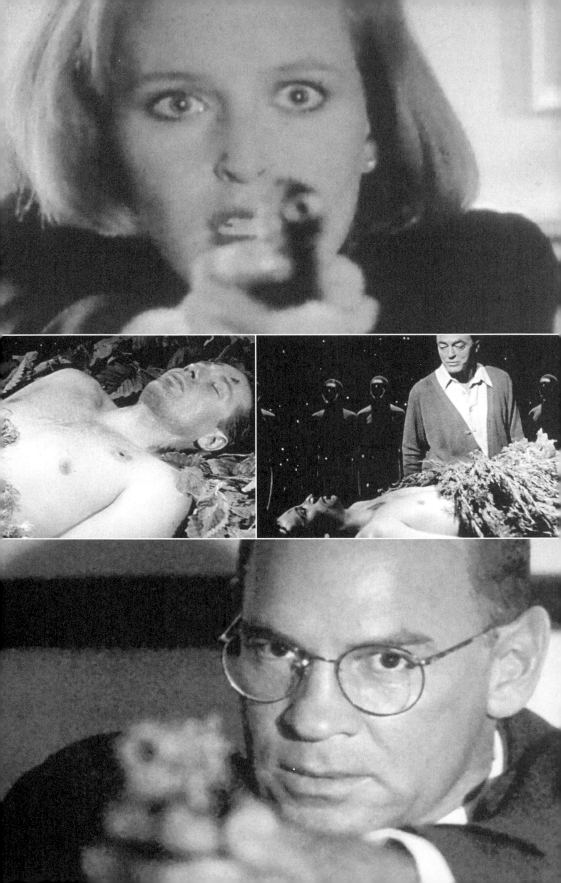

THE BLESSING WAY

EPISODE: 3X01

FIRST AIRED:
September 22, 1995

WRITTEN BY:
Chris Carter

EDITOR:
Stephen Mark

DIRECTED BY:
R. W. Goodwin

GUEST STARS:
Mitch Pileggi (AD Walter
   Skinner)
Peter Donat (Bill Mulder)
Floyd Red Crow Westerman
   (Albert Hosteen)
Melinda McGraw (Melissa Scully)
Sheila Larken (Margaret Scully)
Nicholas Lea (Alex Krycek)
William B. Davis (The Cigarette-
   Smoking Man)
John Neville (The Well-Manicured
   Man)
Tom Braidwood (Frohike)
Jerry Hardin (Deep Throat)
Alf Humphreys (Dr. Mark
   Pomerantz)
Dakota House (Eric)

Michael David Simms
   (Senior Agent)
Rebecca Toolan (Mulder's Mother)
Don S. Williams (1st Elder)
Forbes Angus (MD)
Mitch Davies (The Camouflage Man)
Benita Ha (Tour Guide)
Ian Victor (The Minister)
Ernie Foort (Security Guard)
Lenno Britos (Hispanic Man)

LOG LINE:
With the Cigarette-Smoking Man pursuing the secret files that prove the existence of alien visitation and experimentation—and Mulder still missing—Scully finds her own life and career in jeopardy.

PRINCIPAL SETTINGS:
Two Grey Hills, New Mexico; Washington, D.C.

SYNOPSIS:
Albert Hosteen, the tribal elder Scully had brought Mulder to in the previous episode ("Anasazi") to decipher the encrypted MJ Documents, relates in voice-over an ancient Native American saying that "something lives only as long as the last person who remembers it." Because of that, Albert warns, some would seek to change history by eliminating those who know it.

Suddenly the Cigarette-Smoking Man and soldiers burst into Albert's home. "I want Mulder and I want those files!" he demands as the soldiers brutally club both Albert and his grandson. Scully arrives once they've left, going to the boxcar where Mulder was last seen and finding only smoldering wreckage. Soon after, her car is stopped by troops, who take her printed copy of the files, which document the government's knowledge of alien visitors.

Back in Washington, Scully is told she is to be suspended for "direct disobedience." Believing Mulder to be dead, she tells Skinner she knows the men who killed Mulder and his father won't be punished. When Skinner says they will, she says icily, "With all due respect, sir, I think you overestimate your position in the chain of command." Scully returns to Mulder's desk, only to find the DAT tape containing the secret files gone.

Nicholas Lea, who plays Alex Krycek, was the former boyfriend of Melinda McGraw, who plays Melissa Scully. Asked how it felt to help shoot his girlfriend at the end of "The Blessing Way," he said, "I was just hoping she would speak to me when we got home."

The Cigarette-Smoking Man meets with other shadowy men in a private club, assuring them that the matter of the missing files is being handled and that the media attention will amount to "nothing more than a few scattered obituaries."

Scully visits her mother, breaking into tears. "I've made a terrible mistake," she tells her. "Dad would be so ashamed of me." She's later visited by the Lone Gunmen's Frohike, who shows her a news clipping about the Thinker—the computer hacker who first accessed the files—who has been murdered, execution-style.

Back in New Mexico, buzzards lead the Native Americans to Mulder, who's found buried under debris and badly injured, having escaped the boxcar, staying alive in underground tunnels. "Only the holy people can save the FBI man's life now," Albert says. "He is in their hands." In dreams Mulder is visited by Deep Throat, who urges him to go back and finish his work, and his father, who—echoing Albert's words—says, "You are the memory, Fox. It lives in you. If you were to die now the truth will die, and only the lies survive us." In his stupor, Mulder also sees an image of the aliens in the boxcar, being killed by a cyanide canister.

Returning to the FBI office to tell Skinner about the Thinker's death, Scully is scanned by a metal detector, which registers a small implant under the skin at the base of her neck. Removed by a doctor, the device looks like a tiny computer chip.

After three days, Mulder rouses. "Like a rising sun, I sensed in him a rebirth," Albert notes. Scully confides to her sister, Melissa, about the chip. Melissa encourages her to try to access the memory of her abduction, but Scully resists the hypnotherapy. Returning to her apartment, she sees Skinner suspiciously coming out of it, hurriedly speeding off. In her own dreams Scully sees Mulder, awakening with a start.

At the funeral service for Mulder's father, Scully encounters an older gentleman seen earlier with the Cigarette-Smoking Man, dubbed the Well-Manicured Man. He warns her that she's in real danger of being killed, perhaps by someone she knows. The man adds that his colleagues—a "consortium representing global interests"—are "acting impulsively." When she asks what his business is, he merely replies, "We predict the future, and the best way to predict the future is to invent it."

Mulder's mother returns home from the funeral to find Fox waiting for her. Elsewhere, Scully receives a call from Melissa but is wary due to the Well-Manicured Man's warning. Going to meet her instead of waiting at the apartment, Scully encounters Skinner, who takes her to Mulder's place so they can talk. Not trusting him, Scully pulls her weapon and holds Skinner at gunpoint. Meanwhile Melissa, mistaken for Scully, is shot entering Scully's apartment by the renegade Agent Krycek and another man, who have mistaken her for Dana.

"I came here to give you something," Skinner tells Scully, who eyes him skeptically. "I've got the digital tape." At that moment there are footsteps at the door, and Skinner uses the distraction to draw his own gun. It's a stalemate.

To be continued . . .

Forbes Angus played X's scientific accomplice in "Soft Light," and returns here as a doctor who removes an implant from Scully's neck.

BACK STORY: Despite this episode's enormous popularity, for David Duchovny "The Blessing Way" remains "a little bit of a disappointment" in terms of the pivotal role he thought the trilogy could have played in regard to Mulder's character. "I felt like that was probably the episode where I would have as an actor gotten to do a lot more, but as Chris wrote the show it became kind of a symbolic journey rather than a real one, and it was like other people took Mulder's journey for him," Duchovny says.

"I like the psychology, and I like the thinking that went into the episode as a viewer. As an actor, I felt like an opportunity passed me by. If I had to do any episode over again, it would be that one," he says, calling it "the greatest missed opportunity we had. You build a character over two years, and then tell the story through other people. I felt like it was removed, and if I had to do it over again I'd make that more personal."

"The Blessing Way" also introduces the Well-Manicured Man, the distinguished-looking older man to whom the Cigarette-Smoking Man must answer. He sits at the center of the Shadowy Syndicate, the conspiratorial cabal who are the string-pullers behind the government conspiracy. We see them here for the first time, in a smoke-filled room in a luxurious club in New York City.

Chris Carter disagrees, saying that being the "absent center" in the episode—as Duchovny has described it—was Mulder's proper role after the sweeping events that took place in the second season cliffhanger "Anasazi." "Sometimes being that character . . . someone who allows the other characters to say the things that need to be said about this journey, is the right way to do it, because for the character to say it himself becomes for me dramatically uninteresting," he suggests. For that reason, "The Blessing Way"—as the middle part of the trilogy—had to shift the dramatic weight from Mulder to Scully, Carter says, in order to set up what occurs in "Paper Clip."

Visual effects producer Mat Beck considers the lengthy sequence where Mulder hallucinates perhaps his most difficult assignment of the year. "That floating stuff was just a bitch," he says, noting that there were "four solid minutes of visual effects" and a lot of moving elements. "Brevity is the soul of visual effects," Beck adds, slightly altering an old adage.

The New Mexico locations were created at a rock quarry in Vancouver painted red with 1,600 gallons of paint. "It was just an incredible find," locations manager Louisa Gradnitzer says, with even the weather cooperating on the day of filming, as the sun broke through to truly approximate the Southwestern United States—one area deemed virtually impossible to duplicate in lush Vancouver. After painting the quarry, visual effects then inserted second-unit footage actually shot in New Mexico to complete the illusion.

Moreover, the reservation scenes were filmed at an abandoned mining town that had been flooded years earlier, making the ground rocky and barren. While there, the production team noticed the old mine eventually used as the setting where the thousands of files were housed in "Paper Clip." A Navajo sand painter was flown in to do the paintings—creating four of them in two days—and a real medicine man brought in as a technical adviser after some Native Americans complained about cultural inaccuracies in "Anasazi." Chris Carter subsequently attended a Native American peyote ritual in researching the episode, which he named after an actual chant.

The producers also considered it a major coup casting John Neville (whose credits include the title role in *The Adventures of Baron Munchausen*) as the latest in the show's string of uniquely named characters, the Well-Manicured Man.

"The Blessing Way" is loaded with irony and references to earlier moments in the series—among them having Krycek, played by Nicholas Lea, shoot Melissa Scully, portrayed by his then-girlfriend Melinda McGraw (with whom he'd worked previously on *The Commish*). Lea recalls that his attentiveness to her at the time prompted ribbing from the crew, since between takes he kept asking if the woman who had just been shot was comfortable or wanted a pillow. Mulder also talks in his sleep about wanting sunflower seeds, having discussed inheriting his father's taste for them in the second season episode "Aubrey."

A tag at the end of the episode reads "In Memoriam. Larry Wells. 1946–1995." Wells was a costume designer on the series.

lly and Skinner remain squared off at gunpoint, and the
gure at the door—whose footsteps were heard at the end of
e previous episode—turns out to be Mulder, who enters with
s gun drawn. Now it's a three-way standoff, and Skinner
ctan gives in. Sk ys th the evi-
ce, and M ter " Your c tte-smo frienc
led m f r for tha e." S r in ts the tape is

PAPER CLIP

EPISODE: 3X02

FIRST AIRED:
September 29, 1995

WRITTEN BY:
Chris Carter

EDITOR:
Heather MacDougall

DIRECTED BY:
Rob Bowman

GUEST STARS:
Mitch Pileggi (AD Walter
  Skinner)
Walter Gotell (Victor Klemper)
Melinda McGraw (Melissa Scully)
Sheila Larken (Margaret Scully)
Nicholas Lea (Alex Krycek)
William B. Davis (The Cigarette-
  Smoking Man)
John Neville (The Well-Manicured
  Man)
Tom Braidwood (Frohike)
Dean Haglund (Langly)
Bruce Harwood (Byers)
Floyd Red Crow Westerman
  (Albert Hosteen)
Rebecca Toolan (Mrs. Mulder)
Don S. Williams (1st Elder)

Robert Lewis (ER doctor)
Lenno Britos (Hispanic Man)

LOG LINE:
Mulder and Scully seek evidence of alien experimentation by Nazi war criminals while Skinner tries to bargain with the Cigarette-Smoking Man for their lives.

PRINCIPAL SETTINGS:
Washington, D.C.; West Virginia

SYNOPSIS:
Albert Hosteen speaks in voice-over about the birth of a white buffalo—"a powerful omen" in Native American lore, he says, meaning that "great changes were coming."

Scully and Skinner remain squared off at gunpoint, and the figure at the door—whose footsteps were heard at the end of the previous episode—turns out to be Mulder, who enters with his gun drawn. Now it's a three-way standoff, and Skinner reluctantly gives up his weapon. Skinner says he has the evidence, and Mulder tells him, "Your cigarette-smoking friend killed my father for that tape." Skinner insists the tape is "the only leverage we've got to bring these men to justice."

Scully's mother goes to the hospital, finding Melissa in an induced coma. Elsewhere, Mulder and Scully take a picture he'd found of his father taken in the early 1970s to the Lone Gunmen, who identify one of the men shown with him as Victor Klemper—one of several Nazi scientists allowed to escape to the United States after World War II in exchange for their research knowledge, under a secret deal dubbed Operation Paper Clip. That program, they add, was supposed to have been scrapped in the 1950s. At that point Frohike enters, telling Scully about her sister's condition.

The Well-Manicured Man and other members of the Shadowy Syndicate grill the Cigarette-Smoking Man for committing "a horrible mistake" in shooting the wrong woman, demanding that he produce the missing tape, which he says he will do by the next day.

Mulder and Scully visit Klemper, who cryptically advises them to journey to a mining company in West Virginia. He then calls the Well-Manicured Man to tell him of the visit. "Mulder is alive," the Well-Manicured Man announces. Knowing that the hospital is being watched and that Scully is in danger, Albert carries a message to Scully's mother, and prays over Melissa.

> In this episode we learn new birthdates for Mulder (10/13/61) and his sister, Samantha (11/21/65), as shown on the file folder Mulder discovers in the mine. It is also hinted that Fox Mulder was the original target of abduction, not his sister. Trivia buffs will note that Fox Mulder now shares a birthday with his creator, Chris Carter, and Samantha Mulder shares a birthday with Chris Carter's wife.

Skinner meets with the Cigarette-Smoking Man, saying he may have located the tape, cagily adding that it could fall into the wrong hands. "Do you want to work a deal? Is that what this is? I don't work deals," the Cigarette-Smoking Man snarls. Skinner merely says he should know of "certain potentialities."

At the mining site, Mulder and Scully find countless cabinets of medical files hidden there, including one for Scully and another for Mulder's missing sister, Samantha, with Mulder noticing her name has been pasted over his own. Suddenly the lights go out, and diminutive figures rush past Scully. Mulder ventures outside, and sees a massive spacecraft hovering over the facility. Scully observes a sharply defined alien silhouette, but in a flash of light, it's gone.

At that moment several armed men arrive, firing at Mulder as they chase him back into the mine. "We got a small army outside," he says, before the pair escape through a secret door. Meeting at a cafe, Skinner tells them he wants to trade the tape for their safety and reinstatement to the bureau. Mulder says they need the evidence to expose the truth and learn about his father and sister. "Is that answer worth your lives?" Skinner asks.

"It's obviously worth killing us for," Mulder replies.

Scully says they've lost control of the situation, maintaining that the truth is no good if they're dead and that she wants to see her sister. Mulder defers to her, and she tells Skinner to make the trade. If they don't honor the deal, Skinner assures them sternly, "I'll go state's evidence and testify, or they'll have to kill me, too."

Skinner stops to see Scully's mother at the hospital, pursuing a mysterious man into the stairwell, where he's ambushed by Krycek and two other men who pummel him and take the tape. When Krycek's accomplices leave him in the car, he realizes they mean to eliminate him, springing from the vehicle moments before it explodes.

Mulder and Scully return to see Klemper but are met by the Well-Manicured Man, who tells them he's dead. After the 1947 Roswell crash, he explains, Nazi scientists were brought to the U.S. to conduct experiments, trying to create an alien/human hybrid. Genetic data were gathered from millions of people through smallpox vaccinations, and Mulder's father—having threatened to expose the project—was kept silent via Samantha, who was abducted as insurance against him speaking out. "Why are you telling me this?" Mulder asks, even as Scully cautions him against trusting the man.

"It's what you want to know, isn't it?" he responds dryly.

Krycek calls the Cigarette-Smoking Man at the club, telling him he's alive and warning against any further attempts on his life. Meanwhile, the Cigarette-Smoking Man assures his compatriots that the digital tape was destroyed in a car bomb explosion and that no deal will be made with Skinner regarding Mulder and Scully.

This episode provides further insight into the Mulders' divorce: Bill Mulder lived in West Tisbury (Martha's Vineyard). Mrs. Mulder lives in Connecticut.

Unable to use a real white buffalo calf for this episode, the crew were forced to photograph a very light-colored calf and bleached it optically in postproduction.

Mulder goes to his mother, asking if his father had asked her to decide between him and Samantha. "No, I couldn't choose," she admits reluctantly, weeping. "It was your father's choice, and I hated him for it. Even in his grave, I hate him still."

The abandoned mining company building featured in this episode actually lies next door to the quarry where the second-season finale, "Anasazi," was filmed. The building served as headquarters for the rock quarry, which was painted red for that episode.

The Cigarette-Smoking Man meets with Skinner, telling him the tape is gone and that his own life may be in jeopardy. "This is where you pucker up and kiss my ass," Skinner counters, saying Albert has memorized the tape's contents and related it to twenty other men under his tribe's narrative tradition. "So unless you kill every Navajo in four states," Skinner informs him, "that information is available with a simple phone call." As the Cancer Man sits speechless, Skinner adds, "Welcome to the wonderful world of high technology."

Melissa Scully has died, and Dana mourns at her bedside. Mulder says they've both lost so much, but that he still believes the truth is out there—and can be found through their work on the X-Files. "I've heard the truth," Scully says with grim determination. "Now what I want are the answers."

BACK STORY: Mitch Pileggi still considers this one of the show's finest episodes, especially savoring the rather cathartic moment when Skinner tells the Cigarette-Smoking Man to "pucker up and kiss my ass." "That will be one of my favorite lines forever," he says. The scene also tends to draw enormous applause from fans when shown prior to introducing Pileggi at *The X-Files* conventions.

Stunt coordinator Tony Morelli, the show's "all-purpose bad guy," was one of the two men who joined Krycek in assaulting Skinner in the stairwell. Pileggi is fond of pointing out that his character did get a few licks in before being overcome, and that it took three men to subdue him. For his part, Nicholas Lea has playfully joked about giving his off-screen pal a rematch somewhere down the road.

What special effects chief David Gauthier calls "the mother of all mother ships" was actually a 180-foot-wide truss, adorned with 6,000 pounds of lighting, which the special effects crew managed to fly 275 feet in the air on a massive crane, creating the image of light streaming through from the outside. Because the contraption wobbled, however, the actual craft seen briefly by Mulder coming over the mountain ended up being entirely computer-generated, another case of visual and special effects working hand in hand.

The "aliens" glimpsed briefly running past Scully were mostly played by eight- and nine-year-old children, who quickly tired of their Halloween getups and soon began complaining. "They are so excited at first," notes Carter, who also used kids in suits during "Duane Barry," which he directed. "Then you get those costumes on them and about a half-hour later they're saying, 'Can I go home now?'"

In another example of the show's staggering attention to detail, the props department generated two drawers' worth of medical files using real DNA samples that were borrowed from a lab. With the mixture of Nazi scientists and the father-to-son legacy, Duchovny likens the mythic elements of these three episodes to another trilogy, *Star Wars*, as well as *Raiders of the Lost Ark*. There's also a touch of *Sophie's Choice* in the abduction of Samantha Mulder and the revelation about how and why she, and not her brother, was taken.

During filming, Duchovny had a hard time not chuckling when Tom Braidwood rushes up to hug him as Frohike, who had thought that Mulder died. During rehearsal Duchovny told Braidwood he should try to act the way Spock did when he discovered that Kirk was still alive in an episode of the original *Star Trek* series, "Amok Time."

"Paper Clip" carries a memoriam to Mario Mark Kennedy, 1966–1995, a major fan of the show who'd organized online sessions on the Internet. Kennedy died as a result of injuries he received in a car accident.

WHAT WORLD WAR II NAZI CRIMINAL IN "PAPER CLIP" GIVES MULDER AND SCULLY A CLUE WHERE TO FIND THE MASSIVE FILES HIDDEN IN AN ABANDONED MINE?

The Lone Gunmen tell Mulder that Victor Klemper performed outrageous "medical experiments" on prisoners of war and Jews in the concentration camps. The U.S. government supposedly sheltered him from the Nuremburg trials in order to exploit his "expertise"; according to Langly it was Klemper's knowledge of the human body's limits that enabled the Americans to win the space race. Klemper appears in a group photo taken at the mine, along with Mulder's father.

stocky youth plays a video game in an arcade when a
rawnier youngster, Darin Oswald, comes up and says he had
n playing there. The bully knocks Darin to the ground, at
ch point the lights go out. "Oh, man, you shouldn't have
e that," says Zero, Darin's friend. Unnerved, the bully
ds for his car but it shorts out and soon he begins spas-
g wildly as Darin watches him through the door. Mulder and

D.P.O.

EPISODE: 3X03

FIRST AIRED:

October 6, 1995

WRITTEN BY:

Howard Gordon

EDITOR:

Jim Gross

DIRECTED BY:

Kim Manners

GUEST STARS:

Giovanni Ribisi (Darin
    Peter Oswald)

Jack Black (Bart "Zero" Liquori)

Ernie Lively (Sheriff Teller)

Karen Witter (Sharon Kiveat)

Steve Makaj (Frank Kiveat)

Peter Anderson (Stan Buxton)

Kate Robbins (Darin's mom)

Mar Andersons (Jack Hammond)

Brent Chapman (Traffic Cop)

Jason Anthony Griffith (First
    Paramedic)

Bonnie Hay (Night Nurse)

LOG LINE:

Mulder and Scully investigate a series of deaths related to a teenage boy who can control lightning.

PRINCIPAL SETTING:

Connerville, Oklahoma

SYNOPSIS:

A stocky youth plays a video game in an arcade when a scrawnier youngster, Darin Oswald, comes up and says he had been playing there. The bully knocks Darin to the ground, at which point the lights go out. "Oh, man, you shouldn't have done that," says Zero, Darin's friend. Unnerved, the bully heads for his car, but it shorts out, and soon he begins spasming wildly as Darin watches him through the door.

Mulder and Scully arrive at the crime scene, where the boy is the fifth victim of an apparent lightning strike in that area. "Looks like his heart was cooked right in his chest," Mulder observes. The sheriff, Teller, is hostile to the agents' presence, suggesting that lightning was the cause. Mulder, however, isn't so sure, given that of 60 people killed by lightning strikes each year, 4 have died in this area alone. Beyond that, Mulder notes that all the victims are young men, adding to the bizarre nature of such a coincidence. "After all that we've just seen," Scully says, referring to previous episodes, "I hope you're not thinking this has anything to do with government conspiracies or UFOs."

The "Astadourian Lightning Observatory" is named for Mary Astadourian, Chris Carter's executive assistant. "Darin" Oswald is named for story editor Darin Morgan.

At the arcade Mulder and Scully meet Zero, who points out the game the latest victim was playing. All the high scores are by "D.P.O."—the same initials as the lone survivor of the five lightning strikes, Darin Oswald.

At the garage where he works, Darin encounters his boss's wife, Mrs. Sharon Kiveat, who's clearly uncomfortable around him. Her husband, Frank, says the FBI are coming to see Darin, and as they question him Mulder's cellular phone suddenly starts smoking. "It just got hot all of a sudden," he says.

"Bummer," Darin responds nonchalantly, walking away from them.

Alarmed by the FBI's presence, Zero goes to see Darin, who doesn't share his concern, instead calling up lightning to fry cows. "I'm in the mood for a little barbecue," he mumbles, getting hit by lightning and seeming to enjoy it.

Finding the dead cows, Teller brusquely suggests to Mulder and Scully that "your business here is finished," but Mulder finds a shoeprint melted into the ground. "This is the first lightning strike I've ever seen that left behind a footprint," Mulder says. The footprint has antifreeze in the boot's sole, providing a link to Darin because he works at the garage.

Darin amuses himself by changing traffic signals—eventually causing a crash among passing cars—while the agents "go see if the shoe fits," as Mulder puts it, finding that Darin wears the same shoe size as the imprint. In Darin's room they also find a picture of Sharon Kiveat hidden in a skin magazine.

The yearbook in Darin Oswald's closet contains photographs of X-Files director Kim Manners and prop master Ken Hawryliw on the page with Sharon Kiveat.

At the scene of the car crash Darin makes Frank collapse, and when the paramedics' equipment doesn't work, the boy uses his hands to jolt Frank's chest and get his heart beating again. "Rescue Nine-one-one," Darin says with a grin.

Mulder tries to question Sharon Kiveat at the hospital where her husband's been taken, but she's reluctant to talk. A glance at Darin's chart, meanwhile, shows an electrolyte imbalance that may explain his conductive powers. "He is lightning," Mulder says, "and we've got to get to him before he strikes again."

Questioning Darin but lacking the evidence to hold him, they go to see Sharon Kiveat, who admits Darin had a crush on her. Later, she began receiving unusual phone calls, and Darin told her he had "dangerous powers." The agents are surprised to find that Teller has released Darin. Darin, who believes Zero has betrayed him, goes to the arcade and zaps him with a lightning bolt. The agents return to the hospital to protect the Kiveats, and the power goes out. "He's

here," Mulder says.

Darin confronts Scully, her gun drawn. It's a standoff, but Sharon Kiveat leaves with him as he asks. Teller intervenes outside, and Sharon Kiveat flees while Darin kills the sheriff. Mulder pulls the woman to safety as lightning strikes Darin again, rendering him unconscious.

Restrained in a psychiatric hospital, Darin's tests are now normal, and the DA has "no idea how to begin building a case" against him. Darin stares blankly at the TV, changing channels without using the remote control until the episode itself clicks off.

BACK STORY: Director Kim Manners experienced a personal tragedy on the third day of filming this episode when his best friend and the friend's son died in a drowning accident in Mexico. "It blew my mind," Manners admits. "Shooting that was a shattered experience for me. I was not there in mind, but in body only." There was some consideration of having another director replace him, but Manners insisted on seeing things through.

Writer Howard Gordon also contends that the episode may have suffered somewhat contextually in that this stand-alone hour had to follow the epic nature of the "Anasazi"/"The Blessing Way"/ "Paper Clip" trilogy. "After you've had an unbelievable meal, where you've been dealing with the death of Scully's

WHAT WAS DARIN OSWALD'S FAVORITE GAME IN "D.P.O."?

Darin Peter Oswald is so annoyed to have his "Virtua Fighter II" game taken over when he leaves for a bathroom break that he kills the pushy pizza delivery boy with a lightning bolt.

sister and the death of Mulder's father—huge, huge issues—and the next week you find yourself in a video arcade in Oklahoma, it was sort of set up some way for disappointment," he says.

The episode itself drew its inspiration from a one-line concept card, "Lightning Boy," which had been tacked on a board in Carter's office as a possible episode since the first season. "Chris had an idea called 'Lightning Boy,' with nothing more than that there was a kid who could control lightning. We weren't even quite sure what he could do," notes Gordon, who says the key moment came when he connected the idea of that power as a metaphor for disenfranchised adolescence—answering Carter's constant question, "Why are we telling this story?"

Special effects coordinator David Gauthier rigged a "lightning machine," buried in the ground, for the sequence when Darin is struck. The actor stood on a small stand, with the riggings underneath capable of generating three million candlepower each. Mirrors were used to establish the effect of the lightning flaring up and outward, augmented by sparks and smoke. The machine itself actually produced enough heat to singe the grass.

The character of Teller was named after half of the magic/comedy duo Penn and Teller, notorious skeptics who doubt all aspects of the paranormal and had met with Carter about doing an episode of *The X-Files*. Although he couldn't find an appropriate vehicle for them, the skeptical sheriff seemed a fitting tribute. In terms of the cast,

putting the picture of Sharon Kiveat in an erotic magazine was a bit of an inside joke as well since the actress who played her, Karen Witter, once modeled for *Playboy*.

The old farmhouse featured as Darin's home is owned by a 94-year-old man named Vin who also let the producers use his cows as extras. When location manager Todd Pittson assured him he'd be paid for use of the cows, Vin—who keeps the beasts merely as pets—simply shrugged and responded, "They're here anyway." Built early in this century, the distinctive looking house has also appeared in such films as *Jumanji* and *Jennifer 8*.

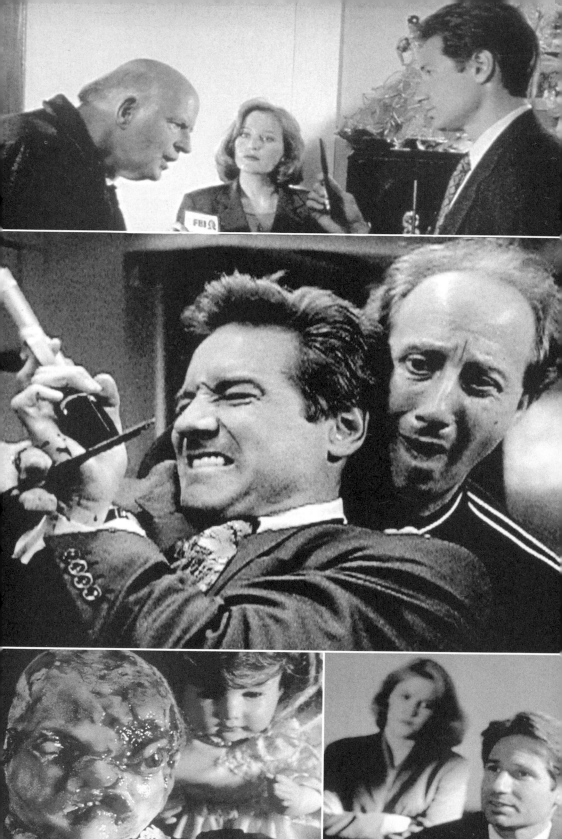

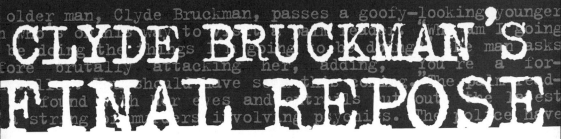

CLYDE BRUCKMAN'S FINAL REPOSE

EPISODE: 3X04

FIRST AIRED:
October 13, 1995

WRITTEN BY:
Darin Morgan

EDITOR:
Stephen Mark

DIRECTED BY:
David Nutter

GUEST STARS:
Peter Boyle (Clyde Bruckman)
Stu Charno (Puppet)
Frank Cassini (Detective Cline)
Dwight McFee (Detective Havez)
Alex Diakun (Tarot Dealer)
Karin Konoval (Madame Zelma)
Ken Roberts (Clerk)
Jaap Broeker (The Stupendous Yappi)
David McKay (Young Husband)
Greg Anderson (Photographer)

LOG LINE:
Mulder and Scully enlist the help of a man who can see when people will die while searching for a serial killer who preys upon fortune-tellers.

PRINCIPAL SETTING:
St. Paul, Minnesota

SYNOPSIS:

An older man, Clyde Bruckman, is in a liquor store. Walking out, he passes a goofy-looking younger man who's on his way to visit a fortune-teller. "Why am I going to be doing the things I'm going to be doing?" the man asks before brutally attacking her, adding, "You're a fortune-teller. You should have seen this coming."

The woman is found with her eyes and entrails cut out, the latest in a string of murders involving psychics. The police have summoned help, but they're unfamiliar with Mulder when he and Scully arrive; rather, they've called upon a TV psychic, the Stupendous Yappi, who prances around picking up "readings" before stopping abruptly. "Someone is blocking me," he says, to the shock of both Scully and Mulder, asking the latter to leave because of his negative energy. "I can't take you anywhere," Scully quips.

Bruckman is an insurance salesman, who

urges a young couple to buy a comprehensive life insurance policy because he foresees the husband's gruesome demise. The couple sits stunned and scared by Bruckman's revelation. "Mister, you really need to work on your closing technique," says the husband. Later, when Bruckman finds the body of the fortune-teller in a Dumpster, he tells Mulder and Scully details about it he couldn't possibly know. While skeptical about the Stupendous Yappi, Mulder suspects Bruckman can "see things about this crime." They take him to the crime scene and going into a sort of trance, Bruckman tells them they'll find another body the next day, which they do near a landmark Bruckman described.

Bruckman is reluctant to get involved, saying the killer will continue to kill whether he helps or not. "If the future is written," Mulder asks, "then why bother to do anything?"

"Now you're catching on," Bruckman replies flatly.

Testing Bruckman's abilities, Mulder realizes he can tell how people are going to die but has little practical information about the case. He does take them to the woods, where they find another body, oddly explaining that he became obsessed with how people die in the 1950s when singer the Big Bopper died after a coin flip won him a seat on an airplane—along with Buddy Holly and Ritchie Valens—that subsequently crashed. En route, Mulder and Bruckman have this memorable exchange:

Bruckman: "You know, there are worse ways to go, but I can't think of a more undignified one than autoerotic asphyxiation."

Mulder: "Why are you telling me that?"

Bruckman: "Look, forget I mentioned it. It's none of my business."

Bruckman says the killer will kill more people before he's caught. He even foresees Mulder's death. He envisions Mulder chasing the killer, who sneaks up behind him and slits his throat. Bruckman then gets a

The real Clyde Bruckman was a screenwriter for Buster Keaton and Harold Lloyd in the days of silent film; he committed suicide. Dwight McFee makes his fourth appearance as an X-Files guest actor, as Detective Havez; his character's name is based on another silent movie writer, Jean C. Havez. Detective Cline (Frank Cassini) is named for Eddie Cline, who directed several Buster Keaton comedies. The man under the wheels of Scully's car is named Claude Dukenfield; this is the real name of W. C. Fields (William Claude Dukenfield.) Finally, the name of Bruckman's hotel, "Le Damfino," echoes the name of a boat used by Buster Keaton in his movie The Boat.

WHAT DESSERT DID MULDER STEP IN DURING A SEQUENCE IN "CLYDE BRUCHMAN'S FINAL REPOSE"?

Banana cream pie. Clyde Bruckman foresees Mulder's encounter with the Puppet during a kitchen fight. In his vision, the Puppet attacks just as Mulder steps in a pie. Despite Mulder's urging him for more details, Bruckman is fixated on the flavor of the pie.

note from the killer saying he's going to murder him but has questions for him first. "I'll be dead before you catch this guy no matter what you do," Bruckman tells the agents.

Scully guards Bruckman in the hotel where they've taken him to protect him while the killer visits another psychic. Though she's doubtful, Bruckman tells Scully he sees them in bed together, in "a very special moment neither of us will ever forget." Rushing to investigate the latest murder, Mulder and Scully pass the hotel bellhop, who is in fact the killer. When he brings room service to Bruckman's room, they touch the same object and recognize each other, chatting calmly. The bellhop tells Bruckman he doesn't understand why he's committed such horrible acts. "Because you're a homicidal maniac," Bruckman responds. Surprised emerging from the bathroom, the agent left with Bruckman is killed.

Scully suddenly realizes she'd seen the bellhop at the other crime scenes and that he's the murderer. Mulder chases him just as in Bruckman's vision, but as he sneaks up behind him Mulder spins and blocks the knife. Mulder loses his footing, but Scully arrives and shoots the bellhop just in time. "Hey," the bellhop says, with a look of genuine surprise, "that's not the way it's supposed to happen."

They return to find Bruckman dying from an overdose of pills. Scully sits at his bedside, deeply moved, just as he pictured she would. Bruckman has left her a note, asking if she would like the small dog that belonged to his neighbor, an old woman who passed away the night before. That night Scully ponders the day's events at home as she pets the dog, seeing a TV ad for the Stupendous Yappi's psychic hotline. Scully picks up the phone, pauses, and then heaves it against the set, which goes black.

BACK STORY: David Duchovny immediately points to this hour as one of his favorites during the third season. "I loved 'Clyde Bruckman,'" he says.

Clyde Bruckman, in his poker game with Scully, is holding the Dead Man's Hand—aces and eights. This is the same hand Wild Bill Hickok was holding when he was shot to death in Deadwood, South Dakota. But Wild Bill was holding only two pair; Clyde has him beat with a full house.

The part of the Stupendous Yappi was written specifically for Duchovny's stand-in, Dutch-born actor Jaap Broeker, who briefly reprised the role in another Darin Morgan–scripted episode later in the season, the equally bizarre "Jose Chung's *From Outer Space*." "He [Morgan] saw me on the set and came to me and said, 'Do you mind if I write you a part?' I thought that he was joking," Broeker recalls, noting that some time later Chris Carter walked by and said, "Hello, Yappi" after the script was turned in.

Broeker took a week off from his stand-in duties to prepare for the role. "We had just a blast doing it," he says. "It was great. I'm grateful to Darin, and to David and Gillian." Anderson did have one problem with Broeker's appearance, frequently laughing when he darted up to her with his hyperactive eyebrows arched.

"Clyde Bruckman" ran more than 10 minutes too long in its first cut and thus had to be pared down considerably, including two scenes between Peter Boyle and Gillian Anderson. "So many gags were lost. It's a shame," says continuity/script supervisor Helga Ungurait. Morgan experienced the same problems with his first script, "Humbug," and made a point not to repeat it on subsequent episodes. "After 'Humbug,' I was always conscious of being too long," he notes. "'Clyde Bruckman' was the disaster, because it was humongously long."

Morgan adds that he drew his inspiration for the episode in part from his own dark mood at the time he wrote it. "I was feeling somewhat suicidal, so I thought I'd have the main character commit suicide at the end," he says dryly. The joke about "autoerotic asphyxiation" grew out of previous gags about Mulder's interest in erotica as well as a book Morgan had read on homicide investigations, which actually had a section on autoerotic asphyxiation, which is often misinterpreted as suicide. Looking at the pictures, Morgan concluded, "There's just no dignity there. It's just a terrible way to be found dead."

Boyle wasn't familiar with *The X-Files* and didn't realize just how demanding the part would be, having been drawn to the episode after reading the script. As a result, director David Nutter spent two to three hours over that weekend with Boyle, talking to him about the show and his character. Nutter calls it "one of the most enjoyable shows I've ever done," adding that the record for running long still belongs to another episode he directed, "Beyond the Sea," which ran 16 minutes over.

Chris Carter has resisted casting big-name guest stars on the show despite interest from some performers who are fans of the series. The producer's mantra remains "It's only as scary as it is believable," feeling that extremely recognizable actors make it more difficult to lose oneself in the show's world. Boyle is a marquee actor, Carter concedes, but such a gifted character actor that he didn't upset that dynamic.

Visual effects producer Mat Beck and special makeup effects maven Toby Lindala worked out an elaborate scheme for the stages of the dream scene in which Bruckman decomposes. The skeleton rib cage was composed of copper pipe, so as heat wore away the bogus skin, gelatin melted around the ribs. Eight different stages were put into play to create the effect, fading from the actor in makeup to a dummy made up by Lindala and finally a completely computer-generated skeleton, assembled in a series of morphing shots.

"Of course, half of it worked and half of it didn't," Beck says of initial plans for the process, adding that the episode "was another down-to-the-wire one" in terms of time, with a mad scramble to rerecord the sound on that sequence—when Bruckman says "And then . . . I wake up"—inserting the pause just right so the moment worked as intended in the script.

Stu Charno, who appeared in this episode as the Puppet/killer, is married to Sara Charno, who was previously a writer on the show.

WHO WAS CLYDE BRUCKMAN'S FAVORITE MUSICIAN?

The Big Bopper. It was the death of his boyhood musical hero that first got Bruckman thinking about the remarkable and unique series of coincidences that led to the Bopper's death in a plane crash with Buddy Holly. According to Bruckman, his psychic ability to foretell the manner of a person's death stemmed from this seminal event.

ut to death, and his wife, Danielle, swears she'll never
h says flatly when they come for him. Strapped into the
venge all the petty tyranny and the cruelty I have suf-
ie. As he continues to rant, the warden simply says, "Fry
nd Scull... ...e prison, ...e ...d... been found
ugh the pri...n ...at Neech would be reincarnated, Mulder
e explained." ...amining the ...uard' ...ody Scully finds it

THE LIST

EPISODE: 3 X 0 5

FIRST AIRED:

October 20, 1995

WRITTEN AND DIRECTED BY:

Chris Carter

EDITOR:

Heather MacDougall

GUEST STARS:

Bokeem Woodbine
  (Sammon Roque)

Badja Djola (Napoleon
  "Neech" Manley)

John Toles-Bey (John Speranza)

Ken Foree (Parmelly)

April Grace (Danielle Manley)

J. T. Walsh (Warden Brodeur)

Greg Rogers (Daniel Charez)

Mitchell Kosterman (Fornier)

Paul Raskin (Jim Ullrich)

Denny Arnold (Key Guard)

Craig Brunanski (Guard)

Joseph Patrick Finn (Chaplain)

LOG LINE:

A death row inmate makes good on his promise to return from the dead and kill five people who wronged him.

PRINCIPAL SETTING:

Leon County, Florida

SYNOPSIS:

Prisoner Neech Manley is about to be put to death, and his wife, Danielle, swears she'll never love another man. "Gotta go now," Neech says flatly when they come for him. Strapped into the chair, Neech says, "I will return to avenge all the petty tyranny and the cruelty I have suffered," announcing that five men will die. As he continues to rant, the warden simply says, "Fry him," and the switch is thrown.

Mulder and Scully reach the prison, where a guard has been found dead in Neech's cell. Word spread through the prison that Neech would be reincarnated, Mulder notes, and the guard's death "cannot be explained." Examining the guard's body, Scully finds it decomposing with maggots around the face, eating at the flesh. Another inmate, Speranza, says Neech has returned. "The man was electric," he says. "Pure energy."

In Neech's cell, two flies crawl on the

stained pillow. Wandering out into the hall alone, Scully is grabbed by a man in the shadows. "I know who he's gonna kill," he says. "There's a list. One of the cons has it. A man named Roque." Shaken, Scully leaves, but later a prisoner opens a paint can and finds the head of one of the guards inside, with maggots on it as well.

The medical examiner tells Scully the first victim's lungs were filled with larva of the green bottle fly and that the man suffocated

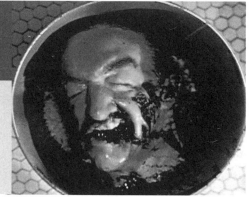

WHAT X-FILES PRODUCER MADE A CAMEO APPEARANCE IN "THE LIST"?

Joseph Patrick Finn's name appeared twice in the credits for this episode: once at the beginning, in his role as line producer, and once at the end, in his role as the prison chaplain.

or drowned. Mulder questions Roque, who wants a transfer out of the prison in exchange for the three remaining names on Neech's list. The warden, who insists he won't make a deal, enters his office to find the guard's headless body sitting in his chair.

Perusing Manley's diary, Mulder notes that he was obsessed by reincarnation, but Scully remains doubtful. Asked if Neech has come back, his widow, Danielle, says, "I think if anyone could, it'd be Neech." At the prison, a guard takes Roque into the showers, where the warden waits for him, wanting to know who's on the list. "You're number five," Roque says defiantly after the warden punches him. "How's it feel to be on death row, Warden?" Roque is later found dead in the showers, while the guard who warned Scully, Parmelly, is seen kissing Danielle.

Mulder doubts that Roque was on Neech's list and asks for the name of the executioner, which the warden reluctantly provides. They find the man dead in his home, his face and neck decomposed and covered with maggots like the other victims.

Speranza, the other prisoner, says he's seen Neech since his death and that Roque wasn't on his list. The agents visit Manley's former lawyer, Danny Charez, while the warden tells Speranza he'll get his case reopened if he'll "call off the dogs." Alone, Charez rests on his couch, looking up to glimpse someone forcing a pillow down onto his face. Later, Parmelly comes to Danielle's house. She's angry that he's there because she knows the FBI is staking out the place. "A woman gets lonely, sometimes she can't wait around for her man to be reincarnated," Scully muses, believing Parmelly to be responsible for the killings. Told of Charez's death, Scully wonders if he's the fifth victim, which both Mulder and the warden seem to doubt.

Danielle awakens, seeing Neech by her bed. She follows with a gun, finding Parmelly. "You're him," she says, shooting him before the agents can enter. As with Roque, the warden takes Speranza to the showers. "Neech's list got one man left to die," the convict says, as we hear the warden beating him.

Assuming the case to be over, the agents prepare to leave, but Mulder stops the car, saying it doesn't make sense "laying it all on Parmelly." "It's over," Scully says, not entirely convinced herself. "Let's just go home." Slowly, reluctantly, they drive off, even as the warden passes them, swatting at a fly that lands in the back seat. Looking in his rearview mirror, the warden sees Neech behind him, grabbing his throat as the car careens into a tree.

The warden lies dead, a single fly crawling near his mouth.

BACK STORY: Carter admits to going over budget (as he puts it, "We broke the piggy bank") in building the prison set from scratch, but he justifies the expense by noting that the set has already

been recycled in subsequent episodes (including "Teso dos Bichos" and "Talitha Cumi") as well as rented out to other productions in Vancouver as the only prison set in town.

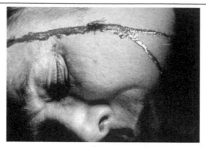

"It's really come in handy. It's already paid for itself and then some," he says. "We use a lot of prisons on this show."

Construction coordinator Rob Maier's crew had just 10 days to build the set, one of the biggest jobs of the year. In addition, each part can be unbolted, taken apart, and reassembled, despite standing nearly two stories high and fully supporting a man's weight on its upper level.

This episode also represented a departure in terms of the show's design, using green colors and underwater sounds to establish the submarine-like atmosphere Carter sought in the jail. "'The List' was an attempt to do something different," says cinematographer John Bartley, who considers the episode unique in terms of its look compared to other installments of The X-Files.

On the downside, virtually everyone would be just as pleased if they never saw or smelled maggots again, including the stars. "So far the maggots have been the hardest to work with," Anderson says, referring to the assortment of creatures featured on the show. "They're just the most disgusting things you can imagine."

Not everyone felt quite so squeamish. Special effects makeup supervisor Toby Lindala didn't have time to do a full-body replica of the first victim found on the autopsy table covered with maggots. As a result, the actor, Denny Arnold, simply had some makeup applied to make him look like a corpse, then had to lie there with actual maggots crawling on him. Lindala recalls the actor taking the ordeal good-naturedly, lying prone on the table and yelling, "If any of those little bastards get anywhere near my mouth, I'm going to eat them!" Rice was used in place of the maggots in some instances, but the bugs actually did have to be placed on the prop bodies.

Despite a lack of flash relative to other stunts performed on the show, stunt coordinator Tony Morelli says the final car crash—when the warden careens headfirst into a tree—was the most harrowing action sequence he undertook during the third season. "I just strapped myself in and went for it," says the former kickboxing champion.

The writing staff points to "The List" as being noteworthy in that nothing really gets solved, inasmuch as Mulder and Scully walk away with the wrong solution even though Mulder isn't entirely satisfied by pinning the crimes on Parmelly. In Carter's case, the fifth time also seems to be the charm: Carter received a Directors Guild of America nomination for "The List," having garnered a prime-time Emmy Award nomination for writing "Duane Barry," the fifth episode of the show's second season, which he also wrote and directed.

Names of fans, friends, high school classmates, and former colleagues frequently find their way into episodes, and "The List" is no exception. Here, the executioner bears the same moniker (Perry Simon) as an NBC executive the producer knew during his days producing for that network.

ACTOR MITCHELL KOSTERMAN RECALLS A MEMORABLE FEAST CATERED BY CHRIS CARTER FOR THE CAST AND CREW WHILE CARTER WAS DIRECTING "THE LIST":

"The lunch break was at six in the evening. We were on the grounds of a shut-down mental hospital, with lots of lawn and leafy trees. There was a crisp white Arab-style tent set up on the grass.

"People were lined up going into the tent. At the entrance there were four people in costumes reflecting the time of the French Revolution. The food being served was roast quail, sea bass, vol au vent, and some kinda mashed-potato-in-a-bird's-nest thingy. Just inside the tent were two large salad and bread tables.

"In the middle of the bread table was a head.

"Well, it was actually some guy with his head poked through a hole in the table. He had a thick accent and was issuing humorous epithets to the diners as they took the bread, and often shouted, 'Let them eat cake!'"

Interestingly enough, it was Mitchell Kosterman's character (the guard, Fornier) who wound up losing his head. . . .

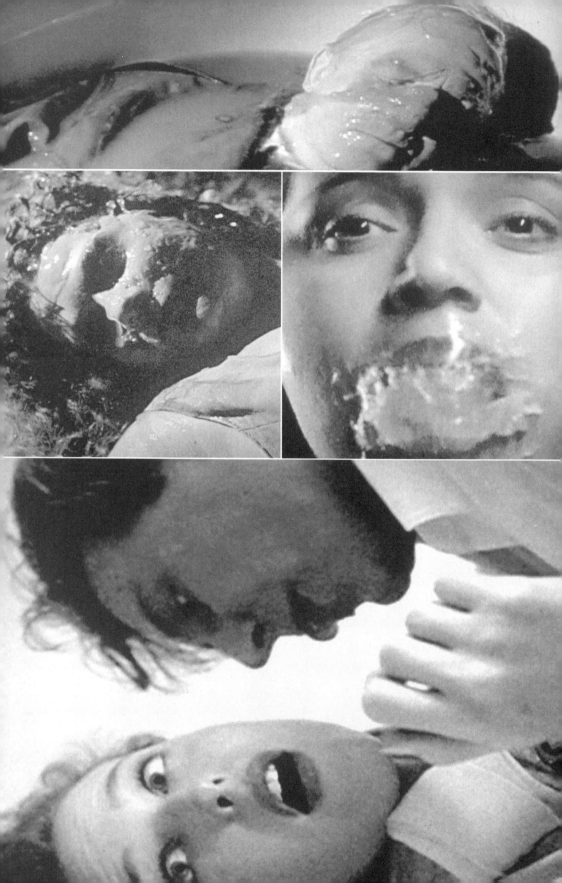

woman, Lauren, sits in a car with a man she's meeting fo:
first time after three months corresponding on-line. Whe:
y kiss she pulls back gasping, her mouth foaming. The nex
, the police find the car with her disfigured body inside.
lder and Scully are call tective Cross, wit
lder saying four wo sly disappeared i
ssissippi and the o bo wa similarly decomposed.

2SHY

EPISODE: 3X06

FIRST AIRED:

November 3, 1995

WRITTEN BY:

Jeffrey Vlaming

EDITOR:

Jim Gross

DIRECTED BY:

David Nutter

GUEST STARS:

Timothy Carhart (Virgil Incanto)

Catherine Paolone (Ellen
   Kaminsky)

James Handy (Detective Alan
   Cross)

Kerry Sandomirsky (Joanne Steffen)

Aloka McLean (Jesse Landis)

Suzy Joachim (Jennifer Workman)

Glynis Davies (Monica Landis)

Randi Lynne (Lauren Mackalvey)

William MacDonald (Agent
   Dan Kazanjian)

Brad Wattum (Patrolman)

LOG LINE:

Mulder and Scully track a serial killer who preys on lonely, overweight women via the Internet.

PRINCIPAL SETTING:

Cleveland, Ohio

SYNOPSIS:

A woman, Lauren, sits in a car with a man she's meeting for the first time after three months corresponding online. When they kiss she pulls back gasping, her mouth foaming. The next day, the police find the car with her disfigured body inside.

Mulder and Scully are called in by a Detective Cross. Mulder indicates that four women previously disappeared in Mississippi and the one body found was similarly decomposed. Because each woman answered a personal ad, he wants to find out if Lauren was also a "lonely heart."

Elsewhere, the killer, Virgil Incanto, chats online with another woman named Ellen. She's afraid to meet him, but he prods her, typing back, "You can't hide behind your computer forever." The session is interrupted by Virgil's landlady, Monica, who says she knows that he's a writer and wonders if he'd look at her work. Virgil agrees to but then abruptly shuts the door in her face.

Preparing to perform an autopsy on Lauren, Scully pulls the drawer out to find that the body has almost totally liquefied, with nothing left but a skeleton. Meanwhile, a friend of Lauren's tells Mulder Lauren had met a man, "2Shy," in the "Big and Beautiful" section of an online chat room. "He knew exactly what to say," she notes, somewhat sheepishly admitting that she saved the letters herself.

Mulder surmises the killer has moved from personal columns to the Internet, having opened an account with a credit card from one of his previous victims. The agents put out a localized online warning, prompting Ellen's friend to dissuade her from meeting Virgil. Lab results find a digestive enzyme, like stomach acid, on Lauren's body, and an absence of fatty tissue. In addition, the medical examiner weighed the body at 122 pounds, when Lauren's friend told Mulder she weighed over 165 pounds.

Kerry Sandomirsky (Joanne) played Tracy, the retarded girl in "Roland"; Glynis Davies makes her third appearance on The X-Files as Virgil Incanto's luckless landlady.

Stood up at the restaurant where he was to meet Ellen, Virgil leaves in desperation, picking up a slightly overweight prostitute. When she refuses to kiss him, Virgil tries to force her, and she claws his hand, revealing red pulp beneath the skin. Another prostitute surprises him as he feeds on the woman, causing Virgil to flee.

Virgil's letters to Lauren include lines from 16th-century Italian poems, prompting Mulder to conclude the killer has an academic background along those lines. The skin sample from under the hooker's fingernails also shows a lack of oils or essential fatty acids, prompting Mulder to theorize that the killer isn't psychotic but rather acting on a physical need, seeking to replenish those chemicals. Scully thinks it's a reach to posit that the killer is "some kind of fat-sucking vampire," but Mulder suggests he may be a genetically different human being. Though Scully acknowledges that scorpions do predigest food by regurgitating onto their prey, she adds, "I don't know too many scorpions who surf the Internet."

Cross assembles a list of 38 potential suspects from academic circles, and they begin checking them. Cross shows up at Virgil's place, and they exchange a look when the detective notices the bandage on Virgil's hand.

Ellen has apologized to Virgil via E-mail, suggesting they try to meet again. The two have dinner, and he manipulates her into driving him back to his apartment. Virgil invites her up, but as they talk in the car he sees the light on in his unit and quickly sends her off—his landlady, Monica, having let herself in when the manuscript she brought him wouldn't fit under the door. To her horror, Monica finds Cross's decomposing corpse in the bathtub, recoiling as Virgil emerges behind her.

Monica's 12-year-old daughter, Jesse, who is blind, goes to Virgil's apartment looking for her mother, dialing 911 after smelling her mom's perfume inside. The FBI now has Virgil's name, but there's no other record of his existence. Mulder suggests they trace him through his computer files, which an agent must gradually reconstruct to reveal names of his chat partners. "These are all his victims," Mulder says, calling the readout "a regular grocery list."

The FBI sends a warning to those on the list and is able to reach all but two, one of them being Ellen. Virgil has gone to see her, and she lets him in, stalling for time when she receives the FBI warning—until Virgil spots an artist's rendering of him that's on the computer reflected in the mirror. Mulder and Scully break into Ellen's place and find her gasping on the floor, with Mulder chasing a figure running down the street that turns out to be merely a teenage graffiti vandal. Virgil is still in the apartment, surprising Scully, who fights back but is ultimately knocked down, fending Virgil off until a shot rings out, dropping him. Ellen, injured but angry, holds the smoking gun.

A week later Virgil sits in detention and appears weak, his skin scaly and flaky. Mulder says 47 women are missing in 5 states and asks if he can give their families peace of mind. "They're all mine," he says dispassionately.

Virgil Incanto's name evokes the Italian Renaissance poets he translates: in Dante Alighieri's (1265–1321) Inferno, the poet's guide through the seven circles of hell is the Roman poet Virgil. The terza rima verses (a rhyme scheme Dante invented) are divided into long sections called cantos. One of the titles Mulder reels off to Detective Cross is "La Vita Nuova" (The New Life), one of Dante's more famous books.

Another title cited by Mulder is Baldassare Castiglione's (1478–1529) book Il Cortegiano, a work on courtly behavior by one of the Renaissance's most famous ambassadors. In the book, two courtiers discuss the best ways of, among other things, wooing a woman.

"When you look at me you see a monster," he tells Scully after Mulder's left, "but I was just feeding a hunger."

"You're more than a monster," Scully replies. "You didn't just feed on their bodies. You fed on their minds." As she exits, Virgil mutters something in Italian, then repeats it in English: "The dead are no longer lonely."

BACK STORY: David Duchovny's photo double, Steve Kiziak, was "discovered" in true Hollywood fashion during the technical survey for this episode. Locations manager Louisa Gradnitzer noticed Kiziak—an electrician's apprentice who'd just moved to Vancouver—coming out of a Starbucks coffee bar, pointing out his unerring resemblance to *The X-Files* star right down to his walk. Then director David Nutter took over. "David Nutter starts yelling, 'Hey you! Stop! We've got to talk to you!' from the window of the bus," chuckles assistant locations manager Rick Fearon.

"I think he thought we were going to abduct him, or try to sell him car speakers," Nutter says.

Some crew members nicknamed "2Shy" the "lick me–kill me" episode. The writers admit they did contemplate whether the notion of Internet lonely hearts might put off a segment of the show's loyal audience, but they credit Chris Carter with keeping his eye focused on telling a good story and steeling himself against being distracted by such considerations. "These chat rooms on the Internet are filled with people who are pretending to be what they aren't," Carter observes. The show examines that phenomenon, he says, commenting not on *The X-Files*' fans but rather on people who might be, to quote the song, "looking for love in all the wrong places."

Nutter also points to a terrific performance by Timothy Carhart as the killer. "I've been really fortunate about getting a character in these

stand-alone shows that can become something quite special," says the director, whose 15 episodes include "Beyond the Sea" (with a memorable turn by Brad Dourif), "Irresistible" (about a death fetishist played by Nick Chinlund), and "Ice."

Despite its dour tone, this show produced another off-camera comedic highlight when Mulder and Scully's stand-ins inadvertently walked into the wrong condominium. The scene called for the two to walk across a patio and through a door, but because all the units looked the same, the pair accidentally stepped into the next-door neighbor's place—several times—while the stunned couple entertained dinner guests. "They (the couple) didn't even say anything," laughs Gradnitzer, who sent the hostess an apologetic card and flowers.

While it might have appeared dire, Anderson describes her bathroom tussle with the killer as "fun." The actress enjoys performing her own stunts when possible, having been unable to do so during her pregnancy and its aftermath, "when I was still getting back into my body." Though she had relatively few chances to roll around with homicidal maniacs during the third season, "when I get the opportunity to I enjoy it."

Some of the substance secreted by the killer was devised by David Gauthier, "doctoring up" a material called Ultra-slime used in such movies as *Ghostbusters*. The main portion, however, came from a veterinary product called J-Lube that was mixed with food products and thus "essentially edible," says Gauthier. He even tested the goo by putting it on the face of assistant Andrew Sculthorp, who calls it "probably the most distasteful thing I've ever had to do."

WHAT VITAL COMPONENT WAS NOT PART OF LAUREN MACKALVEY'S BODY IN "2SHY"?

Agent Scully is surprised to learn from her lab report that most of Mackalvey's body fat (adipose tissue) is missing.

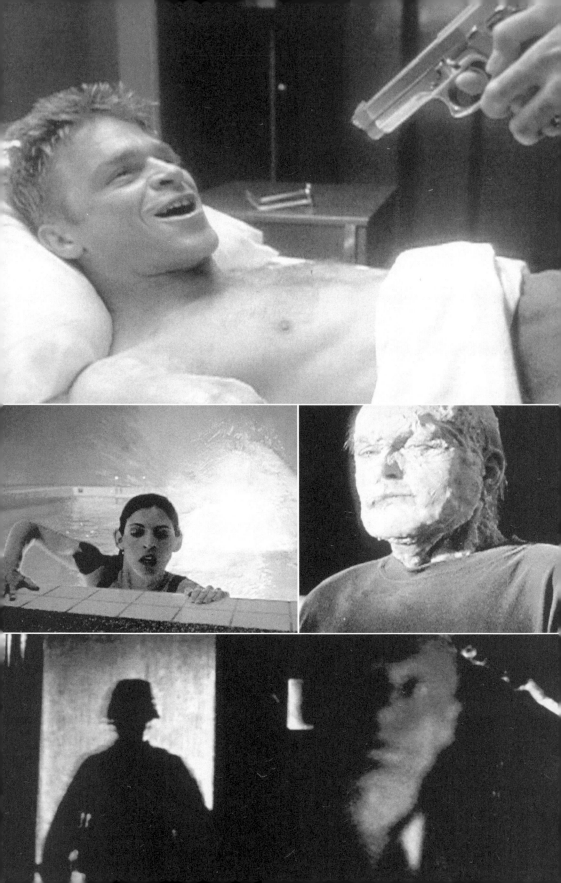

THE WALK

king to a doctor in a military hospital about his three
cide attempts," Lt. Colonel Stans explains obliquely, "He
't let me die." Left alone, Stans heads to the hydrother-
room, bolts the door, and leaps into the scalding water.
bolts, open, allowing stans to be saved
pite being and horribly mulder ully question
ns, who discusses a presence looking like a soldier that

EPISODE: 3X07

FIRST AIRED:
November 10, 1995

WRITTEN BY:
John Shiban

EDITOR:
Stephen Mark

DIRECTED BY:
Rob Bowman

GUEST STARS:
Thomas Kopache (Gen. Thomas
    Callahan)
Willie Garson (Quinton "Roach"
    Freely)
Don Thompson (Lt. Col. Victor
    Stans)
Nancy Sorel (Capt. Janet Draper)
Ian Tracey (Sgt. Leonard "Rappo"
    Trimble)
Paula Shaw (Ward Nurse)
Deryl Hayes (Army Doctor)
Rob Lee (Amputee)
Andrea Barclay (Mrs. Callahan)
Beatrice Zeilinger (Burly Nurse)

LOG LINE:
A suicide attempt and subsequent murders at
a military hospital bring Mulder and Scully
into contact with a quadruple amputee veteran
who may have the power of astral projection.

PRINCIPAL SETTING:
Ft. Evanston, Maryland

SYNOPSIS:

Talking to a doctor in a military hospital
about his three suicide attempts, Lt. Colonel
Stans explains obliquely, "He won't let me die."
Left alone, Stans heads to the hydrotherapy
room, bolts the door, and leaps into the scalding
water. The bolts, however, fly open, allowing
Stans to be saved despite being burned horribly.

Mulder and Scully question Stans, who discusses a presence looking like a soldier that
killed his family and continues to torment
him. The questioning is interrupted by
Captain Janet Draper, the aide to General
Callahan, who asks them to suspend the investigation. Down the hall, amputees meet in a
therapy group. One of them, Rappo, who was
wounded during the Gulf War, gets angry,
saying they're not normal and there's no way
the therapist can know how he feels. The
orderly, Roach, takes Rappo back to his room,
saying quietly that he's worried about the FBI.

Deryl Hayes, playing an Army psychiatrist, was a CIA operative in "Shadows."

Mulder and Scully meet with General Callahan, who seems hostile toward them. Scully thinks he's protecting his men—including another soldier believed to have killed his family, then himself. Mulder, however, can't understand why Stans would try to commit suicide and leave the only door in the room unlocked.

Alone, the general hears the ghostly voice that previously spoke to Stans, which says, "Your time has come, killer," as his answering machine begins making eerie sounds.

Captain Draper takes a swim, but an unseen presence grabs her and yanks her under the water. She's found dead with bruises on her neck and shoulders. Mulder warns the general that his family may be in danger, suggesting the pattern fits that of Stans's phantom killer. Alarmed, the general admits to hearing the strange sounds on his answering machine the night before.

At home, the general's son, Trevor, sees the shadow, and the answering machine there plays the same eerie messages. Scully spots a figure running through the yard, but by the time they get outside he's gone. Back at the hospital, Roach tells Rappo he won't help him anymore. The FBI soon finds Roach's fingerprints on mail addressed to each of the victims. "We've got him," Scully says, arresting Roach.

Elsewhere, the general's son plays in his backyard, until a figure suddenly explodes from the sand, burying the boy underneath.

"I didn't kill anybody," Roach insists. "I'm just the mailman." He points them toward Rappo, a quadruple amputee, who twitches as if in some kind of trance. Roach begins to panic, and they find him dead in his cell, a bedsheet stuffed down his throat. Mulder believes Rappo is practicing some form of astral projec-

The facial shield worn by Col. Stans is actually used for burn patients to protect the delicate subdermal layer of skin exposed by burns. Patients this badly burned lose the protection of their own skin and can become prey to any passing bacterium or virus.

tion, noting that the astral body is said to have greater strength than the corporeal one. Roach needed to acquire objects for Rappo to establish a link to a place, which is why he referred to himself as "Rappo's mailman." Played backwards, the general's messages repeat "Your time has come, killer."

Mulder questions Rappo, accusing him of the murders, but he laughs off the charge. Later, the general sees an image of Rappo, following a trail of blood to find his wife dead. The general goes to see Stans, saying that he was right, that their tormentor "won't let us die."

"I know who he is," Stans says.

The general goes to Rappo, who acknowledges killing his wife, "and the boy, too." Rappo urges the general to shoot him, but he fires over his head, telling him, "You're going to have to suffer like the rest of us." The agents find Rappo in a trance-like seizure while the

Actor Ian Tracey is not a quadruple amputee; in reality, his arms and legs were hidden by clever costuming and placement, while makeup artist Toby Lindala added prosthetics to give him "stumps."

general takes the elevator to the basement, where jets of steam fill the room, revealing a human shape that casts him against the wall. Mulder follows, only to be catapulted across the room by the presence himself.

While this is going on, Stans locks himself in Rappo's room, forcing a pillow over the amputee's face. Mulder sees the shape rushing toward him through the mist, but as Rappo dies it disappears. In voice-over, Mulder says no physical evidence linked Rappo to the deaths but that his family's request for burial in Arlington National Cemetery was denied. War destroyed his body, Mulder observes, as Stans gives the general his mail, then slowly ambles down the hallway. "What destroyed those parts of him that make us human beings, those better angels of our nature, I cannot say."

WHAT METHOD DID GENERAL CALLAHAN'S MYSTERIOUS CALLER IN "THE WALK" USE TO MASK THE MESSAGE LEFT ON THE ANSWERING MACHINE?

The message was recorded backward. In the music industry, "backwards masking" has occasionally been used to hide "secret" messages; more often the "messages" heard when a tape is played backward are coincidental. But General Callahan's tape revealed Sgt. "Rappo" Trimble threatening the general's life.

BACK STORY: The special effects department rigged the shot where the general's assistant drowns in the pool by securing a cable to the bottom that pulled the actress down. Mat Beck and David Gauthier also teamed up to create the image of a wave launching over the woman as she clings to the side of the pool. "Mat and I seem to work relatively closely," Gauthier says. "I get an idea of what he can do, and he has an idea of what I can do." Similarly, one of the crew members was completely buried in sand and then had to burst out of the ground in the scene where the boy gets killed, with Beck optically enhancing the effect after the fact. The sequences where Rappo tosses Mulder and the general across the room utilized a device called an Air-Ram, which employs compressed air and when triggered creates the effect of someone being catapulted.

Beck remembers running into another last-minute buzzsaw on this episode in terms of accomplishing the visual effects in time. "It was Wednesday at ten o'clock [at night], and we had a computer-generated man that did not look good," he chuckles, as technicians worked through the night to correct the image.

Writer John Shiban got the idea for this episode watching an old Marlon Brando movie, *The Men*. "It just popped into my head that the strongest emotion for this guy is just to get up and walk—that's the one thing he can't do, and the one thing he wants the most," he explains. "The astral projection thing just kind of fit. Then came the research."

Shiban also admits there was some concern about killing the general's young son, though "it didn't bother me," he adds with a laugh. "There were certain people on the staff who felt that was extreme, who didn't want to see that. I felt the whole idea behind the story was one of empathy—this guy wanted his CO to feel how he feels: 'You took my whole life away. I've got nothing.' The only way to do that was to take everything away from the man, and what worse thing to lose than a child? It's horrific, but to me that's what a horror story is about."

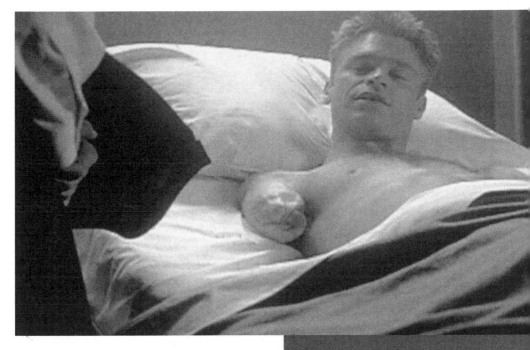

HOW DID "RAPPO" MANAGE TO EXACT HIS REVENGE IN "THE WALK"?

Mulder speculates that the quadraplegic, who lost both arms and legs in the Gulf War, had somehow learned to project his spirit out of his body, a process sometimes called astral projection.

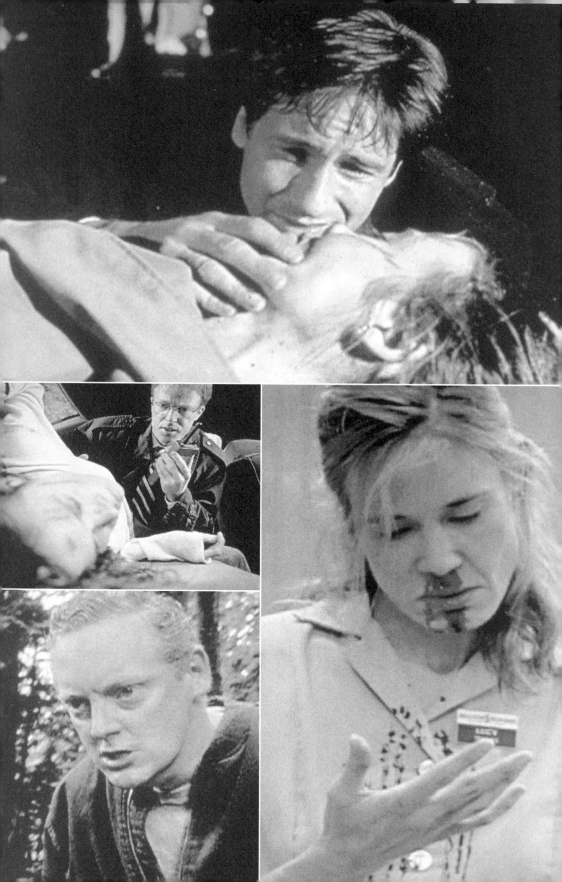

s picture day at a local high school, and the photograph-
's assistant later superimposes his picture with that of
e of the girls, Amy, photographing it again and again. At
ght he enters the girl's house, clamping his hand over her
uth. "Nobody's gonna to spoil us," he says. Elsewhere a
itress, Lucy, spontaneously begins to bleed from the nose,
llapsing to the floor while repeating, "Nobody's going to

OUBLIETTE

EPISODE: 3X08

FIRST AIRED:

November 17, 1995

WRITTEN BY:

Charles Grant Craig

EDITOR:

Heather MacDougal

DIRECTED BY:

Kim Manners

GUEST STARS:

Tracy Ellis (Lucy Householder)

Michael Chieffo (Carl Wade)

Jewel Staite (Amy Jacobs)

Ken Ryan (Agent Walter Eubanks)

Dean Wray (Tow Truck Driver)

Jacques LaLonde (Henry)

David Fredericks (Photographer)

Sidonie Boll (Myra Jacobs)

Robert Underwood (Paramedic)

Dolly Scarr (Fast Food Supervisor)

Bonnie Hay (Woman)

David Lewis (Young Agent)

LOG LINE:

The abduction of a young girl prompts Mulder to seek the help of a woman kidnapped by the same man years earlier and who has the ability to feel what the victim feels.

PRINCIPAL SETTING:

Seattle, Washington

SYNOPSIS:

It's picture day at a local high school, and the photographer's assistant later superimposes his picture with that of one of the girls, Amy, photographing it again and again. At night he enters the girl's house, clamping his hand over her mouth. "Nobody's gonna to spoil us," he says. Elsewhere a waitress, Lucy Householder, spontaneously begins to bleed from the nose, collapsing to the floor while repeating, "Nobody's gonna to spoil us" again and again. Her watch says 10:05, the exact same time Amy was abducted.

Mulder arrives at the missing girl's house, expressing sympathy to her mother and saying he knows how she feels. "I'm sorry," she responds, unaware of Mulder's personal history regarding his sister, "but how could you really know how I feel?"

Mulder admits that Lucy, 30, is "why I came down here," noting that she fainted at the same time Amy was kidnapped and was heard repeating what her abductor said. "That's spooky," says Scully.

"That's my name, isn't it?" Mulder quips, referring to his Academy nickname. Mulder reveals that Lucy was kidnapped at age eight and missing for five years before she escaped, while her abductor was never caught.

Taken to the hospital after her seizure, Lucy insists she knows nothing about Amy's case and is eager to leave. Meanwhile, the kidnapper, Carl Wade, gets a flat tire, but chases away a tow truck driver who stops to help him because he has Amy in the trunk. Two

blood types are lifted off Lucy's work clothes—both hers and Amy's. Lucy also has a criminal record, which prompts suspicion among the other agents, but Mulder maintains that Lucy is a victim, not a suspect.

At a halfway house, Lucy shivers uncontrollably. "It's dark. I can't see," she moans, with scratches on her face that mirror those of Amy, who is seen quivering in a cold, dark room. Mulder takes

Lucy to dinner, but when he asks her if she feels better than Amy does, she snaps that she wouldn't know. "If anyone knows, I'd say you do," he replies, voicing his theory that she can see what Amy sees and asking Lucy to lead them to the girl. Wade, the photographer's assistant/ kidnapper, keeps photographing Amy, who screams at the blinding flash.

Mulder and Scully watch an old videotape of Lucy shot just after her escape from her captor, exhibiting the damage caused by her ordeal. The agents also report a break in the case—with Amy's school pictures missing and Wade having been fired the day after the shoot. Mulder takes the picture to Lucy, who identifies Wade (who'd spent the last 15 years in an institution) as her abductor.

Wade leaves Amy alone, and she pries a board loose, escaping into the woods as Wade returns. He pursues her, and Lucy runs also, mimicking Amy as she falls and hurts her arm. "What's happening to me?" Lucy sobs, later saying that she fees "like it's happening all over again."

Scully arrives with two other agents who have come to arrest Lucy because the blood on her clothes proved to be a DNA match with Amy's blood. When they return, however, Lucy is gone. Mulder repeats that Lucy shouldn't be a suspect, prompting one of the agents, Eubanks, to ask how Amy's blood got on her. "She may have bled it," Mulder says tentatively, suggesting that "some kind of empathic transference is involved." Scully says Lucy could be working with Wade and that Mulder is blinded because he's "so sympathetic to Lucy as a victim—like your sister." Mulder angrily says he's thought of that, but Eubanks interrupts them, as the tow truck driver reports seeing Wade near Easton, where Lucy was found 17 years earlier.

Pursuing a hunch, the agents get Wade's address from a local photo shop, finding the house empty except for Lucy, who trembles in the basement, fueling suspicions that she's an accomplice. She doesn't know how she got there but says it was where Wade kept her long ago. "He hasn't touched her, not yet," she says. "He wants to, but he can't. That's why he takes the pictures." The danger to her will grow, she adds, if Wade thinks he can't have her. Mulder tells Lucy she's the strong one and that Amy needs her strength.

Lucy feels cold and wet, and Mulder realizes Wade is dragging Amy through the river. Hearing the sirens, Wade repeats, "Nobody's gonna to spoil us," forcing Amy under the water as Lucy gasps and collapses in the agents' car. Catching up to Wade, Mulder shoots him fatally and lifts a lifeless Amy from the water. He begins CPR on the girl, to no avail. "Mulder, it's no use," Scully says, but suddenly Amy stirs, coughing up water as Lucy expires.

Mulder rushes back to find Lucy dead, caressing her cheek tenderly as water drips out of her mouth and weeping at her side. Amy is uninjured despite being dragged through the woods for at least a mile, while Lucy drowned, with five liters of water in her lungs. "Lucy may have died for Amy," Scully tells Mulder reassuringly, "but without you they never would have found her." Mulder notes sadly that Lucy, more than helping Amy, finally discovered "the only way she could escape."

BACK STORY: "Oubliette" (derived from the French root "to forget," also referring to a forgotten place or, according to the dictionary, a concealed dungeon having a trap door in the ceiling as its only opening) proved to be David Duchovny's favorite episode of the third season with regard to his own performance.

It was, however, a particularly difficult shoot. Severe weather played havoc with production, as a river the producers intended to use for the climactic sequence became swollen due to heavy rain, rising four to five feet. That forced the crew to move to another location and shoot the scene a week later, in the process losing a day of production, according to producer Joseph Patrick Finn. Costume designer Jenni Gullett also notes that any sort of water shoot presents problems, because multiple costumes are needed for additional takes each time a costume gets wet.

Director Kim Manners points out that Mulder had expressed emotion before over the loss of a family member, but not a stranger, and that actress Tracey Ellis's sensitive portrayal of Lucy helped bring both the character and Duchovny to that emotional crescendo. The episode also marked Manners's first after his difficult personal experience during "D.P.O.," and he found himself affected as well by Ellis's unique quality, which was "so sensitive, like a delicate flower. I really plugged into that, and she really plugged into this role. It was just a great experience."

Fox's standards and practices department did issue a number of

> The brief snatch of music heard over the closing scene is the hymn "Kyrie Eleison," a dirge for the dead.

notes expressing concern regarding aspects of this episode, which as initially written involved the abduction of a 12-year-old girl, which in the network's eyes offered some uncomfortable parallels to the widely publicized Polly Klaas case. "We cast this girl, and after we did the network went, 'Absolutely not'—that she has to look at least fifteen or sixteen," recalls Manners. In addition, the network was "very frightened that we would play her terrified," Manners says, so a point was made of trying to downplay Amy's ordeal.

The actress who played that role, Jewel Staite, had just turned 13 but clearly looked older, and efforts were made through makeup to add to that effect in order to mollify Fox officials. Understanding the network's sensitivity, the producers even auditioned some older girls for the role after Staite had been cast to make sure she could indeed pass for being 15. Happily, it was agreed that Staite fit the bill. "We cast the best actress for the part," says Chris Carter.

An unmarked train car is entered b
doctors work on an unseen figure,
masks burst in, killing the doctor
a body bag.Mulder watches a tape o
anteed authentic" alien autopsy.
network," says Scully. Mulder got
off a satellite dish, but when Muld

side, in a hospital setting, four doctors work on an unse
gure, extracting a strange green fluid. Suddenly armed m
aring masks burst in, killing the doctors and zipping t
oject—glimpsed to reveal an alien form—into a body ba
lder watches a tape of the incident he ordered through t

mber of Japanese men. Inside, in a hospital setting, fou
acting a strange green fluid. Suddenly armed men wearin
zipping the subject—glimpsed to reveal an alien form—int
incident he ordered through the mail, billed as a "guar
, this is even [?] [?] aired on the Fo
ape from a guy [?] Allentown who [?] to have pulled i
d Scully go to s[?] the man they find [?]m dead, killed exe-

NISEI

EPISODE: 3X09

FIRST AIRED:

November 24, 1995

WRITTEN BY:

Chris Carter & Howard Gordon &
Frank Spotnitz

EDITOR:

Jim Gross

DIRECTED BY:

David Nutter

GUEST STARS:

Mitch Pileggi (AD Walter Skinner)

Stephen McHattie (The Red-
     Haired Man)

Raymond J. Barry (Senator
Matheson)

Robert Ito (Dr. Ishimaru)

Tom Braidwood (Frohike)

Dean Haglund (Langly)

Bruce Harwood (Byers)

Steven Williams (X)

Gillian Barber (Penny Northern)

Corrine Koslo (Lottie Holloway)

Lori Triolo (Diane)

Paul McLean (Coast Guard Officer)

Brendan Beiser (Agent Pendrell)

Yasuo Sakurai (Kazeo Takeo)

LOG LINE:

Video of an alien autopsy puts Mulder and
Scully on the trail of a conspiracy involving
Japanese scientists that may shed light on
Scully's abduction.

PRINCIPAL SETTINGS:

Knoxville, Tennessee; Allentown, Pennsylvania; Newport News, Virginia

SYNOPSIS:

An unmarked train car is entered by a number
of Japanese men. Inside, in a hospital setting,
four doctors work on an unseen figure,
extracting a strange green fluid. Suddenly
armed men wearing masks burst in, killing the
doctors and zipping the subject—glimpsed to
reveal an alien form—into a body bag.

Mulder watches a tape of the incident he
ordered through the mail, billed as a "guaran-
teed authentic" alien autopsy. "Mulder, this is
even hokier than the one they aired on the Fox
network," says Scully. Mulder got the tape
from a guy in Allentown who claims to have
pulled it off a satellite dish, but when Mulder
and Scully go to see the man they find him
dead, killed execution-style. Mulder chases an
Asian man who flees the scene carrying a
leather satchel. The man disarms him, but
Mulder pulls a gun from an ankle holster, cap-

Gillian Barber played Beth Kane in "Red Museum." In that episode, the catch phrase was "He is one." In this episode, Barber (as Penny Northern) says of Dana Scully, "She is one."

turing the suspect. "I got tired of losing my gun," he quips tartly.

The suspect speaks only Japanese, and to their surprise Assistant Director Skinner shows up, saying they'll have to release the man because he's a high-ranking Japanese diplomat and that the murder will be handled by another agency. In the satchel, which Mulder withholds instead of logging it as evidence, he finds satellite photos and a list of "Mutual UFO Network" members, one of which, Betsy Hagopian, is circled. Mulder goes to see the Lone Gunmen, who say the photos are of a ship called the *Talapus*. Elsewhere, the man Mulder caught is released at the Japanese Embassy in Washington, but when he gets into a limousine he's killed by a shadowy character referred to in the script as the Red-Haired Man.

Scully, meanwhile, checks up on Betsy Hagopian, finding a number of other women in the house who seem to recognize her. The murdered man was a member of their group, and they tell Scully that she's "one of us," asking if she had an "unexplained event" in the last year when she was missing. "Most of us here have been taken many times," says one of the women, Penny, referring to the "bright white place." Memories begin to seep back, they say, but Scully doesn't want to discuss it and is told she's afraid to remember. All the women have the same mark on their necks from the implant as Scully, and they take her to see Betsy Hagopian, who's dying of a cancer ailment that won't respond to treat-

ment. "We're all dying because of what they do to us," Penny says, suggesting they'll each wind up like Betsy. Scully is clearly shaken.

Mulder goes to Virginia, sneaking onto a ship in the harbor that he discovers to be the *Talapus*. Black-suited armed men drive up and begin searching the boat, forcing Mulder to escape by diving into the water. Climbing out, Mulder peeps through a warehouse window and sees men in white plastic suits working on a large circular object that's partially obscured but which he believes to be a UFO taken aboard the *Talapus*.

Mulder returns to find his apartment ransacked and Skinner waiting inside. He explains that the diplomat was found dead, apparently

killed by someone looking for evidence—the satchel—that Mulder didn't log. The State Department is breathing down his neck, Skinner says, telling Mulder to return that bag. "Whatever you stepped in on this case is being tracked into my office," he says tersely, "and I don't like it." Skinner adds that he's taking himself off the hook this time, and that Mulder is on his own.

Mulder's new phone number is (202) 555-0199

Mulder goes to see Senator Matheson, his former benefactor, who also tells him he must return the satellite photos, while seeking to earn Mulder's trust by informing him about the four Japanese scientists who were murdered. "What am I onto here?" Mulder asks.

"Monsters begetting monsters," the senator replies.

Scully returns, still reeling from her encounter with the women, while Mulder obtains a World War II photo picturing some of the slain Japanese scientists, who were part of a medical corps, 731, that performed horrible experiments. Scully seems to recognize one of the men pictured. Mulder posits that they were trying to create an alien-human hybrid and so the government killed them, which Scully calls "a fantasy." How, Mulder wonders, can she still refuse to believe with all she's seen? "Believing is the easy part, Mulder," she notes. "I just need more than you. I need proof."

"You think that believing is easy?" he counters.

Mulder identifies what the spy photos were tracking—train cars carrying test subjects, which he calls "our government's secret railroad." Mulder goes to a train yard, spotting men transferring what looks like a living alien, covered in plastic, onto a train. After taking the chip found in her in for analysis, Scully watches the alien autopsy video, recognizing one of the Japanese doctors in it—flashing back to her own abduction, recalling him looming over her. Mulder calls from the train station, where the Red-Haired Man stealthily kills a Japanese man apparently sent to meet one of the scientists, Dr. Zama. By the time Mulder gets there, the train has already left.

Turning up at Scully's apartment, X warns that Mulder mustn't get on the train. She calls to tell Mulder it's too dangerous and to "let it go." "I can't," Mulder says, leaping from an overpass onto the car, losing his cell phone—and thus his lifeline to Scully—in the process.

To be continued . . .

BACK STORY: "It was just logistically huge," co–executive producer R. W. Goodwin says of this two-part story, which was actually delayed several weeks—after initially being conceived as a stand-alone episode—to fine-tune and expand the concept as well as allow more time to plan its production. "Just that stunt, with Mulder jumping on top of the train, we worked six weeks on that." The stuntman was cabled, so although he jumped off the overpass to create that feeling he never actually landed on the train. Despite that, stunt coordinator Tony Morelli says the jump itself wasn't particularly difficult compared to some of the other stunts that have been executed on the show.

There was also alarm about using Duchovny in such a potentially dangerous situation, but the actor enjoyed the show. "It was fun to jump on a train, fun to jump off a train," Duchovny says with an arched eyebrow. "It was something I hadn't done."

This episode introduces the red-haired and lovelorn Agent Pendrell (Brendan Beiser), who is named for a street in Vancouver. Agent Pendrell of the FBI Sci-Crime lab proves invaluable in "Nisei," "731," "Apocrypha," and "Avatar." He is more than willing to put in long hours in the lab for the sake of his favorite agent, Scully.

Trained Rangers were used to play the tactical team in the opening sequence, part of a concerted effort to ground the show in reality at all times. "We have a lot of technical advisers, because I try not to fake everything, [but rather] try to make everything as realistic as possible," says props master Ken Hawryliw. Of the trained soldiers, he adds, "They know what they're supposed to be doing, rather than just putting a gun in an extra's hands."

One of the interesting aspects of directing a two-parter, says director David Nutter, stems from the awareness that one of your colleagues will handle the other half. "Knowing that Rob Bowman was going to follow me, my only hope was that I could keep up. He's such a wonderful visual stylist," he says. Each of the directors has a different approach, with Nutter saying

The number of the boxcar in which the alien autopsy takes place is 82594. This recalls the date, August 25, 1994, when Chris Carter first stepped behind the cameras, directing the Emmy-nominated episode "Duane Barry." The date reappears periodically throughout the rest of the third season.

he always seeks to "stay back out of the way" of the material, so that a viewer wouldn't necessarily be conscious of the choices he makes or distracted from the reality the show attempts to convey.

Scully's joke about the hokey Alien Autopsy special on Fox turned out to be ironic, since Fox repeated the special the following night—a scheduling move that wasn't anticipated when the episode was being produced—airing promotional spots for the special during this hour's initial telecast. A 10-year-old boy played the alien on the autopsy table, while his twin sister served as the alien on the train car. "They tolerated all this adhesive," says special effects makeup supervisor Toby Lindala, noting that the girl had no problem with the oversized dark contact lenses used to create the alien eyes. Two new alien heads were also designed for the episode.

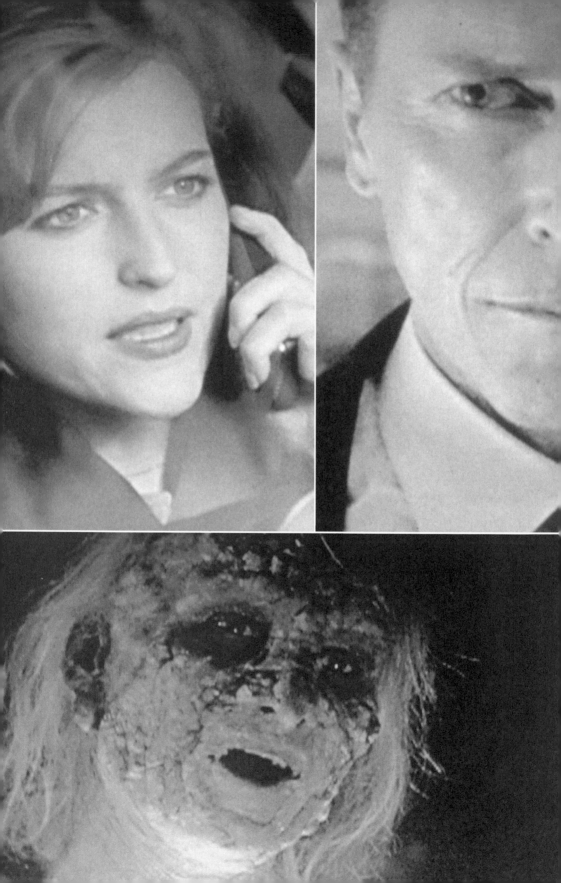

ops round up strange-looking human-old creatures at a site
beled Hansen's Disease Research Facility. One of the crea-
res, his skin horribly deformed, watches from a distance
the others are gunned down in front of a mass grave.Mulder
ngs to the train, while Scully questions X angrily about
 to help him, pulling her gun only to be quickly disarmed.
ere are limits to knowledge, he says, adding that if she

731

EPISODE: 3X10

FIRST AIRED:

December 1, 1995

WRITTEN BY:

Frank Spotnitz

EDITOR:

Stephen Mark

DIRECTED BY:

Rob Bowman

GUEST STARS:

Stephen McHattie (The Red-
   Haired Man)

William B. Davis (The Cigarette-
   Smoking Man)

Michael Puttonen (Conductor)

Robert Ito (Dr. Ishimaru/Zama)

Steven Williams (X)

Colin Cunningham (Escalante)

Don S. Williams (1st Elder)

Brenden Beiser (Agent Pendrell)

LOG LINE:

Mulder is caught on board a speeding train with what might be alien cargo and a government killer while Scully seeks her own solution to the conspiracy.

PRINCIPAL SETTINGS:

Perkey, West Virginia; Washington, D.C.

SYNOPSIS:

Troops round up strange-looking humanoid creatures at a site labeled Hansen's Disease Research Facility. One of the creatures, his skin horribly deformed, watches from a distance as the others are gunned down in front of a mass grave.

Mulder clings to the train, while Scully questions X angrily about how to help him, pulling her gun only to be quickly disarmed. "There are limits to my knowledge," X says, adding that if she wants to know more about the train and who killed her sister, to "find out what they put in your neck." That device, he says, "holds more than I could ever tell you—maybe everything you need to know."

Mulder makes it into the train, telling the conductor who he is and asking for access to the compartment of the Japanese scientist he's pursuing, Dr. Zama. He finds the compartment empty except for several meticulous journals handwritten in Japanese. Meanwhile, Scully returns to Agent Pendrell, who says the chip found inside her seems to replicate the brain's memory function and duplicate mental processes. "You could know a person's every thought," Scully muses. As she suspects, the manufacturer is Japanese, and Pendrell has traced a shipment from the maker to Dr. Zama at a disease research facility in West Virginia.

On the train, the Red-Haired Man who killed the diplomat corners Dr. Zama in the lavatory, and Mulder later finds the scientist dead. Mulder arms the conductor as he leaves to look for the killer. Scully goes to the disease research facility, where she meets several of the deformed creatures huddling in the darkness. "Please, don't hurt us," the leader says, telling Scully that death squads have been coming since the medical staff left, killing hundreds of them. They're lepers, and he takes Scully to a mass grave as a helicopter and soldiers arrive, capturing her.

Mulder goes back to the quarantine car, peering through the pinhole to see an alien-looking form in the darkness. Suddenly the Red-Haired Man wraps a garrote around Mulder's throat, strangling him until the conductor intrudes with the unloaded gun Mulder had given him, locking them in the car. The interruption gives Mulder time to recover, pulling his gun. The attacker claims to be with the National Security Agency and says there's a bomb on the train.

Scully is met by the First Elder—a member of the Shadowy Syndicate seen in earlier episodes—who says the creatures were "victims of an inhuman project" and that the world is now ruled by whoever has the greatest scientists. The Red-Haired Man's cell phone rings, and to his surprise it's for Mulder—Scully calling with the First Elder. "Whatever is on that train is not alien," she tells him. Zama, she says, experimented on human subjects, operating out of a leper colony. The secret railroad was used for those tests, she maintains, and the alien abduction is "just a smokescreen."

The test subject on their train has hemorrhagic fever, she adds, so thousands will die if the bomb detonates.

Mulder is skeptical but finds the bomb, ticking down with just over 100 minutes before it explodes. Mulder tells the conductor to reroute

NUMEROLOGY:

The exit code for the boxcar is 101331, or Ten Thirteen Thirty-One.

them to a place as far from a populated area as possible, where they unhook the car, stranding him and his captive there. As minutes fly by, the Red-Haired Man says their cargo is "a weapon." Mulder surmises that Zama came up with an immunity to biological weapons, the government didn't want the science shared, and the creature in the quarantine car is an alien-human hybrid.

Scully tries to contact Senator Matheson and summon X, finally calling Mulder with only six minutes before the bomb will detonate. From watching the video she's ascertained the car's exit code, which Mulder punches in. As the door opens, the Red-Haired Man strikes Mulder, pummeling him into unconsciousness. As he exits the car, however, a shot rings out, and the man collapses, dead. It's X, who carries a bloodied Mulder over his shoulder to safety as the car and its contents explode.

> The entry code is 1111471, which reappears later as the aircraft registry number on the downed P—51 Mustang in "Piper Maru." Although most of the numbers that appear in The X-Files have some hidden meaning, this number, which first appeared as part of Mulder's badge number in "F. Emasculata," and recurs throughout the third season, has NO significance. It is, if anything, the ultimate in-joke: a sly tease for the fans who hang on every detail.

A week later, Mulder finds himself stymied trying to get information about the car, and even Senator Matheson won't return his calls. He finds a journal, but it appears to be a substitute for the one he'd seen with Dr. Zama's writings, which may have unlocked the secrets. "They're getting away with it, Scully," he says, frustrated.

"They've gotten away with it, Mulder," she responds. "And what they can't cover they apologize for. Apology has become policy." An angry Mulder says he doesn't want the usual formulated responses, but rather "an apology for the truth." Elsewhere, a Japanese man transcribes what appears to be Dr. Zama's original journal, as the Cigarette-Smoking Man leans back, lighting up a cigarette and puffing away with satisfaction.

BACK STORY: Director Rob Bowman, who calls this episode "one of my all-time favorites," set up seven cameras prior to the train car explosion to catch the shot from that many different angles. "When it was over he called me and said, 'Dave, I used them all,'" recalls David Gauthier, who salvaged a bell from the train and had it engraved for Bowman. As for the scenes with Mulder on top of the train, a harness was cabled over the top of the car, with the cable digitally removed by visual effects supervisor Mat Beck.

"Things that stick in my mind are the scenes with David and Stephen McHattie inside the train," says Bowman. Allowing those two actors to play longer scenes using a Steadi-cam was "almost like a stage play" showcasing two fine actors, he notes. "That's a change from what we're usually doing, which is filming little eighths of a page, and let's get out of here."

Bowman also took considerable ribbing after the episode for inadvertently destroying two cameras—a running joke featured later in a gag reel for a Fox executive, where Bowman earnestly says he plans to drive a truck through a trio of cameras and then throw two more cameras at the truck as it goes by.

The mere idea of setting most of the action aboard a train entailed numerous production difficulties. "Any time you use such a large prop as a train it presents a problem," understates producer Joseph Patrick Finn, noting that the show had to build train car interiors for the special car where the alien was kept as well as sleeper cars. The sets were then floated on inner tubes to create the feeling of a rocking movement.

The producers also took a real train car that had been decommissioned and blew it up. In order to produce the desired blast effect, the stainless steel was cut out of the train, which was blown up with 120 black-powder bombs and 45 gallons of gasoline. That prompted considerable concern from the park service where the scene was shot about where all that debris was going to end up, but as usual, the producers cleaned up their mess. A blue-screen visual effects matte shot was used to superimpose the two actors over the explosion, as X carries Mulder to safety.

According to Steven Williams, X's heroic actions in this episode helped endear him more to the show's viewers. "X was starting to get a little bit irritating to the fans," he says. "He'd come on and say some nebulous shit, some ambiguous sort of thing, and people would say, 'Come on! Just give him the information!'"

The mass grave represented one of Toby Lindala's biggest assignments of the year, with 25 masked actors (mostly children) having to fill the open grave on top of an equal number of prop bodies. Lindala and his 8-man crew had to create those 50 different makeup pieces and bodies in just 5 days, adapting some existing masks from previous episodes to get the job done in time. "It was complete pandemonium here," he says. "We had two crews going day and night."

This is also one of the few episodes to substitute another slogan for "The Truth Is Out There" during the opening credits, in this case, "Apology Is Policy." Chris Carter wrote the scene that led to the shift, inspired by U.S. government apologies regarding secret radiation experiments. The opening script was previously replaced with the lines "Trust No One" (in "The Erlenmeyer Flask"), "Deny Everything" ("Ascension"), and a translation of "The Truth Is Out There" into Navajo in "Anasazi."

Carter indicates that there's no set criteria for changing the intro, saying some of the considerations are, "If there's an idea that really interests me, and it contains a wonderful truth, like I believe these things do." In addition, the line should resonate with the show and not be a cliche. "It is also the advertising gene I have in my DNA. I tend to like these pithy epigrams. They appeal to me, and I think they set the show apart from other shows on TV as well," he suggests.

"They help to define what it is. 'The truth is out there' has found its way into the sort of cultural vocabulary, and so have some of these other ones, too."

WHAT IS THE MEANING OF THE EPISODE TITLE "731"?

During World War II a special unit of the Japanese Army experimented on prisoners of war. These prisoners were exposed to disease and extremes of temperature; they were operated on without anesthesia. Like their Nazi counterparts, they may have been given refuge in the United States to continue their experiments. This group was known to top Japanese Army officials as Unit 731.

reverend addresses a congregation in Pennsylvania, say
from his palms. After the sermon a man comes to see him,
and pinning him against the wall, wisps of smoke rising
"bleeding" was a fraud and that he's the 11th stigmatic
motivated murders. At an elementary school in Loveland, Oh
The agents are summoned by a social services worker, who
institutionalized. Mulder and Scully visit Kevin's father

REVELATIONS

EPISODE: 3X11

FIRST AIRED:

December 15, 1995

WRITTEN BY:

Kim Newton

EDITOR::

Heather MacDougall

DIRECTED BY:

David Nutter

GUEST STARS:

Kevin Zegers (Kevin Kryder)

Sam Bottoms (Michael Kryder)

Kenneth Welsh (Simon
   "Millennium Man" Gates)

Michael Berryman (Owen Jarvis)

Hayley Tyson (Susan Kryder)

R. Lee Ermey (Rev. Patrick
   Findley)

Leslie Ewen (Carina Maywald)

Fulvio Cecere (Priest)

Nicole Robert (Mrs. Tynes)

LOG LINE:

Mulder and Scully seek to protect a young boy who displays wounds of religious significance from a killer, causing Scully to question her own faith while being cast in the role of the boy's protector.

PRINCIPAL SETTING:

Loveland, Ohio

SYNOPSIS:

A reverend addresses a congregation in Pennsylvania, saying that miracles really do happen as his palms begin to spontaneously bleed. After the sermon a man comes to see him, grabbing the reverend by the throat with supernatural strength and pinning him against the wall, wisps of smoke rising from his neck.

Examining the body, Mulder says the reverend's "bleeding" was a fraud and that he's the 11th alleged stigmatic slain over 3 years in an international string of religiously motivated murders. At an elementary school in Loveland, Ohio, a young boy, Kevin Kryder, begins to bleed from his hands in class. The agents are summoned by a social services worker, who explains that Kevin has bled before and that his father was institutionalized for believing he had to protect Kevin from evil forces. Mulder and Scully visit Kevin's father.

"He's bleeding again, isn't he?" he asks flatly, saying the boy has been chosen and that dark forces will come to slay him in the form of a powerful man as part of "the great war between good and evil." He also tells Scully she must "come full circle to find the truth," but she

MISSING LINES:

At one point in the conversation between Scully and Mr. Kryder, the boy's father, he begins to speak in tongues. Scully, but not Mulder, can understand him, even when he quotes a line from The Day the Earth Stood Still—"Klaatu barada nikto." This scene was cut from the final version.

doesn't understand. "You will," he says vaguely.

At the shelter where he's been taken, Kevin is abducted by a strange-looking man who tells a ghost story to the children. Mulder notes based on the other children's description, the abductor apparently looks like "Homer Simpson's evil twin." Yet Kevin's mother recognizes the man as Owen Jarvis, whom she had hired to do yard work. Alone with Kevin, Owen says he's his guardian angel. Mulder and Scully burst in, finding Owen but not the boy. "I'm not the one that wants to hurt him," Owen insists, saying he was asked to protect Kevin by God. Turning to Scully, he says, "How can you help Kevin if you don't believe?"—suddenly leaping from a second-story window and escaping.

Kevin returns to his house, and the man seen initially killing the reverend appears looking for him. He finds the boy as Owen intervenes and struggles with the man, who overpowers him, the smoke rising from Owen's throat as he's strangled. When the agents arrive Owen's body is alone, and Kevin turns to a mystified Scully, saying, "Are you the one that was sent to protect me?"

Owen's body isn't decomposing normally, and Scully mentions how she was taught in Catechism about "incorruptibles" whose bodies wouldn't decay. For once, Mulder's the skeptic, telling her not to let faith cloud her judgment. Her examination finds that a print on Owen's neck belongs to Simon Gates, the chief executive of a large company. "A rich and powerful man," Scully muses, remembering the warning from Kevin's father.

Kevin is with his mother when their car breaks down, and Gates arrives, harming Kevin's mother and chasing the boy into the woods. Inexplicably, however, Kevin—who has previously appeared in two places at once—is back in the car with his mother, who runs over Gates before crashing into a ditch. With Kevin's mother dead, Scully vows she'll protect him. Mulder reports that a man fitting Gates's description rented a car under the name Forau—one of the devil's disciples.

Scully sees a cut on Kevin's side as he bathes and wonders aloud if divinity might be involved, but Mulder dismisses the notion. "How is it you can go out on a limb whenever you see a light in the sky, but you're unwilling to accept the possibility of a miracle?" Scully asks.

"I wait for a miracle every day," says Mulder, "but what I've seen here has only tested my patience—not my faith." Hearing a sound, they break open the bathroom door to find Kevin gone, with the wrought-iron bars smoldering and bent outward. Scully goes to see Kevin's father, but he's heavily medicated and unable to concentrate. Seeing a trash can nevertheless provides a clue, and she surmises that coming "full circle" indicates Gates has taken the boy to a recycling center he owns in Jerusalem, Ohio. Mulder is doubtful, instead pursuing a sighting of Gates at the airport. "You think it's you, don't you?" Mulder says to his partner. "You think you're the one who's been chosen to protect Kevin."

In another reappearance of a Twin Peaks star from David Duchovny's days on that show, Kenneth Welsh (Wyndham Earle) stars as the Millennium Man.

Gates tells Kevin he must die "for the New Age to come" when Scully reaches the scene. Gates flees with Kevin up a flight of steps, trying to leap into a huge shredding machine. The boy, however, clings to the side as

Gates is ground up in the blades below. As Scully reaches his side, Kevin simply says, "I knew you'd come."

Two days later, Kevin's hands have healed, and he tells Scully he'll see her again. Scully goes to confession for the first time in six years, asking the priest if he believes in miracles and expressing her own doubts, since only she and not Mulder witnessed them. "Maybe they weren't meant for him to see," the priest responds, telling her that we must sometimes "come full circle to find the truth."

Scully isn't surprised by the revelations, but is afraid, she says, "that God is speaking, but that no one's listening."

BACK STORY: "Revelations" offers a virtually unique case of role reversal involving Mulder and Scully, which Duchovny took as a refreshing change of pace, saying it was easier for him "not to be so emotionally involved in the chase. I found it easier to be the character that kind of sits back and says, 'No, that can't be true.'

"It was fun not to have to drive every scene, but actually to get into the way of every scene rather than having to push it forward. It becomes tiring after three years to step into every scene and have to drive it forward." By contrast, in "Revelations," Mulder, he observes, got to be "the one to say 'Let's put the brakes on,' or to put my hands in my pockets and say, 'Hey, I don't think so.' In that sense, it was fun."

Director David Nutter notes that dealing with faith provided a way to delve further into

The stigmata, or wounds of Christ, have been reported among believers for several hundred years. The best known stigmatic of this century was Padre Pio in Italy. The most famous stigmatic of all is St. Francis of Assisi (1182–1226), the first recorded instance of the phenomenon. He bled from his hands, feet, and side for the last two years of his life.

UNEXPLAINED PHENOMENA

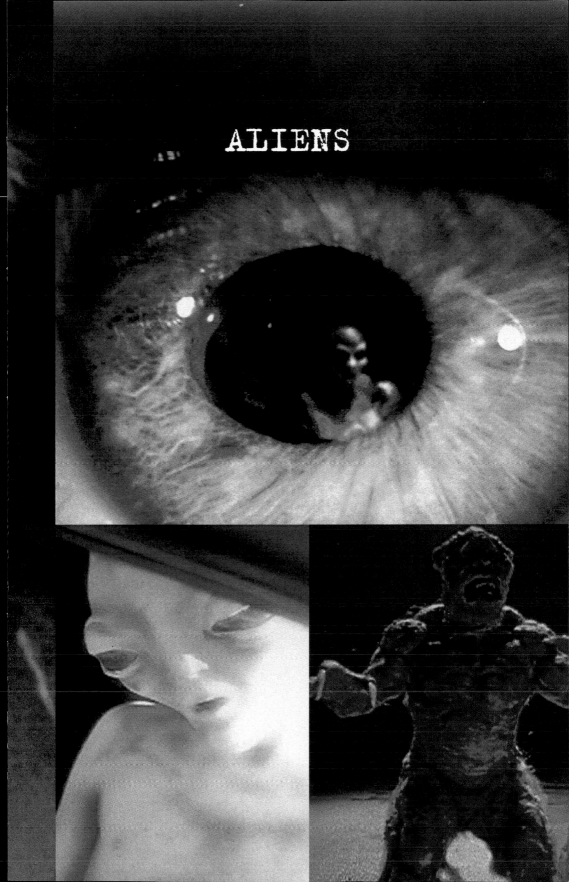

ALIENS

CONSPIRACIES

MONSTERS

Scully's character, showing that there are other dimensions to her. He also felt Anderson delivered a sparkling performance, especially in such quieter moments as the final sequence when she goes to confession. "I really love so much working with Gillian," he says. "She's got such an ability to emote and give from the inside." Nutter also had fun with the ghost story scene, though he admits working with that many kids wasn't a picnic and, in fact, "never really is."

"Revelations" is notable as well in its exploration of religious faith, a topic often perceived as being given short shrift on television—in large part due to network fears about offending a segment of the audience. "It dealt with faith, not religion with a capital 'R' or Catholicism with a capital 'C,'" Chris Carter explains, alluding to his own overriding interest in religion and politics, which has clearly found its way into the show on multiple levels. "To me, the idea of faith is really the backbone of the entire series—faith in your own beliefs, ideas about the truth, and so it has religious overtones always," he says.

"It is a more sensitive area on television because you run the risk of pissing certain people off, but I think we handled it in such a way as to make it about miracle belief, or lack of belief—and we set it against the paranormal, which is, 'Why can Mulder believe in things that go bump in the night, and when Scully believes in a miracle he shuts her down?' I think it was one thing juxtaposed with the other that gave the episode its interest."

The character of the priest did receive some help from a higher power. The finished shot left the producers unsatisfied with the actor's voice, so a new vocal track was added in postproduction using a different performer in Los Angeles.

> ## WHAT MADE KEVIN KRYDER DIFFERENT FROM THE ELEVEN OTHER VICTIMS OF SIMON GATES IN "REVELATIONS"?
>
> Of all the "stigmatics" (persons bearing bleeding wounds similar to the crucifixion wounds of Christ) stalked by Simon Gates, the Millennium Man, only Kevin was a genuine stigmatic.

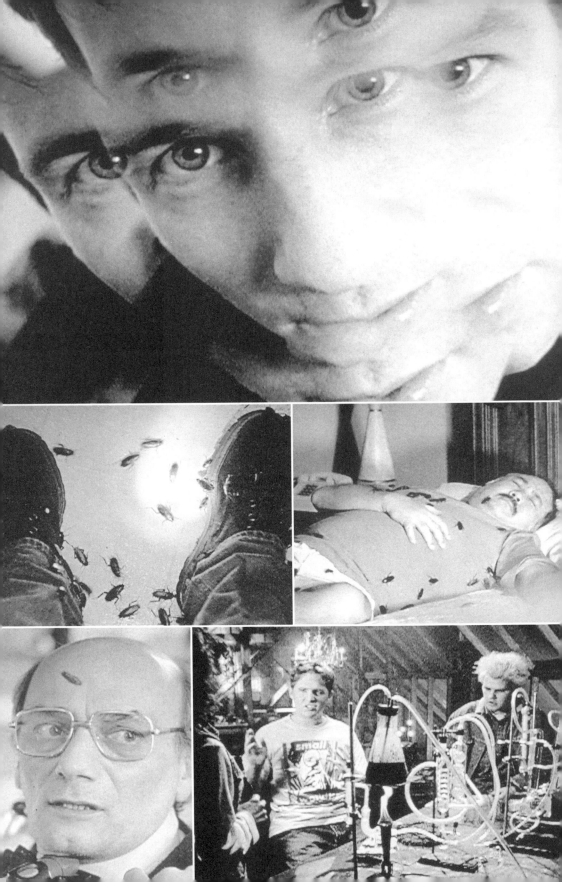

WAR OF THE COPROPHAGES

EPISODE: 3X12

FIRST AIRED:

January 5, 1996

WRITTEN BY:

Darin Morgan

EDITOR:

Jim Gross

DIRECTED BY:

Kim Manners

GUEST STARS:

Bobbie Phillips (Dr. Bambi
  Berenbaum)

Raye Birk (Dr. Jeff Eckerle)

Dion Anderson (Sheriff Frass)

Bill Dow (Dr. Rick Newton)

Alex Bruhanski (Dr. Bugger)

Ken Kramer (Dr. Alexander Ivanov)

Nicole Parker (Chick)

Alan Buckley (Dude)

Tyler Labine (Stoner)

Maria Herrera (Customer #1)

Sean Allan (Customer #2)

Norma Wick (Reporter)

Wren Robertz (Orderly)

Tom Heaton (Resident #1)

Bobby L. Stewart (Resident #2)

Dawn Stofer (Customer #4)

Fiona Roeske (Customer #5)

Tony Marr (Motel Manager)

LOG LINE:

A number of deaths seemingly linked to cockroaches cause widespread panic in a small town.

PRINCIPAL SETTING:

Miller's Grove, Massachusetts

SYNOPSIS:

A man, Dr. Bugger, waxes eloquent about
cockroaches before stomping on one. "Look,
buddy, I just kill 'em," the exterminator tells
the scientist, Dr. Jeff Eckerle, who summoned
him. Suddenly, Bugger grabs his chest and collapses, and later Eckerle finds him lying dead
with roaches crawling all over him.

Mulder is in the vicinity, investigating
accounts of unidentified colored lights in the
sky. He calls Scully, who provides him with a
long dissertation about the unlikelihood of
alien life. "Scully, what are you wearing?"
Mulder replies mischievously. The local sheriff
stops Mulder, but he's quickly called away, saying there's been "another roach attack."
Mulder calls Scully, saying it "appears that
cockroaches are mortally attacking people."
He cites the exterminator's death and two others earlier in the day, noting that these events
were reported by scientists and are "not coming from yahoos out in the boondocks."

Elsewhere, a trio of teenagers do drugs,
with one seeing roaches burrowing under his

The candy Scully eats in the convenience store is called Choco Droppings.

skin. Attempting to rid himself of the roaches he sees, he hacks himself to death with a razor blade. Scully says there's a possible explanation, telling Mulder about Ekbom's syndrome—a similar delusion associated with drug abuse. Mulder catches a roach, and handling it cuts his fingers, leading him to believe the exoskeleton is made of metal. The sheriff wonders if the government has been conducting experiments, perhaps creating "a new breed of killer cockroaches."

The medical examiner asks Mulder if there's danger, and they later find him dead in the bathroom—the orderly saying that he was "covered in cockroaches." Scully, however, has a theory to explain that too, noting that "straining too forcefully" can cause a brain aneurysm.

Mulder goes to the government facility while Scully calls back, saying she's uncovered research about a breed of cockroach attracted to light that might account for the sightings. Mulder, meanwhile, sees the walls in the facility ripple, as roaches burst out of them. The light comes on, and he's joined by the stunning Dr. Bambi Berenbaum, a USDA researcher studying roaches. She's even got a theory that UFOs are nocturnal insect swarms, and when Mulder's phone rings, he quickly says "Not now" and hangs up.

At Mulder's hotel, one of the residents watches a local news report about the cockroaches urging people not to worry while showing men in contamination suits. Mulder calls Scully, telling her about Dr. Berenbaum and her theories. "Her name is Bambi?" Scully repeats twice. Hearing a scream, Mulder finds the man who'd been watching the news dead. The other residents saw roaches crawling on him, but there are none when Mulder arrives. Becoming skeptical, Mulder thinks the man scared himself to death, noting that all Scully's conjectures have been correct. Now, however, Scully isn't so sure, and she decides to come to town.

Scully is reading Breakfast at Tiffany's, a reference to David Duchovny's appearance on "Celebrity Jeopardy!" The Final Jeopardy question referred to this Truman Capote book; Duchovny guessed wrong and lost the game.

Mulder takes a cockroach to Bambi, who says it looks like a micro-processor, implying the creature might be mechanical. Mulder goes to an expert in the field, Dr. Ivanov, a wheelchair-bound scientist who creates insect-like robots. Ivanov says most space travelers would likely be robots and that anyone who envisions the grey-skinned, big-eyed aliens we've come to know "has been brainwashed by too much science fiction." Mulder can only shrug, as a bug literally crawls across the screen.

Scully finally arrives, finding a panicked mob ransacking a convenience store. "Haven't you heard about the roaches?" a woman

tells Scully, who yells at them to calm down, until a fight over bug spray prompts everyone but Scully to race outside. As he leaves Dr. Ivanov's office, Mulder captures a roach. "Greetings from planet Earth," he says.

Animal trainer Debra Coe used approximately 300 cockroaches for this episode, during which there was only one casualty. According to Coe, one cockroach-actor died from old age.

According to Bambi, however, it's just a typical cockroach. Scully calls, saying Dr. Eckerle was researching methane and has been importing animal dung, which may explain the infestation of a new breed of cockroach, since roaches are dung-eaters.

Mulder goes to see Dr. Eckerle, who, crazed with fear, pulls a gun. Scully pulls up and encounters Bambi, who asks if she wants help. "No, this is no place for an entomologist," Scully says, popping an ammo clip into her gun. Mulder's phone rings, and the skittish Dr. Eckerle fires at him, releasing the methane. The agents race outside as the facility explodes, and they rise slowly, covered with dung. "Crap," says Mulder.

The sheriff later tells them about fires, looting and insecticide poisoning the night before. Dr. Ivanov shows up and meets Bambi, as the two wander off together. "Smart is sexy," Scully quips as Mulder watches

them go, adding that their children might be smart enough to stop the next invasion of artificially intelligent space-roaches. "I never thought I'd say this to you Scully, but you smell bad," Mulder deadpans.

At his computer, Mulder types up his thoughts about the case, wondering how we'd react if such creatures visited Earth. Just then Mulder reaches for a snack but is startled to see a strange, alien-looking roach on the plate. Mulder grasps an X-File, looks at the insect quizzically for a moment . . . and then squashes it.

BACK STORY: This hour represented a creative reunion of sorts between writer Darin Morgan and director Kim Manners, who worked together on "Humbug," the acclaimed second-season episode about circus freaks.

Perhaps the most obvious question relates to what it's like to try and elicit performances from an army of cockroaches, but the director found his six-legged stars to be remarkably cooperative. "We were amazingly lucky," he marvels. "Every shot I wanted to get, they did."

The show kept the bugs in a "roach corral" to prevent them from infesting the stu-

The name of the town, Miller's Grove, is reminiscent of the site of Orson Welles's famous War of the Worlds hoax, involving insect-like Martian invaders supposedly attacking "Grover's Mill," New Jersey. The broadcast caused a panic similar to the one seen in the convenience store.

dio, and time and again the little guys behaved like true show-business troopers. "We were shooting the bathroom sequence," Manners remembers, "and we let this cockroach out from underneath the camera, and the little sonofabitch ran right underneath the stall. I just said, 'Cut it! Print it!' Then we get the toilet paper roll, and the cockroach started at this end and walked all the way across the roll and went straight toward the actor," just as it was supposed to do.

"But that's not the best one," he continues, describing the shot when the cockroaches are supposed to climb up on the toilet tank behind the guy who's sitting there. "We couldn't hurt the cockroaches—believe it or not, you can't hurt a cockroach—so we're saying to the handlers on the other side of the wall, 'Be careful, don't hurt them, but get them in there.' I had like five of them I wanted to run to the top of the tank.

"After about four takes as a joke I said to Debbie Coe, our wrangler, bring the bugs over here. I stuck my head in the bucket and I said, 'Now listen you little (expletive), I'm gonna give two cues: The first one is 'Camera action' and the second one is 'Action.' That's when you little (expletive) run to the top of the tank.' I said, 'Action!' and they were right there. An absolutely perfect shot. It's a true story, and it worked."

Crew members verify the moment with amazed bemusement. "When I saw Kim Manners talking to a bucket of cockroaches, that was a highlight for me," confirms cinematographer John Bartley with a broad smile.

WHAT WAS THE NAME OF THE EXPERIMENTAL FUEL RESEARCH STATION MULDER VISITED IN "WAR OF THE COPROPHAGES"?

Alt-fuel. The firm's motto was "Waste is a terrible thing to waste."

Anderson, who popped a cricket in her mouth during the making of "Humbug," happily points out that she was spared any further six-legged encounters in this episode. "The closest I got was the chocolates in the store. That was it," she says with a smile, adding that "War of the Coprophages" was one of her favorite episodes of the third season, along with another Morgan episode, "Jose Chung's *From Outer Space*."

As his starting point, Morgan had read about an artificial-intelligence researcher at MIT who built robots in the shape of large insects. The writer liked the idea of aliens sending robots to Earth, since people "usually think of that in terms of aliens with big heads." Morgan then wedded that idea with stories about mass hysteria, including a famous case from the '40s that he was going to have the sheriff discuss before ultimately cutting the scene to keep the episode from running long again.

Incredibly detailed plastic and rubber cockroaches were made for the show. "You could put one next to a real roach and no one would

know the difference," says props master Ken Hawryliw, whose department also worked for weeks creating "piles and piles" of bogus dung using an organic (but not that organic) substance. Similarly, all of the robots in Dr. Ivanov's lab were built from scratch, modeled after drawings of similar robots the crew was shown.

Morgan came up with the town name, Miller's Grove, by playing around with Grover's Mill, the town mentioned in Orson Welles' famous hysteria-inducing *War of the Worlds* radio broadcast. As for other memorable names, Dr. Bambi—who became an immediate subject of derision along the Internet—was played by actress Bobbie Phillips, who had a recurring role as well on the ABC series *Murder One*. Phillips also appeared in *Showgirls* and the Showtime anthology series *Red Shoe Diaries*, which, of course, also features David Duchovny.

High-school jock Boom eulogizes
offer their sympathies, saying
blond virgin to sacrifice next.
and Boom screeches his car to a
while Terri and Margi giggle on
a flower. Mulder and Scully argu

rgi and Terri reference to the sacrifice a blond vi
n, prompting the detective to storm away, "don't suppo
e s a virgin, do you?" Mulder asks, "to which Scully repli
ippily, "I doubt she's even a blond." A local man, Bob Spit
terrupts the service, ranting about satanism, which might

SYZYGY

dead friend while two pretty blond girls, Terri and Ma
"the cult" believed to have killed him is said to be aft
e if we weren't virgins we wouldn't be so scared," Terri s
. The next morning Boom is found dead dangling from a cl
precipice abo e, pla ing. He l ves e, h loves me not"
r directions as the pull into Co ty, "the Perfect Har

EPISODE: 3X13

FIRST AIRED:

January 26, 1996

WRITTEN BY:

Chris Carter

EDITOR:

Stephen Mark

DIRECTED BY:

Rob Bowman

GUEST STARS:

Dana Wheeler-Nicholson
  (Det. Angela White)

Wendy Benson (Margi Kleinjan)

Lisa Robin Kelly (Terri Roberts)

Garry Davey (Bob Spitz)

Denalda Williams (Madame
  Zirinka)

Gabrielle Miller (Brenda Jaycee
  Summerfield)

Ryan Reynolds (Jay "Boom"
  DeBoom)

Tim Dixon (Dr. Richard W.
  Godfrey)

Ryk Brown (Minister)

Jeremy Radick (Young Man)

Russell Porter (Scott Simmons)

LOG LINE:

Two high school girls born on the same day are involved in a series of deaths thanks to an odd alignment of the planets that causes strange behavior in all the townspeople, including Mulder and Scully.

PRINCIPAL SETTING:

Comity, Caryl County

SYNOPSIS:

High-school jock Boom eulogizes his dead friend while two pretty blond girls, Terri Roberts and Margi Kleinjan, offer their sympathies, saying that "the cult" believed to have killed him is said to be after a blond virgin to sacrifice next. "Maybe if we weren't virgins we wouldn't be so scared," Terri says, and Boom screeches his car to a halt. The next morning Boom is found dead dangling from a cliff, while Terri and Margi giggle on the precipice above, playing "He loves me, he loves me not" with a flower.

Mulder and Scully argue over directions as they pull into Comity, "the Perfect Harmony City," meeting the attractive Detective Angela White at a funeral service for the latest victim. White says the boy is the third high school student found dead in as many months, and that local suspicion is that a satanic cult is involved. Scully expresses her skepticism, noting that most such accounts are imagined, down to Margi and Terri's reference to the sacrifice of a blond virgin, prompting the detective to storm away. "You don't suppose she's a virgin, do you?" Mulder asks, to which Scully replies snippily, "I doubt she's even a blond."

A local man, Bob Spitz, interrupts the service, ranting about satanism, which might be dismissed until Margi and Terri clasp hands and Boom's coffin begins to smoke and then burn as people flee the chapel. Mulder

Grover Cleveland Alexander High School is a reference to a question David Duchovny missed on "Celebrity Jeopardy." David said later he thought he was still on the sports section. He confused the pitcher (Alexander) with the president (Cleveland).

and Scully interview Margi and Terri separately, and the two offer virtually identical word-for-word accounts of a satanic ceremony where a baby was going to be sacrificed. Scully notes that the stories are "common, almost cliched." Checking the latest body, however, Mulder and White notice a burn mark on the chest they think resembles a goat or "horned beast," though Scully doesn't see it.

Mulder goes to Detective White's house, apologizing for Scully's behavior while suggesting that she join him to "help me solve the mystery of the horny beast." They take a picture of the body to an astrologer, Zirinka—a pragmatic businesswoman who's convinced the town's gone nuts, which she attributes to "a rare planetary alignment" of Mars, Uranus, and Mercury.

Margi and Terri watch basketball practice, lusting after one of the guys, Scott, who has a girlfriend named Brenda. They shriek when another player, Eric, inadvertently spills a table of drinks on them. "Hate him, hate him, wouldn't want to date him," they chime in near unison. The ball bounces behind the bleachers, and when Eric goes to retrieve it the lights suddenly go out, the motorized bleachers retract and crush a screaming Eric behind them.

Investigating the latest murder, Mulder tells Scully he was following a lead with Detective White, and she's clearly annoyed. "We have differing opinions, but I didn't expect you to ditch me," she snaps. The agents go to the woods, where Spitz and other townsfolk are digging up a backyard looking for a mass grave. Scully calls the effort "rumor panic," but when the searchers find a bag belonging to the local pediatrician with bones inside, they rush to his house.

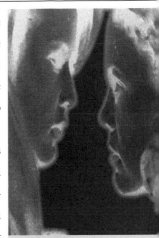

The doctor, seen inside wearing makeup and a fluffy woman's robe, says he sold the bag, and analysis shows the bones belong to a Llasa Apso named "Mr. Tippy" who belonged to Terri. To the doctor's chagrin, Mulder says he smells his favorite perfume, and a strangely hostile Scully calls him on the carpet, labeling his conduct "highly objectionable" while announcing she'll return to Washington so he can work with Detective White.

A "syzygy" is an astronomical alignment of three celestial objects: the sun, the Earth, and either the moon or a planet.

At a birthday party for Terri and Margi, Brenda plays with a Ouija board, which, to her dismay, when asked who she's going to marry spells

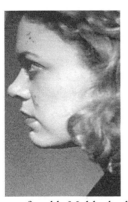

out "S-A-T-A-N." Brenda rushes to the bathroom, where she finds Terri and Margi chanting inside as the door slams behind her. In his hotel, Mulder somewhat pathetically drinks a screwdriver by spooning orange juice concentrate into a vodka bottle, watching an old movie (as does an antsy Scully) that inexplicably is on every channel. White shows up, upset that her cat is missing, taking a swig of vodka herself and forcing an uncomfortable Mulder back onto the bed. "Maybe we can solve the mystery of the horny beast," she says, kissing him as Scully comes in, looking disgusted. "There's been another murder," she says.

Brenda has been impaled on mirror glass, while Scully and Mulder bicker heading to the crime scene. Asked if his insistence on driving is a macho thing "because you're the guy," Mulder quips, "No, I was just never sure your little feet could reach the pedals."

Terri and Margi seek to console Scott, who rebuffs them. "Hate him," Terri says, but instead of repeating her as in the past, Margi simply strides away. The psychic tells Mulder the planets come into conjunction like this once every 84 years, and that this year Uranus is also in the house of Aquarius, which could spell disaster for the town located at a geological vortex, she says, culminating when the planets perfectly align on that day, January 12. Two people born at the same time on that day in 1979 (as Margi and Terri are) would be under the influence of "a grand square," when "all the energy of the cosmos would be focused on you."

Margi goes to Scott alone, but Terri barges in and accuses her of blowing her off for "shoulder time" with him. As the two square off the room begins to vibrate, with garage-door springs shooting back and forth. Both girls are wounded, but they pause to see Scott has been fatally impaled. Margi calls Mulder and tells him that Terri is the killer, while Terri tearfully informs Scully that the reverse is true. The agents talk, agreeing to bring both girls to the police station, where all hell breaks loose—desks shaking and guns firing off on their own. Mulder grabs Margi, dragging her down the hall, locking the two girls in the same room. The whole building shakes, but at 12:01 A.M., it all suddenly stops.

The mob breaks into the station, but the two girls are found sitting in the corner together sobbing. Mulder wonders about the possibility of two girls, born on the same date, finding themselves the focus of unseen forces beyond our grasp.

Getting back in the car, Mulder and Scully speed through a stop sign, and in a rare turn as passenger Mulder is told to shut up when he protests. "Sure. Fine. Whatever," he says, echoing Scully's comments from before.

BACK STORY: Some hard-core fans on the Internet were critical of this episode, not realizing that Mulder and Scully's uncharitable and at times hostile behavior toward each other partly stemmed from the planetary forces that also affected Margi and Terri. "Chris wanted to keep it kind of abstract," admits director Rob Bowman.

Denalda Williams (Madame Zerinka) previously appeared in "Irresistible" as a clerk who took a job application from Donnie Pfaster. Garry Davey makes his fourth appearance on The X-Files—previously he was in "Eve," "Roland," and "End Game."

During their bickering Scully even asks why Mulder always has to drive, and he responds by ribbing her about her height and inability to reach the pedals. "I thought it was hysterical," says Anderson—who stands not quite 5'3"—noting that the scene grew out of longtime nitpicking by fans about such matters, among them the fact that Mulder usually drives the car. Carter, in fact, made the exact same joke about Anderson's "little feet" long before the episode aired at a *The X-Files* convention in Pasadena, California. "Those are comments that have come on the Internet from the beginning," Anderson continues. "They're always picking apart aspects of the show that have nothing to do with the show per se."

Carter remains somewhat bemused by reaction to this episode. "There were all sorts of hints that no one got," he notes, beginning with the camera panning past a road sign that said "Leaving Comity"—which literally means "social harmony." "That's one of the risks you run, that people become so hopeful and familiar and comfortable with something that when you turn it on its head, they don't understand it." Others got it but simply objected because of their desire for Mulder and Scully to get together on a more social level, despite Carter's insistence

that such a relationship won't occur. At least one group of fans in San Francisco savored the show, printing up T-shirts that say "Sure. Fine. Whatever."

The script originally called for Stanley Kubrick's *A Clockwork Orange* to be playing on every channel as Mulder and Scully played with the remote controls in their hotel rooms, but the footage proved so expensive the producer settled for clips of the *Keystone Kops*, which in retrospect worked better in Carter's eyes. "As is often the case, what you're compelled to use is better than what you (initially) wanted," he observes, reflecting the show's philosophy of making the most of available resources.

WHAT WAS WRONG WITH MULDER'S HOTEL ROOM TV IN "SYZYGY"?

Every single channel showed the same Keystone Kops movie.

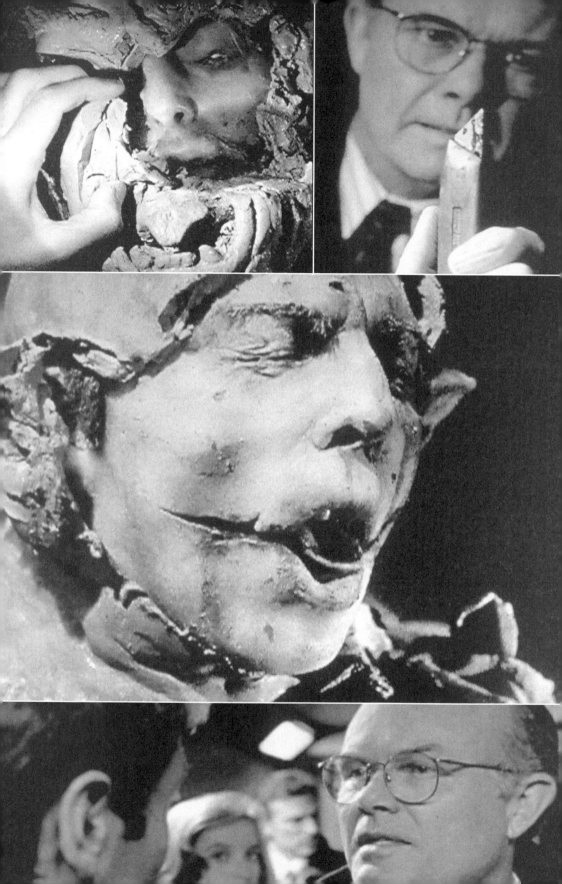

an extension art program students sketch a nude model;
ever, one of them, John Mostov, sketches a grotesque gar-
le that bears no resemblance to the model, smudging bloo
the canvas after cutting himself. The model leaves late
finds   turning   aming a
ething slas at   The FB breaks in late arrestin
tov,   bites   hauser,   of   ents As they dra

GROTESQUE

EPISODE: 3 X 14

FIRST AIRED:

February 2, 1996

WRITTEN BY:

Howard Gordon

EDITOR::

Heather MacDougall

DIRECTED BY:

Kim Manners

GUEST STARS:

Mitch Pileggi (AD Walter Skinner)

Levani Outchaneichvili (John
    Mostow)

Kurtwood Smith (Agent
    Bill Patterson)

Greg Thirloway (Agent
    Nemhauser)

Susan Bain (Agent Sheherlis)

Kasper Michaels (Young Agent)

Zoran Vukelic (Model)

LOG LINE:

A serial killer maintains an evil spirit was responsible for his actions, as Mulder's own sanity comes into question when the murders persist.

PRINCIPAL SETTING:

Washington, D.C.

SYNOPSIS:

At an extension art program students sketch a nude model; however, one of them, John Mostow, sketches a grotesque gargoyle that bears no resemblance to the model, smudging blood on the canvas after cutting himself. The model leaves later but finds his car door jammed shut, turning and screaming as something slashes at him. The FBI breaks in later, arresting Mostow, who bites Nemhauser, one of the agents. As they drag him out the senior agent, Bill Patterson, finds a bloody razor blade.

Going over the case, Mulder notes that Mostow is a Soviet emigrant—who came to the United States after spending years in an asylum—suspected in the murders of at least seven men. Mostow insists that a spirit possessed him during the murders. Another body is found after Mostow's arrest, mirroring undisclosed details of the same pattern of mutilation. Mostow has scrawled a gargoyle image on the floor of his cell. "It killed those men," he says, adding when told of the latest murder, "It found somebody. Somebody new. Just like it found me."

Patterson, Mulder's former mentor, snidely asks if he suspects the involvement of "little green men" or "hounds of hell." The agent notes that his unit spent three years working the case and that his profile led to Mostow's arrest. Mulder is nevertheless hostile to Patterson,

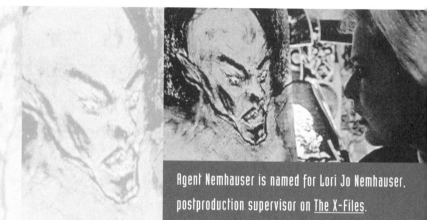

Agent Nemhauser is named for Lori Jo Nemhauser, postproduction supervisor on The X-Files.

noting that he objected to his belief that "if you want to catch a monster, you've got to become one yourself." Checking Mostow's studio, Mulder finds sculpted gargoyles in a secret room, with human corpses inside them. Elsewhere, a glassblower is attacked with the same signature facial mutilation.

Nemhauser confides to Scully that Patterson may have requested Mulder's involvement—that he actually admires his former protegé. Mulder reads up on gargoyles, and Patterson finds him in the library, insisting that Mostow is insane and he's wasting his time. He also expresses disappointment in Mulder, saying he was "clearly mistaken" in the notion Mulder might have "put your feet back on the ground."

Going to Mulder's apartment, Scully is alarmed to find he's papered the room with gargoyle drawings. Mulder awakens in Mostow's studio, chasing a figure through the darkness and plummeting over a railing after the figure slashes at him with a blade.

Scully wonders why he was in Mostow's apartment in the first place at 3 A.M., but Mulder is evasive, saying only, "Whatever attacked me wasn't a person."

Scully believes Patterson is testing Mulder, but when she confronts the agent Patterson tells her, "Let Mulder do what he has to do." Mulder visits Mostow, wondering why the figure didn't kill him as it did the others, punching the prisoner when he won't provide information on how to find the creature. "It can find you," Mostow notes defiantly. "Maybe it already has."

Scully finds a blade at the crime scene with Mulder's prints on it, and the murder weapon is missing from the evidence room. Skinner questions Scully about the weapon, and though she doesn't answer when he asks if she's worried about Mulder, her expression gives her away. "So am I," Skinner says.

Mulder awakens suddenly from a nightmare, returning to Mostow's studio, where he discovers a new body in a pool of blood. Receiving a message from Nemhauser that cuts off suddenly, Scully

IN "GROTESQUE," WHAT ANIMAL LEADS MULDER TO JOHN MOSTOW'S SECRET SCULPTURE STUDIO?

When he and Scully investigate Mostow's apartment, Mostow's cat startles Scully. Mulder follows it and discovers a secret room containing several grisly statues.

calls the number and is surprised when Mulder answers. She asks about the knife, but Mulder insists he didn't take it. Finding Nemhauser's body encased inside a gargoyle sculpture, Mulder turns to see Patterson. "You killed him, Bill," he says slowly, the realization dawning that Patterson lived in Mostow's head for three years and that the violence lived on inside him—with Patterson requesting Mulder in the hope that he would stop him.

Scully enters suddenly, pulling her gun and telling Mulder to drop his, which allows Patterson to flee to the rooftop. He ambushes Mulder, and the two struggle until Patterson is shot, collapsing to the ground wounded. Two weeks later Patterson, like Mostow, yells from his cell that he's innocent. In voice-over, Mulder notes that the agents "work in the dark" but sometimes falter and let the monsters without turn within—leaving them "alone staring into the abyss," he says, the image of the gargoyle appearing, "into the laughing face of madness."

BACK STORY: Kim Manners identifies this as his favorite third-season episode, with a great script and stellar guest performances by Kurtwood Smith and Levani Outchaneichvili. "I thought 'Grotesque' had it all," he says, also singling out Duchovny's performance in exploring the precipice of madness. According to the director, "David did some fabulous work in 'Grotesque.' David really drove himself into this mad world, and I found myself doing it too." For his part, Manners listened to the music from *Jacob's Ladder* over and over, until his wife, as he remembers it, finally asked, "'Do we have to listen to that (bleeping) CD again? It's so depressing.' But it's a way to accomplish these things—to get into the head, into the psyche of these scripts," he says.

"I'm very proud of that episode," says Howard Gordon, "because I think it illuminated a lot of Mulder, but also all of this—that there really is this thin line between madness and sanity. We sort of walk around and act civilized, but there's this thin membrane between us and people who walk into McDonald's and start shooting things up."

John Mostow and Bill Patterson weren't the only ones disturbed by gargoyles. A Catholic hospital proved reluctant to let the crew affix gargoyle figures to the exte-

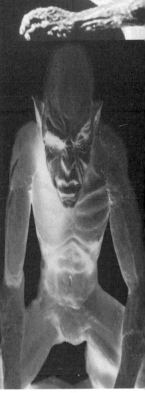

rior of the building for the teaser sequence, considering them a symbol of evil. An appropriate building (Heritage Hall, an old post office) was finally located, but crew members found themselves panicked upon returning from their Christmas holiday to discover the sidewalk next to the building had been ripped up by city workmen in the precise spot the camera would focus in on as it craned past the gargoyle down to the street—what Manners calls "my hero shot"—a mere three days before the sequence was scheduled to be shot. The city responded immediately, double-timing repairs to restore the sidewalk in time for filming.

Assistant art director Gary Allen created the gargoyle sketches, one of which adorns a wall in the production office's casting room. "He just went nuts," says graphic artist Vivien Nishi, with only a hint of irony. Cinematographer John Bartley was particularly proud of the episode's look, which earned him an Emmy nomination. Mark Snow's score for this hour also generated inordinate attention online, though Snow admits he had to hear about it second-hand. "I'm not online," he says. "If I did that I don't think I'd get a thing done."

Gauthier, a diver on a French vessel in the Pacific Oce
is lowered into the water while his mates talk excitedly ab
finding "the needle in the haystack." They lose contact w
Gauthier, who to his horror sees what looks like a man al
inside a sunken ship whose eyes become a murky black. Gauth
rises and says he's fine, but away from his shipmates his
eyes cloud over with the same silky black membra

thier, a diver on a French vessel in the Pacific Ocean,
lowered into the water while his mates talk excitedly about
ding "the needle in the haystack." They lose contact with
thier, who to his horror sees what looks like a man alive
side ... ... become murky ... Gauthier
... says he ... ... but ... ... has mates his own
... cloud over with the same silky ... membrane. Assistant

PIPER MARU

EPISODE: 3X15

FIRST AIRED:
February 9, 1996

WRITTEN BY:
Frank Spotnitz and Chris Carter

EDITOR:
Jim Gross

DIRECTED BY:
Rob Bowman

GUEST STARS:
Mitch Pileggi (AD Walter Skinner)
Robert Clothier (General
    Christopher Johansen)
Jo Bates (Jeraldine Kallenchuck)
Nicholas Lea (Alex Krycek)
Morris Panych (The Gray Haired-
    Man)
Stephen E. Miller (Wayne Morgan)
Ari Solomon (Gauthier)
Paul Batten (Dr. Seizer)
Russell Ferrier (Medic)
Lenno Britos (Hispanic Man)
Kimberly Unger (Joan Gauthier)
Rochelle Greenwood (Waitress)
Joel Silverstone (Engineer #1)
David Neale (Navy Base Guard)
Tom Scholte (Young Johansen)

Robert F. Maier (WWII Pilot)
Tegan Moss (Young Dana Scully)

LOG LINE:
A French salvage ship finds mysterious wreckage from World War II that unleashes a
strange force causing radiation sickness and
leading Mulder into a web of intrigue.

PRINCIPAL SETTINGS:
San Diego, California; San Francisco, California; Washington, D.C.; Hong Kong

SYNOPSIS:
Gauthier, a diver on a French vessel in the
Pacific Ocean, is lowered into the water while
his mates talk excitedly about finding "the needle in the haystack." They lose contact with
Gauthier, who to his horror sees what looks
like a man alive inside a sunken ship whose
eyes become a murky black. Gauthier rises and
says he's fine, but away from his shipmates his
own eyes cloud over with the same silky black
membrane.

Assistant Director Skinner asks to see
Scully, informing her that there have been no
leads in the murder of her sister Melissa and
that after five months—without any leads
from the D.C. police or the Bureau—the case
is to be made inactive. "I don't think there's
anything to read into this," he says, noting that

he'll make an appeal on her behalf. Scully is angry, pointing out that her sister's murder, despite the seemingly available evidence, can't seem "to keep anybody interested."

Mulder tells Scully about the French salvage ship, the Piper Maru, which limped into port in San Diego after being at the same coordinates as the *Talapus*—the ship Mulder believes to have hauled up a UFO. The entire crew has been treated for radiation burns. "There's something still down there," he says.

Going to San Diego, Mulder and Scully check out the irradiated crewmen, all horribly burned, with the doctor noting that such radiation levels don't exist in nature. "Not on this planet," Mulder mutters. One man, they're told, was unaffected: Gauthier, who piloted the ship in while the others were ailing. Visiting the ship, Mulder and Scully are told there's no trace of radiation, though Mulder does detect the black oily substance, seen clouding Gauthier's eyes, on the dive suit as well. The ship's video also reveals a submerged plane, which Scully recognizes as a World War II fighter, a North American B–51 Mustang. "I just got very turned on," Mulder deadpans.

Joan Gauthier comes home to their apartment in San Francisco and tries to leave when her husband is behaving strangely, but he grabs her. When Joan does leave we see the silky substance is now in her eyes.

Scully goes to Miramar Navy Air Base to see an old family friend, Major Johansen. Seeing children at play reminds her of days with her sister when their father was in the service. She asks about the missing plane, but Johansen insists he doesn't remember. At Gauthier's apartment, Mulder finds papers strewn about and a dazed Gauthier as well as the address for a salvage broker. Gauthier has the oily substance all over him and no memory of anything after the dive. Mulder visits the office of the salvage broker, but the "secretary" is uncooperative. He waits outside, tailing her after she leaves just as armed men raid the office.

Kimberly Unger, who plays Joan Gauthier, formerly appeared as a radar operator in "Fallen Angel," with a memorable line: "Sir, the meteor seems to be hovering above a small town in Wisconsin." Robert Clothier, who plays General Johansen, formerly appeared in the second season episode "Red Museum" as an old man in a truck who led Mulder and Scully to a field of cows being injected with bioengineered hormones.

Scully is stopped leaving the base, and Johansen gets in her car, confessing that he was sent to find a sunken plane after World War II as a submarine officer aboard the Zeus Faber. "We bury our dead alive, don't we?" he muses, recounting how men on the sub died of radiation sickness until he led a mutiny against the captain, who's seen with the same membrane over his eyes. Only 7 of 144 crew members survived, Johansen says, and the plane was carrying an atomic bomb bound for Japan. Scully relays this information to a skeptical Mulder.

Mulder tracks the woman from the salvage office, who turns out to be the salvage broker J. Kallenchuk, to the airport, and boards a flight for Hong Kong, as does Joan Gauthier. In Hong Kong, Mulder handcuffs himself to Kallenchuk, accusing her of selling classified government secrets. Mulder drags Kallenchuk to her office, where an armed Alex Krycek waits inside. Krycek, who is supplying the secrets from the digital tape he acquired at the start of the season, pushes the woman outside while she's still cuffed to Mulder, as gunshots ring out and the cuff goes limp. Krycek escapes through a window, and Mulder grabs the key and gets out just before armed men break into the room. Racing down the hall, the men encounter Joan Gauthier, who in a blinding flash leaves them all horribly burned.

Skinner, warned earlier by mysterious dark-suited men who say they "work for the intelligence community" not to reopen Melissa Scully's case, is shot at point-blank range in a Washington coffee shop. The shooter says in Spanish, "*Chupa dura, amigo*"—meaning literally "Suck hard, friend"—spitting on him before running away. Scully gets a call saying that Skinner is being rushed to the hospital.

Krycek prepares to board a plane for Washington, but Mulder surprises him, slamming a phone receiver into his face. "This is for me," he says, headbutting him while taking his gun and sticking it in his belly, "and this is for my father." Aside from revenge, Mulder wants the digital tape, which has all the government's information on UFOs. Krycek pleads for his life, saying the tape is in a locker in

Mulder and Krycek take flight 1121 back to the U.S.; again, this is creator Chris Carter's wife's birthday, November 21.

D.C. and he'll get it for Mulder if he lets him go. Mulder tells Krycek he will go to D.C. with him, but permits him to go clean his bloodied face. As Mulder waits outside, Joan Gauthier enters the bathroom, hoisting Krycek effortlessly off the ground. "Feel better?" Mulder asks when Krycek comes out.

"Like a new man," he says, his own eyes glazing over with the black membrane.

To be continued . . .

BACK STORY: "Piper Maru" was named after Gillian Anderson's daughter, whose middle name means "calm and gentle" in Polynesian. The reference also fit well given the episode's context, since the term also loosely translates to the Japanese word for ship.

Anderson considers this one of the more emotionally difficult episodes she had to play during the season. "'Piper Maru' was challenging," she says, citing her scenes with the colonel, which forced Scully to deal both with feelings about losing her sister and growing up as a navy brat. "There was something about it—having to pull from the past . . . how it brought the present and the past together. It was just good to play."

Story editor Frank Spotnitz was assigned the idea by Chris Carter based on some images he had conceived of and wanted to connect within the episode. "He just knew he wanted a guy in the cockpit of a World War II plane banging against the glass," explains Spotnitz, who at first struggled with writing the script. "He didn't know how he got there, was this guy alive or dead, was it an illusion. Then he wanted a flashback to World War II aboard a submarine. I was stuck on that story for weeks. I had no idea how I was going to connect those, or when that image was going to come.

"Finally, I was flying back from *The X-Files* convention in

Minneapolis and I thought about Scully having not dealt with the death of her sister, and the idea of bringing in Krycek. I didn't have any paper, so I started writing on the back of an airline magazine, filling up all the white space. In the space of that flight I pretty much outlined the story." Nicholas Lea's name also didn't appear until the closing credits, trying to preserve the sense of surprise regarding Krycek's return.

Filming the underwater sequences using the Newtsuit—a 900-pound deep-sea diving apparatus resembling the suits worn by lunar astronauts—provided its own highlight, working in conjunction with a company that performs underwater salvage expeditions. Among those particularly enamored with the underwater sequences was special effects coordinator David Gauthier—a certified diver (he and director Rob Bowman vacationed after the season in Micronesia) for whom the French character first inhabited by the alien presence was named. The diving scenes were principally shot in a 12-by-12-by-24-foot tank, with the actor seen inside the plane remaining underwater within the shell of the cockpit for two hours while filming that scene, breathing through a diving regulator.

A cruise ship terminal stood in for the airport, due to construction at Vancouver's airport.

WHAT IS SO SPECIAL ABOUT THE NAME OF FRENCH DIVER GAUTHIER IN "PIPER MARU"?

He is named for special effects wizard David Gauthier of the Vancouver X-Files crew. Long term X-Philes have learned to watch the end credits as closely as the opening credits for clues to character names.

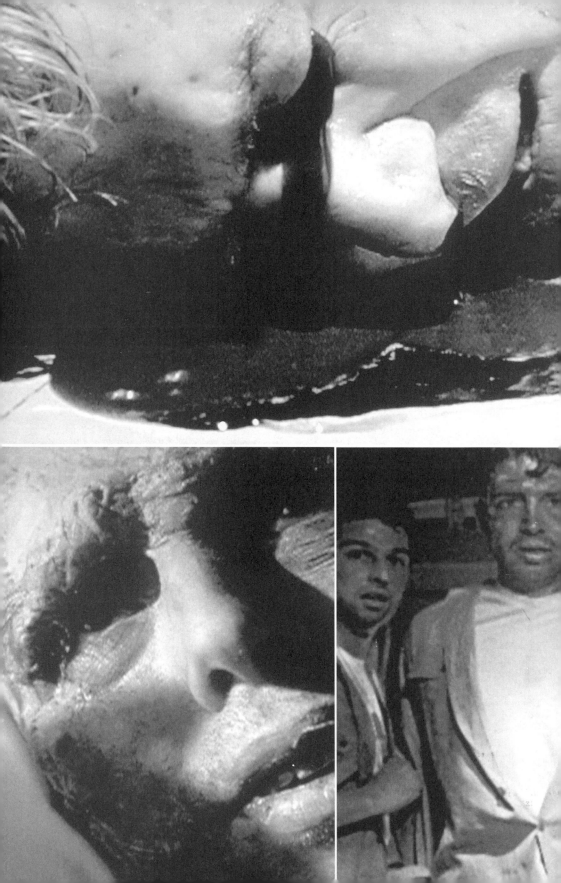

s August 19, 1953, and a sick, burned crewman in Pearl
bor Navy Hospital tells three young government men about
ordeal—how he and others were locked up with the captain
their submarine on a salvage mission and how the men were
ng. The captain had the telltale black membran over his
s, and after being knocked unconscious a black oil oozed
of him down a grate into the lower depths. "For the first

APOCRYPHA

EPISODE: 3 X 16

FIRST AIRED:

February 16, 1996

WRITTEN BY:

Frank Spotnitz and Chris Carter

EDITOR:

Stephen Mark

DIRECTED BY:

Kim Manners

GUEST STARS:

Mitch Pileggi (AD Walter Skinner)

John Neville (The Well-
Manicured Man)

William B. Davis (The Cigarette-
Smoking Man)

Tom Braidwood (Frohike)

Dean Haglund (Langly)

Bruce Harwood (Byers)

Nicholas Lea (Alex Krycek)

Kevin McNulty (Agent Brian Fuller)

Barry Levy (Navy Doctor)

Dmitry Chepovetsky
(Government Man #1)

Sue Mathew (Agent Linda Caleca)

Don S. Williams (Elder)

Lenno Britos (Hispanic Man/Luis
Cardinal)

Frances Flanagan (Nurse)

Brendan Beiser (Agent Pendrell)

Peter Scoular (Sick Crewman)

Jeff Chivers (Armed Man)

Martin Evans (Major Domo)

Harrison R. Coe (Government Man #2)

Craig Warkentin (Government Man #3)

LOG LINE:

Mulder pursues Krycek and the mystery of the
sunken World War II wreckage, while the
shooting of Skinner brings Scully new clues to
her sister's murder.

PRINCIPAL SETTINGS:

Washington, D.C.; Black Crow, North Dakota

SYNOPSIS:

It's August 19, 1953, and a sick, burned crewman in Pearl Harbor Navy Hospital tells three
young government men about his ordeal—
how he and others were locked up with the
captain of their submarine on a salvage mission and how the men were dying. The captain
had the telltale black membrane over his eyes,
and after being knocked unconscious a black
oil oozed out of him, down a grate into the
lower depths. "For the first time, we saw the
enemy that was killing us," the sailor says, later
grasping one of the government men. "That
thing is still down there!" he shouts, entreating

him to "make sure the truth gets out. I can trust you to do that, can't I, Mr. Mulder?" Mr. Mulder doesn't answer, looking to another young government man, who lights up a familiar-looking cigarette. "You can trust all of us," he replies casually.

Back in the present, Scully rushes to the wounded Skinner in the hospital, while Mulder and Krycek arrive in Washington. They rent a car but another vehicle runs them off the road. Mulder is dazed, but when Krycek is yanked from the car and asked about the videotape, a blinding light appears, frying his two attackers. The Cigarette-Smoking Man looks over the burn victims, whose condition is critical. The doctor says he's never seen anything like this before. "I have," the Cigarette-Smoking Man says tersely. "Have the bodies destroyed."

Mulder awakens in the hospital with Scully at his side, telling him about Skinner and showing him DNA results indicating that the man who shot Skinner and the one who shot her sister, Melissa, are one and the same. In New York, the Shadowy Syndicate meets to discuss "disturbing reports" about the French salvage ship. "It seems we have an information leak, gentlemen," one elder says, noting that their Washington associate, the Cigarette-Smoking Man, has been asked to account for this.

Skinner tells Scully he recognized the man who shot him as being with Krycek when the third attacker took the UFO digital tape from him in the hospital stairwell. For his part, Mulder has collected a sample of the oil found on the diving suit as well as on Gauthier and his wife, Joan. He hypothesizes that it's a medium employed by "some kind of alien creature that uses it to body jump"—an entity that waited on the ocean floor 50 years for another host to bring it to the surface, traveling from Gauthier to his wife and then to Krycek. The question, Mulder says, is "what does it want."

Still holding Krycek's key to the locker, Mulder has the Lone Gunmen go to an ice rink and retrieve an envelope, but the cassette case within turns out to be empty. Elsewhere, the Cigarette-Smoking Man sips a drink as Krycek enters, tossing him the tape. "Where is it?" Krycek asks serenely.

During the "Lone Gunmen on ice" scene, you will note the ease with which Byers handles himself. Bruce Harwood (Byers) once trained as a professional ice skater.

"I've been expecting you," the Cigarette-Smoking Man answers casually, telling him, "I have what you want."

The Cigarette-Smoking Man meets with the syndicate, who aren't pleased that he's acted unilaterally in moving the salvaged UFO to another location. The Well-Manicured Man is perturbed by the Skinner shooting as well, which another elder calls "very serious exposure for us."

"I'll take care of it," the Cigarette-Smoking Man says, glaring at the Well-Manicured Man, who frets about the threat to "our project's future." Mulder finds the outline of a New York phone number scribbled on the envelope, calling the syndicate office and speaking to the Well-Manicured Man, who asks to meet him in Central Park. Back in Washington, Scully learns that the shooter is a mercenary named Luis Cardinal who may have already fled the country. Scully insists they keep looking, with one agent asking how without a sign from God. "I've seen stranger things, believe me," Scully snaps, storming out.

The Well-Manicured Man tells Mulder the object in the ocean was a UFO, a "so-called Foo Fighter" downed during World War II. Complications arose during the salvage operation, and a cover story about a third A-bomb bound for Japan was concocted. Mulder says Krycek has the tape and realizes Well-Manicured Man doesn't know where he is either. "Anyone can be gotten to," the man says, prompting an alarmed Mulder to urge Scully to check immediately on Skinner. She finds him in an ambulance being transferred to another hospital, encountering an armed Luis Cardinal, whom she corners in the street. "You shot my sister!" she screams, her gun pointed at him, while a frightened Cardinal offers her Krycek in exchange for his life. Although tempted, Scully doesn't fire, and the police arrest Cardinal, who tells her Krycek is headed to an abandoned missile site in North Dakota where Mulder thinks they'll find the salvaged UFO. At the site the agents descend into a silo, finding a burned man. "He's here," Mulder says, as several armed men arrive, capturing them outside silo door 1013.

The Cigarette-Smoking Man waits outside. "You led him here, didn't you?" Mulder says, yelling as he's dragged away that "You can't bury the truth!" Inside, the Cigarette-Smoking Man eyes the silo door, behind which Krycek convulsively coughs up the black oil, which seeps purposefully into a strange-looking grid on what appears to be an alien craft.

IN "APOCRYPHA," WHAT SINISTER FIGURE AGREED TO MEET MULDER IN CENTRAL PARK FOR AN EXCHANGE OF INFORMATION?

The Well-Manicured Man, seeking the whereabouts of rogue agent Alex Krycek as well as the tape he is carrying, agreed to an "exchange of information" in which he learned more than Mulder did.

Using a cane, Skinner returns to work. Mulder thanks him for putting himself at risk, but Skinner insists he was just doing his job. "This isn't my crusade," he says. Mulder finds Scully at Melissa's grave, bringing news from Skinner that Cardinal was found dead in his cell, and suggesting that if those who took his life haven't gotten to Krycek yet they soon will. Scully ponders Johansen's words, observing that the dead do speak from beyond the grave in the form of conscience, demanding justice. "Maybe we bury the dead alive," she muses.

Meanwhile, far away, Krycek futilely pounds the silo door, hopelessly entombed deep underground.

BACK STORY: The alien spaceship occupied nearly an entire soundstage, according to art director Graeme Murray, with the ship itself shaped like a large triangle—30-feet long on each side—built out of wood. "It was meant to have kind of that stealth look," says Murray, noting that Carter has indicated that any alien vessel should approximate the appearance of some craft that could be perceived as an experimental plane originating on Earth.

Nicholas Lea underwent a true ordeal in lensing the last scene, when Krycek oozes the black oil out of his mouth and nose into the alien craft. The actor had to wear a mask with tubes wired into it that would leak the substance out, compelling Lea to spend considerable time suspended atop the vast ship hunched over the alien grid as the liquid dripped out. "He wasn't particularly pleased with it," Toby Lindala admits.

"It was horrible," says Lea, acknowledging that he could have let a double do the scene but insisted on undergoing the process himself. Applying the prosthetic mask took over an hour, and after shooting the sequence once Lea was called days later and told the scene had been lit too darkly and needed to be filmed again. Still, Lea says he tries to have fun when he's doing the show, "even"—as he told a convention in San Diego—"when you're puking up stuff out of your eyes."

Lindala adds that an earlier effect, when the black ooze drips out of the submarine captain's head, represented a major technical accomplishment—utilizing a full dummy head of the actor that contained six different hoses feeding into each facial orifice. "The quality of work from our shop has really evolved," he says, citing an increase in puppetry as well as remote-control articulation as the show has progressed.

After handling a variety of stand-alone episodes ranging from horror to comedy, director Kim Manners had his first opportunity to contribute to the larger lore of the series in this installment. "That was the first mythology episode that I've ever done, and I loved it," he says. "They're more character-driven. I seem to get the monster of the week."

Because Mat Beck was having difficulty digitally creating the eye effect, the look was generated by introducing an oily substance into water, with Beck then taking that footage and digitally inserting it into shots of the actors' faces. "No one had to wear contacts," David Gauthier explains.

"We shot it four different times," Beck adds. "When you can get the shot practically [as opposed to digitally], you always try to."

A slightly less special effect involved the Lone Gunmen, who proved more than a little shaky on ice skates. That was despite their status as native Canadians, which caused the writers to just assume they would know how to skate. "It's true, I'm afraid," says Dean Haglund, who plays Langly. Haglund says he spent most of his childhood cross-country skiing but that he had never skated. The actor-comic subjected himself to a five-day crash course, taking the "crash" part a bit too literally. Assistant director and part-time actor Tom Braidwood says it had been "a long, long time" since he'd skated, so he bought skates and went out and practiced on weekends in anticipation of his big (albeit brief) scene. Though Braidwood says he enjoyed skating again, he admits with a laugh that he's "terrified of falling," proudly adding, "I didn't fall once."

The silo number where Krycek is stranded, 1013, is one of those that recur on *The X-Files*, since the date is Chris Carter's birthday as well as the name of his production company.

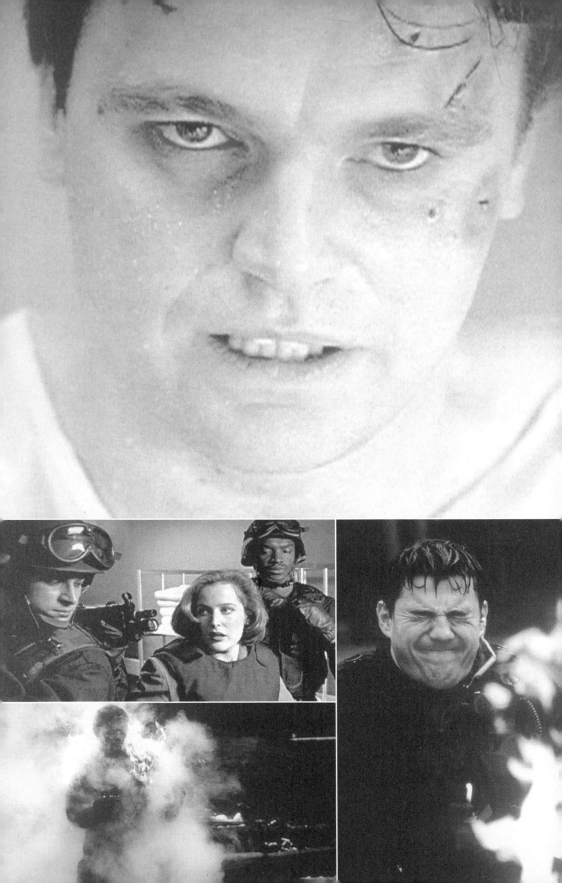

average-looking guy is in a supermarket, filling his bas-
t with high-carbohydrate bodybuilding drinks and waiting in
e calmly before a squad of FBI agents arrests him. "You
ink you can hold me?" he asks as they usher him into a car,
lking to the d   til the oncoming
ck the driver   shes. The driver
lls forward, a   into them as the

PUSHER

EPISODE: 3X17

FIRST AIRED:

February 23, 1996

WRITTEN BY:

Vince Gilligan

EDITOR:

Heather MacDougall

DIRECTED BY:

Rob Bowman

GUEST STARS:

Mitch Pileggi (AD Walter Skinner)

Robert Wisden (Robert "Pusher" Modell)

Vic Polizos (Agent Frank Burst)

Roger R. Cross (SWAT Lieutenant)

Steve Bacic (Agent Collins)

Don Mackay (Judge)

Brent J. D. Sheppard (Prosecutor)

D. Neil Mark (Deputy Scott Kerber)

Julia Arkos (Holly)

Meridith Bain-Woodward (Defense Attorney)

Ernie Foort (Lobby Guard)

Darren Lucas (Lead SWAT Cop)

LOG LINE:

Mulder and Scully investigate a man possessing the power to bend people to his will and who engages Mulder in a scary battle of wits.

PRINCIPAL SETTING:

Loudoun County, Virginia

SYNOPSIS:

An average-looking guy is in a supermarket, filling his basket with high-carbohydrate body-building drinks and waiting in line calmly as a squad of FBI agents surround him. "You think you can hold me?" he asks as they arrest him and usher him into a car. He talks to the driver in a soothing voice until the oncoming truck the driver is looking at simply vanishes. The driver pulls forward, allowing the truck to crash into them as the suspect braces himself against the door.

The surviving agent on the case, Frank Burst, tells Mulder and Scully about the suspect, known only as Pusher, who called him confessing to a string of murders over two years, each looking like a suicide. "It was a game. He was bragging," Burst says.

Mulder sees the word "RONIN," a masterless samurai, fingerpainted on a police car at the scene and checks mercenary magazines, finding an ad that says, "I solve problems.

In the scene where Robert Modell is infiltrating FBI headquarters, two of the "extras" passing in the background are Foo Fighters' drummer Dave Grohl and his wife, Jennifer. The Foo Fighters' "Down in the Park" appears on The X-Files—themed CD, Songs in the Key of X.

OSU"—the Japanese word "osu" meaning "to push." Suggestion is a powerful force, Mulder notes, and the suspect may be bending people to his will; however, Scully points out there's a difference between TV commercials or hypnosis and inducing someone to drive in front of a truck.

Mulder and Scully stake out a pay phone listed in the ad, and Pusher calls, daring Mulder to "follow my little bread crumb trail . . . prove your worth." A clue leads them to a golf course, where under Pusher's influence an agent douses himself in gasoline and sets himself ablaze as a helpless Mulder, Scully, and Burst look on. Mulder finds Pusher in a car nearby, weakened and bathed in sweat. "Betcha five bucks I get off," he says.

Mulder testifies at the hearing, saying Pusher, whose name is Robert Patrick Modell, talks people into injuring themselves. Seemingly swayed by Modell's power, however, the judge lets him go. Outside the courtroom, Mulder tells Modell his shoe's untied. "Made you look," Mulder whispers. "How do you do it?"

Research uncovers that Modell applied to the FBI and claimed to have studied under ninjas in Japan. "Are we talking kung fu movies here, Mulder?" asks an impatient Scully, contending that most of Modell's claims are lies or exaggerations and that he's simply a little man who wants to feel big. Modell goes to the FBI building to access information about Mulder, walking past the security guards by wearing a phony badge that just says "PASS." When Skinner notices him, Modell manipulates a woman into spraying the FBI assistant director with mace and kicking him repeatedly as Modell calmly escapes. Asked about the incident, the woman says it was "like he was with me inside my head," and though she can't explain it, Scully now agrees with Mulder's theory. Raiding Modell's apartment, the agents find the refrigerator full of CarboBoost and medication for epilepsy. Mulder conjectures that a brain tumor may have given Modell psychokinetic powers, with the protein drinks a means of replenishing his energy.

"Maybe he's dying," says Mulder, "and he wants to go out in a blaze of glory," adds Scully, finishing the thought. Modell calls, and as Burst tries to stall so they can trace his location the suspect talks the agent into having a fatal heart attack, telling Mulder he's read his file and is looking for "a worthy adversary." Tracing Modell to a hospital, Mulder—fearing that their quarry may turn armed agents against each other—goes in alone wearing a miniature camera. "Can I get the Playboy Channel?" a nervous Mulder quips.

Mulder hears shots fired, finding a technician and guard dead. A computer monitor shows that Modell does indeed have a tumor, and he appears with a gun as the camera blacks out, prompting Scully to rush in after Mulder, whom she finds squared off at a table with Modell, the gun between them. Modell forces Mulder to play Russian roulette, pulling the trigger at Modell and then his own temple before pointing the gun at Scully. "You're stronger than this, Mulder, fight him," Scully says, pulling an alarm that seems to temporarily break Modell's concentration as Mulder—momentarily freed from his mental grasp—turns and shoots him.

Modell lays hospitalized in a coma from which he'll never awaken. The tumor had been operable until the very end, they're told, but he refused treatment. "It was like you said," Mulder observes. "He was always such a little man. This was finally something that made him feel big." Scully briefly takes Mulder's hand, saying they shouldn't let him take another minute of their time.

BACK STORY: Mitch Pileggi wasn't particularly thrilled, he admits, about Skinner having "this little woman" brutalize him, especially after the character had been roughed up so much in previous episodes. "I was feeling a little uncomfortable with him getting his ass kicked so much, and I think the fans were, too," he notes.

Writer Vince Gilligan set out to establish a

WHERE DID SELF-STYLED ASSASSIN ROBERT "PUSHER" MODELL ADVERTISE FOR CLIENTS?

In the pages of American Ronin magazine, dedicated to martial arts and "soldiers of fortune." He was so anxious to make sure Mulder didn't miss this clue that he scrawled it in blood on the side of a police car.

tense cat-and-mouse game between Mulder and Modell, aka Pusher. "The only conscious thing I wanted to do from the start was get them together as much as I could," he says, though the big

WORLD WEEKLY INFORMER

DEPRAVITY RAMPANT ON HIT TV SHOW

Girl raised by squirrels for 15 years found begging for peanuts in park

HE'S BACK!

Flukeman found washed up in Martha's Vineyard

WHAT WAS THE LEAD STORY OF THE <u>WORLD WEEKLY INFORMER</u> THAT ROBERT MODELL PICKED UP AT THE CHECKOUT COUNTER IN "PUSHER"?

The Flukeman. Supposedly his body has washed ashore on Martha's Vineyard, former home of Mulder's father.

issue in the script ended up being the last act, when Pusher compels Mulder to play Russian roulette.

"I can't believe we got away with it, because the first note back from the network was, 'You can't have Russian roulette,'" Gilligan recalls. "I said, 'What do you mean? That's the whole end of the script!'" Fox's standards department even sought to reinforce their point by consulting the other networks, which claimed they'd never had a Russian roulette scene in a one-hour drama, despite its use in such movies as *The Deer Hunter*, which prompted concern as well when it was shown on television.

"That was their worry: They said they didn't want to give any impressionable kids any ideas," Gilligan says. "My argument to that was I didn't invent Russian roulette. You can make an argument like that more convincingly for a movie like *The Program*, where they came up with the idea of kids lying down on the white stripe in the street."

On a lighter note, in the script Mulder originally asks if the tiny camera he straps on picks up the Discovery Channel, but Duchovny—tapping into Mulder's penchant for joking about erotica—went with the Playboy Channel instead.

Other self-referential moments appear in this episode as well, if you know where to look (and, perhaps, have a big-screen TV and freeze-frame on the VCR). In the opening sequence, Pusher looks at a fictitious tabloid, *World Weekly Informer*, which features an artist's rendering that looks suspiciously like the Flukeman—the humanoid parasite featured in the second season episode "The Host"—on its cover. The text screams, "HE'S BACK!," with a separate headline that says "Depravity Rampant on Hit TV Show." That inset picture actually features props master Ken Hawryliw with a strip-o-gram artist taken on his birthday. "We do a lot of tabloids on this show," notes Hawryliw, who pictured another crew member on a separate cover as a man who wed a gorilla.

In addition, a production assistant on the show, Danielle Faith Friedman, appears in a blink-and-you'll-miss-it turn as the cover model on one of the *American Ronin* magazines Mulder wades

through seeking clues regarding the killer. "You have to fill the frame with something," adds art director Graeme Murray. "You might as well have fun with it." Makeup artist Fern Levin says the show was one of her most difficult assign ments because "everyone was bruised and banged up," with Skinner taking a beating as well as the detectives in the car crash.

The visual effects department had to make a last-minute fix, meanwhile, when it was realized that a sign in the courtroom which should have read "LOUDOUN COUNTY" was actually spelled "LOUDON COUNTY." "We moved the letters around and stuck a 'U' in there" using the computer, Mat Beck says.

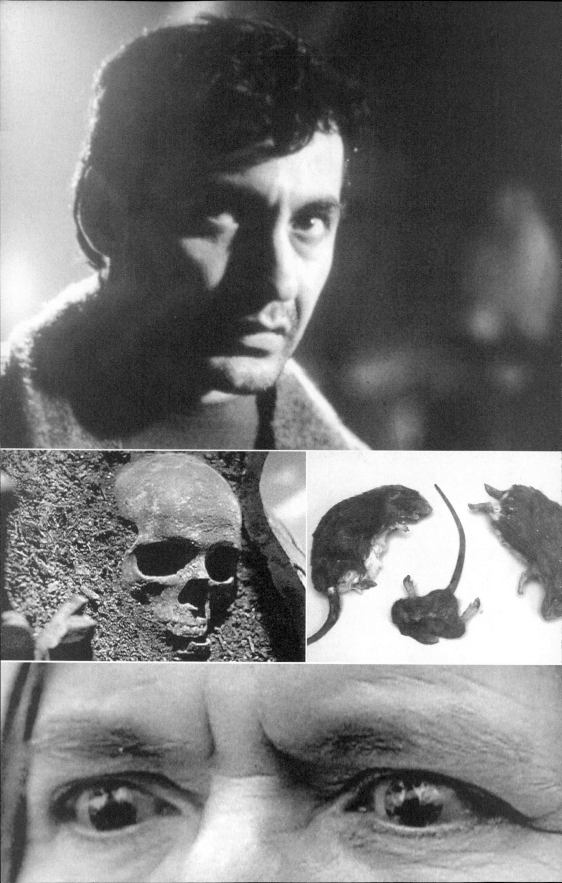

TESO DOS BICHOS

Amaru urn, reputed to hold the remains of a female shaman
unearthed at a ... logical di... h Ecuadorian high
...ds. Dr. Roosev... U... scien... rde... rkers
load the piece ... ut the an coordinating t ... i. Bilac
...es that the l... ... dia... b... the... s...ng the body
a female shama... is ...ac...d t... ... tri... he warns, as a...
... shaman watch... ro... a...ov... Th... w...nt ...llow us to dis

EPISODE: 3X18

FIRST AIRED:

March 8, 1996

WRITTEN BY:

John Shiban

EDITOR:

Jim Gross

DIRECTED BY:

Kim Manners

GUEST STARS:

Vic Trevino (Dr. Alonso Bilac)

Janne Mortil (Mona Wustner)

Gordon Tootoosis (Shaman)

Tom McBeath (Dr. Lewton)

Ron Sauve (Tim Decker)

Alan Robertson (Carl Roosevelt)

Garrison Chrisjohn (Dr. Winters)

LOG LINE:

The unearthing of an ancient Ecuadorian arti-
fact results in a series of deaths potentially
linked to a shaman spirit.

PRINCIPAL SETTING:

Boston, Massachusetts

SYNOPSIS:

An Amaru urn, reputed to hold the remains of
a female shaman, is unearthed at an archaeo-
logical dig in the Ecuadorian highlands. Dr.
Roosevelt, a U.S. scientist, orders the workers
to load the piece, but the man coordinating the
dig, Alonso Bilac, notes that the local Indians
object. "They're saying the body of a female
shaman is sacred to the tribe," he warns, as an
old shaman watches from above. "They won't
allow us to disturb her." Roosevelt ignores
Bilac's protest, and in his tent that night—as
tribe members, including Bilac, drink a yellowish fluid from a ceremonial bowl—the silhouette of a jaguar can be seen pouncing on
Roosevelt, his screams echoing into the night.

Three weeks later, at the Hall of Indige-
nous Peoples in Boston's Museum of Natural
History, where the urn has been taken, a security guard slips in a puddle of blood and one of
the researchers can't be found. Mulder and
Scully are told that the tribe, the Secona, have

protested to the State Department about the urn and the head researcher, Dr. Lewton says he thinks the researcher was killed for working on that project. Lewton acknowledges talk about a curse—that those who disturb the bones will be devoured by a jaguar spirit—but maintains it is merely designed to exploit those fears.

Dr. Lewton is named for Val Lewton, who directed the original Cat People movie.

A graduate student, Mona Wustner, tells the agents that Bilac had lobbied on behalf of the Secona. When Mulder and Scully see him, Bilac acts dazed, saying whatever happened will continue until the bones are returned. "Your investigation is a waste of time," he says distantly. "That is something I can assure you of." Scully sees Bilac as a prime suspect, but Mulder is intrigued by the rumored curse.

As he's leaving the museum, Dr. Lewton's car won't start, and he lifts the hood to find blood on his engine. Suddenly something is upon him, dragging him away screaming. Scully finds rats in the engine at the crime scene, questioning an evasive Mona about Bilac. Searching in the nearby woods, a drop hits Mulder's face, and what he assumes to be rain is in fact blood dripping from human entrails hanging from a branch above.

Mona goes to see Bilac, who looks ill and behaves strangely, drinking the yellowish liquid, a hallucinogen called Yaje that he calls "the Vine of the Soul." Hostile, he orders her out. At work, Mona calls to tell Scully of her encounter with Bilac. Hearing noise, she goes into the bathroom, where the toilets vibrate menacingly, as Mona lifts one of the lids to see damp rats trying to clamber out.

Scully discovers the Yaje at Bilac's house, calling Mulder at the museum, where he's gone seeking Mona. Mulder follows a trail of blood into the bathroom, where Bilac sits, looking exhausted. Mona is dead, he says, indicating that the Amaru—a spirit "more powerful than any man"—will not be appeased. "This is not something you can put in handcuffs," Bilac says. Checking the bathroom, the agents find dead rats in every toilet. They also discover their first body, Mona's dog, who apparently died from eating a cat that consumed a poisoned rat. Citing the presence of rats at various crime scenes, Mulder suggests the spirit may be transmigrating into other animals. "So what are we talking here, Mulder?" asks a dubious Scully. "A possessed rat? The return of Ben?"

On the contrary, Mulder thinks the rats were "trying to escape from something." Bilac, meanwhile, is missing from the room where he was being held, with tracks leading to a vent that empties into steam tunnels beneath the museum. Mulder finds a drop of blood, saying Bilac might have escaped into the vent, adding ominously, "Unless he was dragged." In the tunnels Mulder stumbles across Lewton's mutilated body, as cats congregate around them. One feline attacks Scully, as Mulder pulls it away and the two escape through the vent, where they discover Bilac's corpse.

All the bodies are recovered, but the cats beneath the museum can't be found. After five deaths, the State Department has agreed to return the Amaru urn to Ecuador. The deaths, Mulder says, were ruled animal attacks without further explanation. Bilac, he adds, "learned there is a world beyond our own, unseen but powerful, and as real as the urn itself." Some things, he continues, "are better left buried," as the old shaman watches the urn being returned to its proper resting place.

BACK STORY: Many of those involved with this episode came away disappointed with the finished product, among them David Duchovny and director Kim Manners. Duchovny did make one change he liked in the scene where Mulder and Scully begin to crawl into the tunnel under the museum, as Mulder rather ungallantly mutters, "Ladies first," which wasn't in the shooting script.

Duchovny notes that the line was included origi-

Ron Sauve, who plays the security guard, first appeared as a sewage plant manager in "The Host," uttering the memorable line, "Fifty thousand people a day call my office on the porcelain telephone."

nally and then deleted, but he decided to put it back. "I thought it was funny," he says, adding that he'd "prefer not to remember anything else about that episode," considering it one of the season's least memorable as well as a headache from a production standpoint. For that reason, Manners awarded the crew with "Teso dos Bichos Survivor" T-shirts after production was completed, with the words "Second Salmon" on the back—a reference to the script, which changes color with each revision. In this case, the script underwent so many changes (a dozen different drafts) that they ended up with a salmon-colored version twice.

Manners (who, in characteristically blunt fashion, refers to the episode as "Teso dos Bitches") lays the blame on the premise. "When I read that script I said, 'Guys, pussycats are not scary,'" he says. "An interesting thing happened, because I voted for the jaguar to reappear in the steam tunnels in Act IV. The jaguar's scary. Cats aren't, and they're also stupid. Cockroaches are smarter then cats," he adds, having some experience with the former in "War of the Coprophages." "They're so fluffy and pretty. You don't make a cat a killer."

For her part, Gillian Anderson admits that a scene in which she wrestles with a stuffed cat—due to her allergies when it comes to the real thing—provided one of her season lowlights. The show's animal wrangler, Debbie Coe, did come up with a creative way to prevent any rats from being injured during filming of the scene where hundreds shimmy out of toilets, putting little ladders inside the bowls so the rodents could clamber up them rather than have to climb over each other.

Remarkably, an actor named Frank Welker—who has created voices and sound effects for innumerable animated and science fiction movies—provided all the animal sounds heard in this episode. "We didn't use a single animal voice," says co-producer Paul Rabwin, who also wrote and performed the chant that's featured.

Inclement weather wound up changing the venue of the teaser sequence, at least in terms of the legend that appears. "The weather can cooperate as well as be difficult," says producer Joseph Patrick

Finn, noting that it started to snow during the excavation scene—shot at a gravel pit in a regional park—and thus "really added to the scene." The scripted setting, however, had to be abruptly shifted from the Amazon rain forest—which never gets that cold—to the Ecuadorian highlands, where snow does fall.

Costume designer Jenni Gullett did considerable research on Native American tribes to outfit the cast for the teaser sequence, going to "all the ethnic stores in Vancouver" to buy clothes and accessories. The outfits were then "dirtied down and sandpapered," she says, to produce a worn and weathered look.

In terms of *X-Files* continuity, there's a line about Dr. Lewton having sunflower seeds in his intestine. "A man of taste," says Mulder, referring to his own expressed fondness for that snack in "Aubrey" during the second season.

Finally, the title itself prompted considerable speculation, since there are other more creative—and lascivious—translations than the one writer John Shiban intended. "Teso," he explains, in archaic Portuguese refers to "burial mound," and "bichos" refers to "small animals." Shiban named the episode after an actual chant. "Apparently, in some countries there is some euphemism involved with it that I found out about after," he says.

In Colombia and Venezuela, for example, "bichos" is slang for "balls," as in "You have big bichos," Shiban notes with a laugh. "The network came back later and said, 'We hear rumors this means something.' Then, coming back from Vancouver, the driver of the limousine was from Colombia and he said, 'Aw, I know what that means.'" The writer shrugs, adding, "I figure it's good for ratings."

HELL MONEY

EPISODE: 3X19

FIRST AIRED:

March 29, 1996

WRITTEN BY:

Jeffrey Vlaming

EDITOR:

Stephen Mark

DIRECTED BY:

Tucker Gates

GUEST STARS:

B. D. Wong (Det. Glen Chao)

Lucy Alexis Liu (Kim Tsin)

James Hong (Hard-Faced Man)

Michael Yama (Mr. Tsin)

Doug Abrahams (Det. Neary)

Ellie Harvie (OPO Staffer)

Derek Lowe (Johnny Lo)

Donald Fong (Vase Man)

Diana Ha (Dr. Wu)

Stephen M. D. Chang (Large Man)

Paul Wong (Wiry Man)

LOG LINE:

The deaths of several Chinese immigrants missing internal organs leads Mulder and Scully to a mysterious game with potentially fatal consequences.

PRINCIPAL SETTING:

Chinatown, San Francisco, California

SYNOPSIS:

A terrified Chinese man hurries through the crowded streets of San Francisco's Chinatown. When he enters his apartment he confronts a figure with a flashlight who warns him that it is now time to pay the price. The Chinese man swipes at the figure with a switchblade in his attempt to flee but turns, only to confront three figures dressed in black and wearing ghostly masks. Later, a funeral home security guard spots the same three figures near the crematory oven. As faint cries bring the guard closer to the oven, he peers inside to see the face of the Chinese man.

At the crime scene, Mulder and Scully working with Detective Glen Chao, find the Chinese characters meaning "ghost" scratched inside the oven. With the help of Detective Chao they are also able to identify some burnt paper as "hell money," used to pay off spirits during the Festival of the Hungry Ghosts. They are able to use the "hell money" as a means to identify the body in the oven as Johnny Lo, a recent Chinese immigrant. While searching Lo's apartment Mulder finds blood stains under the newly laid carpet.

An older man, Hsin, tends to his ailing daughter who needs an operation he cannot afford. This is what motivates Hsin to go to the smoke-filled room full of Chinese men, where a dark-suited man displays a satchel full of cash and two vases. One vase is empty and the other is full of red tiles and a single white tile. The empty vase is passed around and each man deposits their personal tile into

> Chinese magic is based not on the four Western elements of fire, earth, air, and water, but on the five elements of earth, fire, wood, metal, and water. Each element corresponds to an important body part: fire, for example, corresponds to the heart. Thus when a luckless player in The Game draws a "fire" tablet, everyone understands that he has drawn the "heart" symbol and is doomed.

the vase. The dark-suited man pulls a tile that corresponds to one of the men in the audience. The man selected then gets the opportunity to try to pull the single winning white tile from the vase. Hsin is relieved that he has not drawn the unlucky tile as they take away the man next to him. Later that evening the body of the man who pulled that tile is found in a shallow grave by Mulder and Scully.

Examining the body, Scully says the numerous surgical scars suggest the man may have been selling body parts, asking Mulder if he realizes what the human body is worth. "Depends on the body," he replies. Scully questions Chao about a black market for body parts, having found a substance used to preserve human organs on the victim during the autopsy. Told he's not being completely cooperative, Chao becomes angry, citing a code of silence within the community. "To them, I'm just as white as you are," he says.

Chao has information that leads them to interview Hsin, the carpet layer. Seen playing the game earlier, Hsin appears now with a patch over one eye, insisting he had an accident at work. As Mulder and Scully go to leave Hsin's apartment, Detective Chao hangs back and has a quick conversation in Chinese with Hsin. Going home, Chao sees writing on his door and is greeted by the three masked figures inside.

Staking out Hsin's place, Mulder and Scully learn Chao has been attacked and hospitalized. Meanwhile, the doctor shown earlier visits Hsin, who says he wants to quit the game. "You have to keep playing," the doctor says, noting the money could save his daughter's life and breaking the rules would release ghostly fire that will consume him.

Mulder and Scully reach the hospital, but Chao has already left, and Mulder notices that his blood type matches that found in the first victim's apartment. Mulder deduces it was Chao's blood found in the first victim's apartment and that he had ordered the new carpet. They return to Hsin's apartment but only find his daughter Kim who has leukemia. Kim is afraid that her father has done something foolish in order to help her get medical treatment. Kim tells Mulder and Scully that each tile symbol corresponds with a body part.

There really is "hell money." During the Chinese New Year, and on yearly anniversaries of a relative's death, specially printed paper money is burned as a gift to the spirit world. It is also customary to burn paper images or replicas of cars, houses, food, or other offerings to the ancestors.

Mulder and Scully, in an effort to track down the doctor who ordered the organ donor tests, arrive outside a Chinese restaurant. It is not until they see Detective Chao entering the dark restaurant that they know that they have the right place. Meanwhile, as Mulder and Scully are following Chao into the restaurant, Hsin is chosen to try to match his tile for his fate. As Hsin is carried away into the back room, Chao bursts through the crowd in attempt to stop the proceedings. Chao demands that the game end and that Hsin is let go. He knocks over the table where the vase with the tiles was set and sends them crashing to the floor. It is then that Chao realizes that the games are fixed, that there is no winning tile in the vase. Mulder and Scully follow the noise upstairs to the smoky room as the doctor slips into the operating room where a semiconscious Hsin lies on the operating table. Chao breaks in only moments before Mulder and Scully and shoots the doctor before he can operate on Hsin.

Scully interrogates the doctor, saying he preyed on desperation and hopelessness. The doctor maintains hope was his gift to these men. Hsin rests in intensive care, and his daughter is put on an organ recipient list. No one, however, wants to testify against the doctor and Chao has disappeared, as Mulder puts it, "like a ghost." Chao, meanwhile, awakens inside the crematorium oven, and begins writing the symbol for "ghost" as flames fill the frame.

BACK STORY: Chris Carter came up with the notion of doing a show about a pyramid scheme for body parts, which became the basis of this episode, with the props department creating the game from scratch. "What's interesting about that episode is that so many people thought it was a real game," notes story

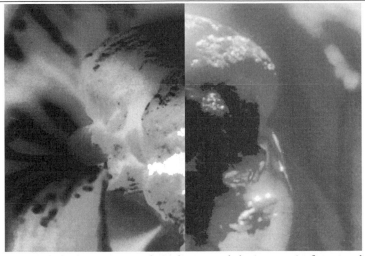

editor Frank Spotnitz, when the central device was in fact utterly fictitious.

In terms of postproduction, "Hell Money" required "a tremendous amount of looping," according to co-producer Paul Rabwin. Michael Yama, who played Hsin, is Japanese, and Lisa Liu, portraying his daughter, spoke Chinese with a Mandarin accent. Once it was realized the two were supposed to be speaking in a Cantonese dialect, all their dialogue in Chinese with English subtitles was redone after the episode with the help of a vocal coach. The rerecorded lines were then dubbed over the original soundtrack. "We did it 'til it sounded right," says Rabwin, who notes that several factors were involved in the decision, among them sensitivity to the Chinese community.

Perhaps the most memorable scene, when the frog pops out of the corpse's chest, proved to be relatively simple by the show's technical standards. The makeup effects crew, under Toby Lindala, used stock molds to rig a fake human torso, placing it over the actor as he lay on the table. For the close-up, the torso only was then placed on a table that had a hole in the midsection, allowing the show's animal wrangler to get underneath and gently push the frog through the opening.

Vancouver's Chinatown stood in for its more celebrated counterpart in San Francisco, as it did for Hong Kong earlier in "Piper Maru." The crematorium scenes were shot within a soundstage.

JOSE CHUNG'S FROM OUTER SPACE

rold, a teenage boy, and his date, Chrissy, are driving
en their car stalls ... out in a ... flash
...t and ... gray ... aliens drag them away ... ore
huge, growling alien interrupts them. Jack, one ...
...s ... that ... "How the hell should
...ow? ... responds. Author Jose Chung ...er

EPISODE: 3X20

FIRST AIRED:

April 12, 1996

WRITTEN BY:

Darin Morgan

EDITOR:

Heather MacDougall

DIRECTED BY:

Rob Bowman

GUEST STARS:

Charles Nelson Reilly (Jose Chung)

William Lucking (Roky Crikenson)

Daniel Quinn (Jack Scheaffer)

Jesse "The Body" Ventura
  (Man in Black)

Sarah Sawatsky (Chrissy Giorgio)

Jason Gaffne (Harold Lamb)

Alex Diakun (Dr. Fingers)

Larry Musser (Det. Manners)

Allan Zinyk (Blaine Faulkner)

Andrew Turner (CIA Man)

Michael Dobson (Sargeant Hynek)

Mina E. Mina (Dr. Hand)

Jaap Broeker (The Stupendous
  Yappi)

Alex Trebek (Man in Black #2)–not
  listed in the credits

LOG LINE:

A novelist interviews Scully about a rumored UFO abduction of two teenagers that seems open to a number of different interpretations.

PRINCIPAL SETTING:

Klass County, Washington

SYNOPSIS:

Harold, a teenage boy, and his date, Chrissy, are driving when their car stalls. The two pass out in a blinding flash of light, and two gray-skinned aliens drag them away before a huge, growling alien interrupts them. "Jack," one alien says to the other, "what is that thing?"

"How the hell should I know?" his compatriot responds.

Author Jose Chung interviews Scully, who apologizes for Mulder's reluctance to speak with him. Chung is writing a book about alien abduction, creating a genre—nonfiction science fiction—he feels will assure him a spot on the bestseller list. Scully asks only that he report the truth, but Chung scoffs, noting that everyone has a different version of what's transpired. "Truth is as subjective as reality," he says.

Scully explains that Chrissy was found with signs of abuse and her clothes inside out, appearing to be a victim of date rape. Harold is apprehended by the police, and he tells authorities that they were abducted. Detective Manners has questioned Harold and doesn't believe his story, but Mulder arrives and isn't so sure, convincing Chrissy to undergo hypnosis, under which she recalls being on an alien ship. Mulder is impressed by her description, but Scully thinks it's "all a little too typical," given the prevalence of abduction lore. Manners tells Mulder he's "really bleeped up this case."

Harold remembers being on the ship, incongruously seeing the gray-skinned alien smoking and repeating "this is not happening" continuously. He also admits that he and Chrissy had sex, which Mulder deems insignificant, but Scully indicates that it at least provides proof it "wasn't an alien that probed her." In Scully's eyes, sexual trauma is more likely than alien abduction.

A witness named Roky comes forward, saying a man in black visited him, telling him he saw Venus, not a UFO, and threatening to kill him if he tells anyone. Roky hands over his manuscript detailing the story, in which he saw two smaller aliens being attacked by a large one named "Lord Kinbote." Mulder acknowledges that Roky is probably delusional but may have seen something, so he has Chrissy hypnotized again, and she seems to support his story. Scully, however, thinks Mulder and the hypnotist are leading her. Manners enters, telling the agents they've discovered an alien body.

Chung also interviews Blaine, a science fiction nut who dreams of being abducted and has his own version of events. He describes seeing "men in black," but it's really Mulder and Scully, the former letting out a high-pitched yelp when he sees the alien corpse, the latter threatening Blaine not to talk. "He said I said what?" asks an incredulous Scully.

Blaine shot footage of the autopsy, which has been turned into a video—hosted by the Stupendous Yappi—entitled *Dead Alien! Truth or Humbug?* "It's so embarrassing," Scully groans, noting that the video was edited so as to obscure the fact that the "alien" was in fact an Air Force major in a costume. Air Force personnel arrive seeking the body, but when they return it's gone. Blaine also says that the man in black took his video and threatened him, as did Mulder. "I

Detective Manners, of the blankety-bleeps, is named for X-Files producer/director Kim Manners.

Alex Trebek, the host of <u>Jeopardy!</u>, of course recalls Duchovny's infamous appearance on "Celebrity Jeopardy." Alex Diakun appears in his third Darin Morgan episode, as the hypnotist. He was the Curator in "Humbug" and the Tarot Reader in "Clyde Bruckman's Final Repose."

didn't spend all those years playing Dungeons and Dragons and not learn a little something about courage," he tells Chung.

After that, Scully admits, Mulder's account of events gets "a little odd." Heading back to the hotel, he encounters the other missing Air Force pilot, who claims he and his partner were flying a UFO as part of a covert government operation but were abducted themselves in the process. Officers come in and take the soldier away, and when Mulder asks about the third alien he replies, "Who? Lord Kinbote?"

Mulder meets the Man in Black at the hotel, who—with the help of *Jeopardy*'s Alex Trebek—suggests that some alien encounters are hoaxes perpetrated by the government. Mulder awakens in Scully's room, and she has no memory of the incident. Subsequently, the agents go to a site where they're told a top-secret plane has crashed, which explains the UFO sightings. Even Manners is shocked to see the two pilots' bodies being carted away. "I know it probably doesn't have the sense of closure that you want, but it has more than some of our cases," Scully says sheepishly.

Mulder visits Chung himself, asking that he not write the book, which will do a disservice to a field of inquiry that's struggled to achieve respectability. Chung says the book will be written, but asks what really happened to the two teenagers. "How the hell should I know?" Mulder says.

Scully reads the book, Jose Chung's *From Outer Space*, describing agent "Diana Lesky" and her partner "Reynard Muldrake," characterized as "a ticking time bomb of insanity." Mulder lies in bed, watching footage of "Bigfoot." Harold, meanwhile, visits Chrissy, who tells him to leave, and as Harold slumps off into the night Chung reminds us that "although we may not be alone in the universe, in our own separate ways, on this planet, we are all . . . alone."

BACK STORY: This episode, not surprisingly, is loaded with in-jokes, beginning with its title. As a practical joke, the writing staff created the wholly fictitious "Jose Chung," an aspiring writer who kept phoning the office (writer John Shiban did the honors) inquiring about an unsolicited script he'd submitted. Chung was repeatedly dismissed, prompting more than a little surprise and confusion from the recipient of those calls when the name suddenly turned up on Morgan's script.

For numerous reasons this episode quickly became a favorite for many members of the cast and crew, including Gillian Anderson, who immediately cites the show as being among her third-season highlights. Anderson also lauds director Rob Bowman for how slickly the hour was produced, while David Duchovny jokes that the little falsetto yelp he lets out at one point comes close to approximating his singing voice.

According to Bowman, allowing everyone to share in the fun was serious business. "There's so many details in the script, I knew the audience wasn't going to understand it unless I told it in a way that they could see into the story— using repetitive staging and anything I could do to give them hooks along the way to remember how things tied together and allow them to be along for the ride," he says. Bowman admits he himself had to read the script "fourteen to fifteen times" before he really

The names of several famous UFO researchers and skeptics show up in this episode: Klass County is named for Philip Klass, who writes books debunking UFO sightings. In his book UFOs Explained he says, "No single object has been misinterpreted as a 'flying saucer' more often than the planet Venus." This line sounds very close to one spoken by former pro wrestler Jesse "The Body" Ventura, one of the Men in Black. The fake alien pilots, "Robert Vallee" and "Jack Schaffer," take their names from UFO authors Robert Schaffer and Jacques Vallee. The MP who arrests Schaffer, Sergeant Hynek, is named for J. Allen Hynek, a researcher who once worked for the U.S. Air Force and who wrote The Edge of Reality: A Progress Report on UFOs.

understood everything and then held a "very detailed meeting" with writer Darin Morgan to go over every aspect of the episode.

Despite its comedic overtones, Bowman points out that the show did have a serious story regarding a conspiracy and cover-up at its core, so he played the hypnosis scenes very soberly. "That's the theme of

WHAT WAS SO FUNNY ABOUT THE NAMES OF JOSE CHUNG'S PROTAGONISTS IN HIS NONFICTION SCIENCE FICTION NOVEL, FROM OUTER SPACE?

"Diana Lesky" and "Reynard Muldrake" are thinly disguised pseudonyms for "Dana Scully" and "Fox Mulder" (Reynard is the French word for fox).

the entire show," he suggests. "One's perception of reality, and how it can be altered by mere words." For all that, Bowman adds, "It was just a kick to do."

Morgan incorporated a number of other inside references into the script as well, such as titling the video *Dead Alien! Truth or Humbug?* ("Humbug" having been the title of his first episode) or naming the foul-mouthed detective after Kim Manners, who directed both "Humbug" and another of Morgan's efforts, "War of the Coprophages." Manners himself has earned a reputation for what might politely be called colorful dialogue. "I swear a lot," he says matter-of-factly. Manners was once an actor and at one point was even going to play the detective himself, but he proved too exhausted from his prior directing assignment to do so. "I had agreed to do it, but for the good of the show my first loyalty is to directing and not acting," he says.

Perhaps foremost, "Jose Chung" provided a breath of fresh air for everyone on the series at a time in the production year when many were beginning to drag and feel their energy fading. Perhaps the biggest revelation to the crew was guest star Charles Nelson Reilly, who captivated virtually everyone and "gave us a lift," as assistant director Tom Braidwood remembers, with his enthusiasm. Reilly's antics included crying "Nurse! Nurse!" each time he needed to consult with the script supervisor and nicknaming everybody, calling costume designer Jenni Gullett and costume supervisor Gillian Kieft by nicknames like "señorita" and "Carlotta," as in, "Okay, señorita, what's next?" Asked about the most interesting guest they costumed during the season, Gullett and assistant costume designer Janice Swayze shout "Charles Nelson Reilly!" almost simultaneously. "He really was delightful," Gillian Anderson concurs.

WHAT ODD CHARACTER FROM "CLYDE BRUCKMAN'S FINAL REPOSE" MAKES A RETURN APPEARANCE IN "JOSE CHUNG'S FROM OUTER SPACE"?

The Stupendous Yappi. The eyebrow-endowed master of self-promotion makes a return appearance flogging the fake "alien autopsy" video based, strangely enough, on Scully's own autopsy of a "gray."

Technical challenges included the alien bondage equipment, which was meant to be revealing without running afoul of Fox's broadcast standards department. Visual effects producer Mat Beck also recalls that this episode provided one of his funniest "fix-its," as one of the missing pilots turned up naked as he walked across the highway, and his unit was called upon to obscure the character's bare butt in order to mollify Fox. "We did a huge flare coming off the car headlights to cover up the butt," Beck says.

The large alien—described in the script as "Behemoth From the Planet Harryhausen," an homage to stop-motion effects wizard Ray Harryhausen—was actually stunt coordinator Tony Morelli in a costume devised by special effects makeup supervisor Toby Lindala. The suit stood more than seven-feet high with stilts built into it, so Morelli's feet were actually situated in the knees. Morelli spent more than 10 hours inside the outfit, rivaling Morgan's own ordeal playing the Flukeman in "The Host." Lindala proudly points out that the suit featured remote-controlled eyes and eyelids, which moved. Beck then digitally manipulated the footage to make the creature look more like a product of stop-motion animation.

"Jose Chung" also marked the only time so far that *The X-Files* theme itself has been employed as dramatic underscore, according to Mark Snow. The composer altered the fifth of the six notes to create a more bittersweet tone accompanying Chung's monologue at the end about loneliness. "This whistle sound has never been used," Snow says, sounding a bit like Detective Manners himself by adding, "The show was so unique I just said, '[Bleep] it, I'm doing it.'"

The manuscript for Jose Chung's book, *From Outer Space*, was simply a copy of the episode's script. From a location standpoint, the Ovaltine, one of Vancouver's oldest cafes, was used in the shot where Mulder meets the pilot and, depending on one's recollection of events, devours slice after slice of pie.

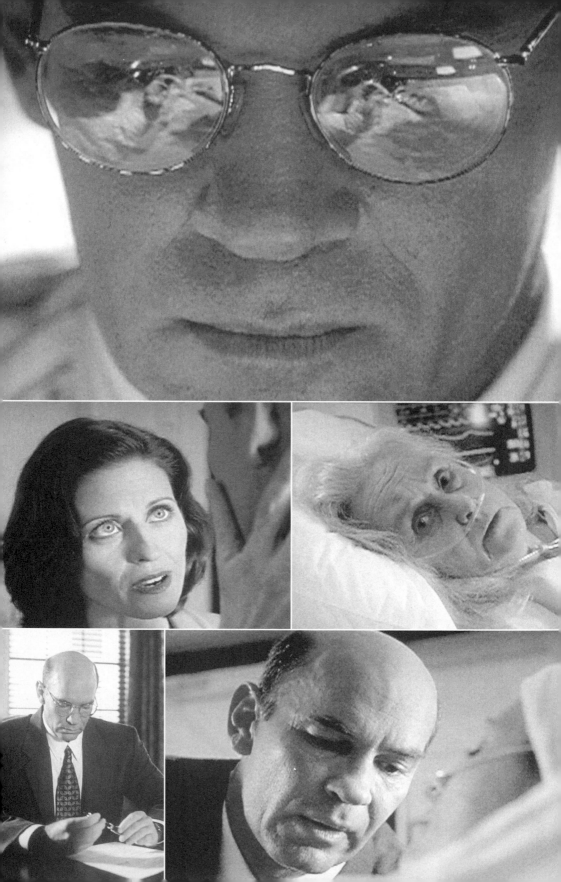

Assistant Director Walter Skinner is presented final
orce papers by his attorney, but he refuses to sign. "After
enteen years, they can wait another day," he says. Seeking
ace at a hotel bar, Skinner meets an attractive young
an, and they go to bed together. Skinner awakens with a
rt from a nightmare in which he sees an old woman looming
r him, finding the woman next to him dead, her head twist

AVATAR

EPISODE: 3X21

FIRST AIRED:

April 26, 1996

WRITTEN BY:

Howard Gordon

STORY BY:

Howard Gordon and David
Duchovny

EDITOR:

Jim Gross

DIRECTED BY:

James Charleston

GUEST STARS:

Mitch Pileggi (AD Walter Skinner)

Tom Mason (Det. Waltos)

Jennifer Hetrick (Sharon Skinner)

William B. Davis (The Cigarette-
   Smoking Man)

Amanda Tapping (Carina Sayles)

Malcolm Stewart (Agent
   Bonnecaze)

Morris Panych (The Gray-Haired
   Man)

Michael David Simms (Senior Agent)

Tasha Simms (Jay "Jane" Cassal)

Stacy Grant (Judy Fairly)

Janie Woods-Morris (Lorraine Kelleher)

Brendan Beiser (Agent Pendrell)

LOG LINE:

In the midst of a marital breakup Skinner
becomes a murder suspect, while a clue to the
case may lie in the form of a strange woman
who appears to him in dreams.

PRINCIPAL SETTING:

Washington, D.C.

SYNOPSIS:

FBI Assistant Director Walter Skinner is presented final divorce papers by his attorney, but
he refuses to sign. "After seventeen years, they
can wait another day," he says. Seeking solace
at a hotel bar, Skinner meets an attractive
young woman, and they go to bed together.
Skinner awakens with a start from a nightmare in which he sees an old woman looming
over him, he finds the woman next to him
dead, her head twisted around.

Skinner tells Mulder at the crime scene there's
no reason for him to become involved. The detective on the case says Skinner wouldn't take a poly-
graph test and that he's a suspect. Scully examines
the body, detecting Skinner's fingerprints and an
apparent vaginal irritation caused by latex. "At
least they were having safe sex," Mulder muses,
adding that he's learned the woman was a prosti-

tute. After he exits, Scully also notices a phosphorescent glow around the victim's mouth.

The agents visit the hooker's madam, who says she took Skinner's credit card number the night before. Scully cites the mounting evidence against him, but Mulder stresses that they owe it to Skinner to find out what happened. "We know that he's put his ass on the line for us a number of times," he reminds her. Skinner has been released, and he's clearly shocked to learn the woman was a prostitute. He glimpses the old woman again, but when he catches up to her it's someone else—his wife, Sharon.

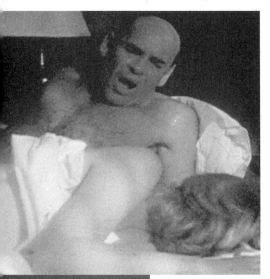

Tasha Simms, who played the mother of one of the Eves in "Eve" and the daughter of a nursing home resident in "Excelsius Dei," returns as Skinner's lawyer.

Sharon Skinner tells Mulder and Scully they've been separated eight months, and that her husband built a wall keeping everyone out. Mulder, she adds, was one of the few work associates he discussed, and she asks flatly if he thinks her husband murdered the woman. "No, I don't think he did it," Mulder says.

At Skinner's office they're told a formal hearing will be held the next day to determine his status, and Scully suggests to Mulder that their boss is "behaving like a guilty man." Scully also discovers that Skinner was receiving treatment for a sleep disorder, dreaming about an old woman who suffocates him. Hypothetically, then, he could have killed the woman in his sleep without realizing it. Mulder notes that the description of the woman sounds like a succubus—mythological spirits known to visit men in the night, sometimes killing other women out of jealousy. That prompts Scully to mention the phosphorescence, but when they check the body it's gone. Mulder suggests the sleep disorder may explain Skinner's behavior—that he doesn't know whether he's guilty or not.

Sharon visits Skinner, saying she wants to help him but that he won't let her. After she leaves he falls asleep, again waking to see the old woman, with detectives at his door saying his wife has been forced off the road and seriously injured.

Pg. 203   TRUST NO ONE

At Mulder's urging Skinner admits he's seen the old woman again, having previously witnessed something during his near-death experience in Vietnam, when she carried him away from the light. He dismissed the vision at the time, having been numbing himself with drugs. "I was no choirboy," he says. "I inhaled." Mulder conjectures that the spirit may be trying to protect him.

Mulder checks Skinner's car—which was used to harm his wife—and has the airbag analyzed. Scully, meanwhile, defends Skinner at his hearing, as she's grilled about whether the assistant director has become "enchanted" by Mulder's notions regarding the paranormal. The FBI dismisses Skinner, and Mulder says they used the X-Files "to put us in check. You remove Skinner and you weaken us."

Mulder, who's found a face on the airbag, believes eliminating Skinner this way to be less obvious than another attempt to kill him. Mulder and Scully go to see the madam, but she's found dead, having apparently either jumped or been pushed off a roof. At the scene, the agents spot a woman named Judy they'd seen with the madam earlier, and ask her to arrange a meeting with the man—the same face pictured on the airbag—who hired the dead prostitute by using Skinner's name. Judy calls the man, telling him to meet her at the Ambassador Hotel in one hour.

At the hospital, Skinner's wife lies in a coma, and he tells her he won't sign the divorce papers, having never told her how she got him through each day. With a start her vital signs change, and Sharon comes out of the coma, as Skinner briefly sees the old woman in her place. "Listen to me . . ." his wife says strangely.

Mulder waits downstairs at the hotel bar while Scully guards Judy in a room. Suddenly a gunman crashes through the door, dazing Scully. Mulder hears gunshots and finds Skinner standing over the would-be killer. In the ensuing investigation the dead man's identity remains

Medieval demonologists and their counterparts, angelologists, had as many categories for supernatural beings as modern taxonomists have for insects or fish. Among them were succubi and incubi. A succubus was a lovely young woman who appeared to men in their sleep and seduced them; an incubus was her male counterpart, who appeared to women. While such a visitation today might be considered downright desirable, in the Middle Ages it was considered an occasion for damnation and regarded with fear and horror. However such visits were regarded, the succubus were always depicted as young and beautiful.

unknown, and Mulder asks how Skinner knew to be at the hotel. "Whatever I believe may have happened, that has no place in an official report," Skinner says, declining to discuss the matter further even off the record. Left alone in his office, Skinner reaches into his drawer—determined to save his marriage—and puts his wedding ring on again.

BACK STORY: In the best-laid plans department, David Duchovny says he suggested showcasing Skinner in an episode but that his ulterior motive backfired. "Actually, I conceived the idea trying to give myself a break," he says with a grin, pointing out that episodes where Mulder and Scully get separated provide one of the few ways he and Anderson "can get a little time off" during production, in that one of them might take a break while the other's shooting. "If we're together, then there's no way," he says. "As it turned out, it was a very heavy episode for me." Still, Duchonvy adds, "It was nice for Mitch, and I think he deserved a nice episode after two years. He did a great job."

Duchovny and the show's publicist snuck onto what was supposed to be a closed set to watch Pileggi shoot his love scene. "He didn't really sneak," Pileggi corrects, laughing loudly. "He just busted right in. He came in and he critiqued us a little bit." As for shooting the scene itself, the actor adds, "We [Pileggi and guest actress Amanda Tapping] basically laid in bed and made out for four or five hours"—surrounded, of course, by crew members trying to light, frame, and photograph the shot.

With Skinner's popularity increasing and in light of the more active role he played in "The Blessing Way" and "Paper Clip," Pileggi contends the episode helped reestablish some of the ground rules regarding where Skinner stands—and doesn't—in relation to the X-Files unit and how far he'll go in fulfilling its mission. "Chris Carter doesn't want to just put him totally in bed with Mulder and Scully," he says, noting that Mulder reached out to Skinner within the episode "and he didn't really take it. He's still a hardass, but fair." Skinner initially discussed his near-death experience during the second season in the episode "One Breath."

Makeup artist Fern Levin used special ink and a fluorescent light to create the appearance of phosphorescence around the corpse's mouth. "I told the actress she was the coolest corpse we ever had," she says. Composer Mark Snow also thinned out his usual score for this episode, feeling such an approach better suited the nature of the drama. "The sound is very unaffected," he explains. "There's less of the scary sounds and more straight-ahead music."

"Avatar" is a Sanskrit word meaning the human incarnation of a deity.

"Avatar" (which in Sanskrit means the descent to Earth of a deity in human or animal form) is also notable for two significant omissions: First, a scene with the Cigarette-Smoking Man (William B. Davis is even listed in the credits, though he has no dialogue), who goes to see Skinner, questioning his allegiance; and a line from Skinner, who, when Mulder says he's finished at the Bureau if he won't trust someone, responds, "That's hard to hear, coming from you." That response was deemed too combative, while the Cigarette-Smoking Man's scene simply fell victim to time considerations. "That was one of those tough choices, where something had to be cut due to length," Carter notes.

Director James Charleston made his debut on the series with this episode, subsequently joining the regular directing rotation. Charleston had been an assistant director on other series, which came in handy, cinematographer John Bartley recalls, the day they shot the dead woman dangling from her alleged suicide leap. A.D. Val Stefoff was out sick that day, and Charleston himself was feeling under the weather. "I told him you never would have gotten through the day without that first A.D. experience," Bartley says.

The episode also demonstrates some of the smaller "fix-its" that get made during postproduction—in this case, when it was noticed that the eyes of Skinner's wife fluttered during her coma scene. The visual effects crew went in and digitally removed the flutter. Although that wouldn't seem to be as elaborate as, say, a morphing shot, making such changes still takes considerable time and effort. "Such a simple, subtle thing, people who don't know think it might be easy," says Mat Beck.

If you scan the credits for this episode carefully, you'll see Skinner's lawyer listed as "Jay Cassal." The character was originally intended to be male so when Tasha Simms was cast, the character was renamed "Jane Cassal"—although not in the credits!

researcher, Dr. Farraday, complains about the rapid extinc-
on of the frog population near Heuvelman's Lake, but his
sertions are dismissed by another scientist, Dr. Bailey
ading back to the car, Bailey realizes he's dropped his
eper, tracking back the lake's edge where he's yanked
reaming into the water Mulder and Scully drive down the
orgia highway with Queequeg Pomerarian Scully acquired

QUAGMIRE

EPISODE: 3X22

FIRST AIRED:

May 3, 1996

WRITTEN BY:

Kim Newton

EDITOR:

Leon Carrere

DIRECTED BY:

Kim Manners

GUEST STARS:

Chris Ellis (Sheriff Lance Hindt)

Timothy Webber (Dr. Paul
  Farraday)

R. Nelson Brown (Ansel Bray)

Mark Acheson (Ted Bertram)

Peter Hanlon (Dr. William Bailey)

Tyler Labine (Stoner)

Nicole Parker (Chick)

Terrance Leigh (Snorkel Dude)

LOG LINE:

Mulder and Scully investigate a series of deaths that may be linked to a lake monster known by the locals as Big Blue.

PRINCIPAL SETTING:

Blue Ridge Mountains, Georgia

SYNOPSIS:

A researcher, Dr. Farraday, complains about the rapid extinction of the frog population near Heuvelman's Lake, but his assertions are dismissed by another scientist, Dr. Bailey. Heading back to the car, Bailey realizes he's dropped his beeper, tracking it back to the lake's edge, where he's yanked screaming into the water.

Mulder and Scully drive down the Georgia highway with Queequeg, the Pomeranian Scully acquired in an earlier episode. "Did you really have to bring that thing?" Mulder asks, with Scully answering that she had no choice because she didn't have enough notice to leave the dog with anyone. Scully, meanwhile, wants to know why they're investigating this missing person case, and Mulder says a Boy Scout leader has also disappeared. Asked if he thinks a serial killer may be at large, Mulder says, "The operative word being 'large'"—as they pass a sign for Big Blue, the Southern Serpent. "Oh, tell me you're not serious," Scully groans.

The agents question Farraday, then the owner of the local bait-and-tackle shop, who cashes in on the folklore with T-shirts and other Big Blue merchandise. Outside, a fisherman hooks what turns out to be the body of the scout leader—or rather, half the body, since it's missing from just above the waist. Scully suggests that the man may have fallen in and been nibbled at by fish, but Mulder says it "looks to me like something took a big bite."

The bait shop owner tromps through the woods in special boots to leave fake dinosaur tracks, getting mired in the mud before he, too, is brutally attacked. Mulder tells the local sheriff the lake should

Heuvelman's Lake was located in Millikan County, named after Rick Millikan, a casting director for the show. Heuvelman's Lake is named after famous monster researcher Van Heuvels, a Dutch "cryptozoologist." His book, In the Wake of the Sea Serpents, is considered a classic on lake monsters. Another classic work echoed in this episode is Berne's pop psychology bible of the 1970s, Games People Play. Mulder's speech about wanting a wooden leg in order to justify not having to work so hard in life comes straight out of the book.

be closed, but the sheriff insists he doesn't have the manpower to patrol its 48 miles of shoreline.

Two teenagers hang out on the dock, seeing a diver suddenly struck, with blood filling the water before his head bobs slowly to the surface. Scully indicates the damage could be attributed to a boat propeller, but Mulder questions the odds of this many accidents happening at one time after Ansel—a photographer obsessed with capturing a picture of Big Blue—also gets swept away. The sheriff agrees with Scully, until he falls into the lake and feels "something big" brush past him. "Close the lake!" he yells, climbing out.

Mulder scans through Ansel's pictures while Scully walks

Queequeg, who bolts off into the woods. Scully chases down the leash, but when she catches up it unravels like a fishing line, and the dog's collar is empty when she reels it in. While Scully sits dejected over Queequeg's disappearance, Mulder notes that sightings of Big Blue have gradually moved closer to shore. They go out on the lake that night, seeing a large blip heading toward them that crashes into their boat, which rapidly takes on water, sinking as they escape onto a large rock. "There goes our $500 deposit," says Scully.

Stranded, Scully wonders why they're in this predicament. Mulder explains that so many of the things they seek are intangible that he truly wants to find this monster—something that exists in a confined space. Scully likens him to the obsessed photographer ("That man is your future," she says), when suddenly they hear a splash in the water, drawing their guns. It turns out to be just a duck.

Mulder coyly asks Scully how she feels about cannibalism, and whether she's lost weight recently. Explaining that she named the dog after a character in *Moby Dick*, Scully compares Mulder to Ahab. "The truth or a white whale? What difference does it make?" she wonders aloud. Their conversation gets interrupted by a loud thrashing, and Scully asks what it could be. "I don't know, but it ain't no duck," Mulder says, as they again pull their guns.

The noise in fact comes from Farraday, who was walking by on the shore—which, in the darkness, had actually been just a stone's throw away. Mulder theorizes that depletion of the frog supply, as Farraday has documented, would force an aquatic dinosaur to seek an alternative food source—namely, humans, venturing closer to shore. The sheriff locates them to report yet another death across the lake, but Mulder insists the monster is in this cove. Hearing a scream, they find Farraday wounded, his leg badly bitten.

Mulder leaves Scully with him while pursuing the beast into the woods, firing as he hears something large rushing toward him through the dark. His flashlight reveals a dead alligator.

In the aftermath, Scully asks how Mulder could be disappointed when he kept the alligator from feasting on the local population. "I guess I just wanted Big Blue to be real," he concedes. "I guess I see hope in such a possibility." Scully says there is hope, that the folklore proves "people want to believe." Reluctantly, Mulder turns away, just missing a serpentine figure as it knifes through the water.

BACK STORY: "Quagmire" is perhaps most notable for the nighttime sequence in the third act where Mulder and Scully get stranded together in the lake.

"I loved that," Anderson admits. "That was so much fun, and I think it was written really well. . . . It was just neat to have us separated from everything and stuck on this island where we could wax philosophical and kind of tell the truth to each other in strange ways."

This is the second episode to feature Tyler Labine and Nicole Parker as "Stoner" and "Chick," two teens on an eternal quest for the perfect high. They first appeared in "War of the Coprophages" inhaling methane.

According to director Kim Manners, the scene involved roughly 10 pages of dialogue—a lot to digest on a weekly series—but provided "some wonderful conversation, and David and Gillian really rose to that," he says.

"It was a quirky little show, and it was a lot tougher than anyone expected it to be," Manners continues. "It was tough for me creatively because it was a blue-sky show, and to try to keep it scary and spooky when you're standing in these beautiful, idyllic surroundings was tough. . . . It's not dark, you don't have the flashlights, you're outside."

The visual effects department generated the lake monster at the last minute, after initial efforts were made to create the image of the creature physically by using, as Mat Beck puts it not-so-scientifically, "a rubber thing" in the water. Outtakes actually show a small crew in a boat dragging a not-very-convincing sea serpent through the lake. "When we saw the actual footage it was like, 'Uh, that's not gonna work,'" adds Beck, who was asked to augment the image digitally before ultimately deciding to scrap it entirely, whipping up the computer-generated Big Blue—as well as the little wake it creates cleaving through the water—in three or four days.

The creature, he says, demonstrates one of the everyday challenges one faces in the world of computer graphics. "If we don't do enough it looks too stiff. If you do too much, it looks like Beany and Cecil," he offers.

"Quagmire" features more than a few sliced and diced bodies, including the half-body model found floating in the water and the head that bobs to the surface. "We've gotten really comfortable with Fast Flex," says Toby Lindala, noting that the durable urethane substance worked particularly well in this episode because the bodies "had to withstand so much water abuse."

Another memorable moment stems from the untimely demise of Scully's dog, Queequeg, who was named for a character in *Moby*

Dick and thus perhaps appropriately meets his end in the jaws of a waterfaring monster. Though killing off a cute little dog always presents some risk in terms of viewer response (people tend to accept butchery of humans more easily than pets), the writers joke that they had all been seeking a way to

The boat that sinks out from under Mulder and Scully is named the "Patricia Rae" after writer Kim Newton's mother.

incorporate the dog in some grisly fashion. "We brought it back just to kill it," deadpans story editor Frank Spotnitz, while creative consultant Vince Gilligan adds, "You can kill a legion of men and women, but no dogs. People go nuts."

Scully acquired the dog, eagle-eyed fans will remember, from an old woman who passed away in the season's fourth episode, "Clyde Bruckman's Final Repose." The Pomeranian later appeared briefly in "War of the Coprophages."

man buries a body in a hole, later killing what appears t
the same man in his kitchen then police arrive to th
n they both look just like t person he'd just killed
til they use a taser gun to apprehend the suspect who now
his horror, the man now his trunk
iting in , Mul wheels a man who co acted hi
onymously he man hands him a newspaper article about th

WETWIRED

EPISODE: 3X23

FIRST AIRED:

May 10, 1996

WRITTEN BY:

Mat Beck

EDITOR:

Heather MacDougall

DIRECTED BY:

Rob Bowman

GUEST STARS:

Mitch Pileggi (AD Walter Skinner)

Sheila Larken (Mrs. Scully)

William B. Davis (The Cigarette-
   Smoking Man)

Tom Braidwood (Frohike)

Dean Haglund (Langly)

Bruce Harwood (Byers)

Steven Williams (X)

Colin Cunningham (Dr. Stroman)

Tim Henry (The Plain-Clothed Man)

Linden Banks (Joseph Patnik)

Crystal Verge (Dr. Lorenz)

Andre Danyliu (County Coroner)

Joe Maffei (Motel Manager)

John McConnach (Officer #1)

Joe DoSerro (Officer #2)

Heather McCarthy (Duty Nurse)

LOG LINE:

Mulder and Scully discover a conspiracy involving mind control through television signals that's responsible for a series of murders in a small town and begins causing Scully herself to behave strangely.

PRINCIPAL SETTINGS:

Braddock Heights, Maryland; Washington, D.C.

SYNOPSIS:

A man buries a body in a hole, later killing what appears to be the same man in his kitchen. The police arrive to find him putting the dead body of the man in his trunk. But they also appear to look like the person he's just killed, until they use a taser gun to apprehend him. To his horror, the man now the person laying in the trunk is his wife.

Waiting in his car, Mulder meets the Plain-Clothed Man, who contacted him anonymously. The man hands him a newspaper article about the murders but won't say who sent him, adding that "more people will die" if Mulder doesn't pursue the case. Going to a psychiatric hospital where the suspect is being held, Mulder and Scully learn the killer murdered five people, thinking he was slaying the same man over and over, and that a babysitter also engaged in an unexplained murder spree in the same neighborhood. The doctor involved, Dr. Stroman, says the man is prone to outbursts.

Checking out the killer's house, Mulder notices a man working on the cable line, and finds hundreds of dated videotapes of cable news. They watch the videos, with Scully hypothesizing that viewing so much violence may have prompted the man's behavior. Mulder, however, calls the link between violence and television "pseudo-science used to make political book," adding that TV couldn't make an otherwise sane man kill five people thinking they're the same guy. "Not even 'Must-See TV' could do that to you," he says. Watching the tapes, Scully steps out for a drink and sees Mulder in a car chatting with the Cigarette-Smoking Man, handing a tape over to him before driving off. Later, Mulder denies taking the car out.

The next day a woman doing the dishes as she listens to the TV. She grabs a rifle after she looks up to see her husband having sex with another woman in their yard. Investigators find only the next-door neighbor dead, however, and in the woman's house they discover more tapes. Mulder also sees the same cable guy, who drives off before he can catch him. Scaling the telephone poll, Mulder pulls out an odd-looking device, while Scully continues to act unsettled and disturbed.

Joseph Patnik, the killer in the teaser, is played by Linden Banks, who played the antiabortion activist Rev. Sistrunk in "Colony." Crystal Verge, who here plays Dr. Lorenz, appeared in "Red Museum" in a red turban, reading instructions "channelled" by Odin. Colin Cunningham, who plays the mysterious Dr. Stroman, was Escalante the leper in "731."

Mulder takes the object he found to the Lone Gunmen, who say it's amazingly sophisticated and emitting some sort of signal. Mulder calls Scully, suggesting that someone is running a test of some kind. Scully responds with paranoia, hanging up and searching the room for listening devices. When there's a knock at her door she fires at it, as Mulder enters after she's fled.

Mulder contacts Scully's mother wondering if she's heard from Dana and tells Skinner he believes she's suffering from some sort of

The writer for this episode, Mat Beck, is the special effects producer for The X-Files. Among other talents, he wrote his master's thesis at Harvard on visual perception.

paranoid psychosis. Skinner notes that she's armed and dangerous, and that Mulder had better locate her before anyone else does. The Lone Gunmen, meanwhile, have finished analyzing the object, which they deem to be a mind control device. Mulder, they ascertain, was probably immune because color is a factor and he's red-green color-blind.

The police call, telling Mulder they've found a body that may be Scully. It isn't, and their inability to reach her mother prompts him to visit Mrs. Scully, where Dana, who is hiding, pulls a gun on him. "He's never trusted me," Scully shouts, to which Mulder replies, "Scully, you are the only one I trust." Mrs. Scully calms her daughter, and Dana is hospitalized, saying she felt the world was out to get her. "Now you know how I feel most of the time," Mulder says gently.

Mulder suggests the video signal takes people's fears and turns them into dementia. Scully relates seeing him talking to the Cigarette-Smoking Man, and Mulder posits that he may be involved. Mulder seeks to contact Dr. Stroman, who treated the man who first killed his wife, but the doctor has left. His forwarding phone number matches the number of the motel where Scully freaked out earlier. Returning to the motel and checking Stroman's room, Mulder notices tell-tale cigarette butts in the ash tray. He uses the phone log to track Stroman to a house. Mulder sees the cable repairman enter, hearing gunshots and finding both men dead. "You're too late, Agent Mulder," X says. When Mulder asks why X would have used a third party to put him on the case if he himself was going to kill them, X responds that those were always his orders and he was hoping Mulder would find them first.

Mulder calls X a coward who works in the shadows, but X simply walks away. "The truth is, you need me, Agent Mulder," he says.

Skinner asks about the killer, and Mulder says he remains "an unknown subject," as his boss observes him skeptically.

Walking down a dark alley X gets into a car, meeting with the Cigarette-Smoking Man, who asks if his work is completed. X says all the personnel and hardware have been "removed," and Mulder's source eliminated. When the Cancer Man wonders about the original source, X merely responds, "That person remains unknown."

BACK STORY: Given its subject matter, this would seem to have been a challenging episode for Gillian Anderson dramatically, but according to the actress it didn't really pan out that way. "It's odd, because it's big emotionally, but I'm not in it all that much because I

disappear for a short period of time," she says. "The stuff that I am in is dramatic, and the challenge is to lay it out in a believable way without going too overboard. Hopefully," she adds, before seeing the completed hour, "it will all cut together okay."

The first meeting between X

A rare continuity error: Scully fires six rounds at the hotel room door; we are later told she fired four.

and the Cigarette-Smoking Man in the closing scene provided a jolt for some viewers, and the producers labored to make sure the sequence had just the right look. "We spent a couple of hours, take after take, of just me coming down the alley," laughs Steven Williams, who adds with some irony that "We spent a couple of hours doing that, and about a half-hour on the dialogue." The character of the Plain-Clothes Man, who serves as what turns out to be a messenger for X at the outset, was concocted because Williams had a production conflict with his other series, *L.A. Heat.* "They gave three

Mulder claims to have been unaffected by the video signal because he is red-green color-blind (and exhibits his tie as incontrovertible proof that he is color-impaired).

of my scenes to another character," confides Williams, who says the producers of his new show are *X-Files* fans who have pledged to try and work around such logistical problems in the future.

Visual effects supervisor Mat Beck, making his debut as a writer, drew his inspiration for the story not only from the debate about television violence but his desire to explore the effect television has on people. "The concept evolved a little bit," he concedes, noting that it was "more complex at first"—as he thumbed through neurology texts studying how the brain interacts with visual media—and ultimately simplified as the episode developed.

Scully's motel room was actually a set constructed within a studio soundstage, as is the office for the Lone Gunmen. The episode also experienced late sound problems that caused postproduction to drag well into the night/early morning prior to its telecast. Co-producer Paul Rabwin provides the voice of a game show host heard in the background.

man, Galen, rants in a fast foo
verybody stays!" he shouts. A gent
e tries to leave Galen opens fir
arksman. "I'm gonna die," Galen s
ouching him and closing the wound.
an has fled the scene. Elsewhere,
sland, where she meets the Cigare

estaurant shooting show   h mystery man, who seems
  from the picture. The   imself, Jeremiah Smith,
etly captured by the Cigarette-Smoking Man's henchmen

TALITHA CUMI

EPISODE: 3X24

FIRST AIRED:

May 17, 1996

WRITTEN BY:

Chris Carter

STORY BY:

David Duchovny and Chris Carter

EDITOR:

Jim Gross

DIRECTED BY:

R. W. Goodwin

GUEST STARS:

Mitch Pileggi (AD Walter Skinner)

William B. Davis (The Cigarette-
Smoking Man)

Peter Donat (Bill Mulder)

Jerry Hardin (Deep Throat)

Roy Thinnes (Jeremiah Smith)

Brian Thompson (The Bounty
Hunter)

Angelo Vacco (Door Man)

Steven Williams (X)

Hrothgar Matthews (Galen Muntz)

Rebecca Toolan (Mrs. Mulder)

Stephen Dimopoulos (Detective)

John MacLaran (Dr. Laberge)

Cam Cronin (Paramedic)

Bonnie Hay (Night Nurse)

LOG LINE:

Mulder and Scully search for a mysterious man with the power to heal whose existence risks exposing a conspiracy involving the presence of aliens on Earth, while various forces seek a strange weapon that comes into Mulder's possession.

PRINCIPAL SETTINGS:

Washington, D.C.; Quonochontaug, Rhode Island; Arlington, Virginia

SYNOPSIS:

A man, Galen, rants in a fast-food restaurant before rising and pulling a gun. "Nobody moves! Everybody stays!" he shouts. A gentle man steps from the crowd seeking to calm him, but when someone tries to leave Galen opens fire, wounding three people before being shot himself by a police marksman. "I'm gonna die," Galen says, trembling.

"Nobody's going to die," the Healing Man says, touching him and closing the wound.

To Mulder's chagrin, by the time he and Scully arrive the Healing Man has fled the scene. Elsewhere, Mulder's mother goes to the family's old summer home in Rhode Island, where she meets the Cigarette-Smoking Man, who reminisces about the good times of years past. He notes that he was a better water-skier than her husband, adding sardonically, "But that could said about so many things . . . couldn't it?" Mrs. Mulder says she's "repressed it all," but the Cigarette-Smoking Man needs her to remember something, and they argue heatedly.

Skinner calls to inform Mulder that his mother has been admitted to a hospital in Rhode Island. She's had a stroke and can't speak, but seeing her son she awakens, scribbling the word "PALM" on a note pad. Later, videotape from the restaurant shooting shows the mystery man, who seems to vanish from the picture. The man, who calls himself Jeremiah Smith, is quietly captured by the Cigarette-Smoking Man's henchmen in his office at the Social Security building and put in a prison cell.

Mulder goes to the beach house, where he's surprised by X, who says he put in the emergency call that saved Mulder's mother after seeing her with the Cancer Man, showing him photos to prove it. Mulder can't imagine why they met, but X suggests the Cigarette-Smoking Man wanted something from her. "It could be something very old," he says. "Certainly something very important."

Jeremiah Smith turns himself in at the FBI building, saying he has no memory of healing anyone or leaving the crime scene. Confused, Skinner and Scully release him. Mulder returns that night to search the beach house, playing with the word "PALM" and writing down the anagram "LAMP," breaking several before finding a strange alien stiletto-like weapon hidden within one.

> In addition to the title, "Talitha Cumi," there are several references to _The Brothers Karamazov_ in this episode. The prison cell dialogues between the Cigarette-Smoking Man and Jeremiah Smith are based directly on "The Grand Inquisitor," in which the Inquisitor justifies keeping his flock in ignorance and slavery because they can't handle freedom. The Cigarette-Smoking Man paraphrases the Inquisitor when he says, "Anyone who can appease a man's conscience can take his freedom from him."

The Cigarette-Smoking Man questions Jeremiah Smith, asking if he realizes the consequences of his actions. People, he says, believe in authority and science, not miracles, and "must never believe any differently if the project is to go forward," adding that "the date is set." Startling him, Smith morphs into the likeness of Deep Throat, wondering how many must die "to preserve your stake in the project."

Upset about his mother, Mulder goes to Skinner demanding the Cigarette-Smoking Man's name. "These men don't have names," Skinner insists, saying the day when he could have helped Mulder in such matters is past. Mulder and Scully go to see Jeremiah Smith at his office, but he bolts into a crowd, disappearing, assuming the likeness of a bearded man.

The Cigarette-Smoking Man returns to the cell to continue the interrogation, and Jeremiah Smith morphs into Mr. Mulder. "I'm

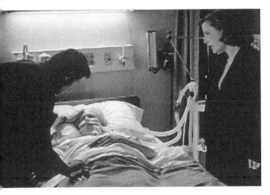

not one of you," the Cigarette-Smoking Man says tersely, to which he replies, "No, all you want is to be a part of it—is to be one of the commandants when the process begins." He then tells the Cigarette-Smoking Man that he's dying of lung cancer, prompting the shaken bureaucrat to accuse him of saying so because "you want to save your life."

"And you?" Jeremiah Smith asks calmly.

The bearded man who eluded Mulder and Scully earlier is in fact the alien bounty hunter Mulder encountered once before (in "Colony"/"End Game"). Having located the prison where Jeremiah Smith is being kept, he morphs back to his original appearance, extending his own alien stiletto. Going inside, however, the Bounty Hunter finds Jeremiah Smith's cell empty.

Mulder learns his mother may not recover, crying at her bedside.

In the hall outside he sees the Cigarette-Smoking Man, preparing to light up. "Are you gonna smoke that, or do you want to smoke this?" Mulder says, grabbing him and sticking a gun in his face. The Cigarette-Smoking Man notes that he's known Mulder's mother since "before you were born, Fox" and maintains that she sought him out because he may have information regarding the whereabouts of Mulder's sister. Checking computer files, meanwhile, Scully finds multiple Jeremiah Smiths listed who all look exactly alike.

X intercepts Mulder in the parking lot, asking that he hand over the alien weapon. "It's the only way we can kill them," Mulder suggests, which X confirms by saying, "A simple gunshot won't do." He adds that those who want the weapon will kill Mulder to acquire it, even if that means turning him into a martyr and his work into a crusade. "What we're talking about is colonization. The date is set, isn't it?" Mulder asks.

Suddenly, X strikes him, and they grapple brutally before going for their guns. Mulder backs away slowly, saying X won't find the weapon if he shoots him. "You're a dead man, Agent Mulder," X says panting from the struggle. "One way or another."

Scully gets home, and Jeremiah Smith comes to her apartment, saying the man she met before was an imposter sent to kill him and that he has information for Mulder about "an elaborate plan, a project and his sister." Mulder calls Scully, saying she's in danger and to meet him off the interstate. Jeremiah Smith, who accompanies Scully, tells Mulder he's come at great risk, and Mulder wants to take him to see his mother. Just then headlights shine upon them, as the alien bounty hunter exits a car, his own weapon drawn. "He's here to kill me," Jeremiah Smith says, as Mulder grasps his stiletto, tensing to act.

To be continued . . .

BACK STORY: The exchange between Mulder and the Cigarette-Smoking Man, when he mentions knowing the agent's mother before he was born, not surprisingly generated considerable speculation even within the show as to whether the shadowy character—in a *Star Wars—*

like twist—might really be Mulder's biological father. "Oh, people will say that," Chris Carter sighed prior to shooting.

For his part, David Duchovny considers that a very real possibility in adding to the series' epic mythology, and William B. Davis says he has contemplated such a scenario in the past and that such thoughts were guiding him in part when he played those scenes. "It has been in the back of my mind," he admits.

"I know that I've talked about it with Chris," Duchovny concurs. "Once Cigarette-Smoking Man started becoming a real character, that became an option." The actor adds that any *Star Wars* analogies would be a bit misguided, given that George Lucas borrowed from a wide variety of myths in developing that trilogy and that the source could be any one of a dozen stories.

Many postings on the Internet grumbled about the prospect of the Cancer Man perching anywhere near Mulder's family tree. "I didn't anticipate the response, but I'm happy for the response, to be honest," Carter observes. "What it does is it creates questions and certainly suspicion. It draws the audience in, just in the way you want it to. . . . I'm not going to say what it means," he adds in appropriately cryptic fashion. "It could mean anything."

Angelo Vacco is a production assistant in The X-Files L.A. production office. He appeared as a gas station attendant in the second-season episode, "F. Emasculata." Hrothgar Matthews also appeared in "Our Town" as a mental patient.

Fox's concern about violent content in television programming ultimately did result in the fight between Mulder and X being trimmed to comply with Fox's broadcast standards department. Even with stunt doubles doing much of the work, Steven Williams wrenched his shoulder during the filming, prompting director Bob Goodwin to treat the actor to the services of a masseuse afterwards.

From a technical standpoint, the alien stiletto works using a pneumatic tube by running a hose up the actor's sleeve to trigger the device. "Low-tech solutions are always the best," says props master Ken

Hawryliw. Similarly, co-producer Paul Rabwin again provided the sound effect for the device—vocally making a phffft sound—as he did with its first use in "Colony"/"End Game" during the second season. Rabwin, who made the sound after a technician spent hours putting together an effect that didn't quite cut the mustard, genially calls that oft-told anecdote "my claim to fame."

The fast food restaurant, Brothers K, is named after *The Brothers Karamazov*, the inspiration for the Cigarette-Smoking Man–Jeremiah Smith inquisition. The episode's title, which means "Arise Maiden" in the ancient Aramaic language, comes from the healing of a young girl that takes place within that story.

The reference to the Cigarette-Smoking Man water-skiing represents another inside joke based on William B. Davis's real-life skills as a championship-level water-skier. In addition, the time is twice listed in the legend as 11:21 P.M., which many fans will recognize as the birthday of Carter's wife, Dori, a number (along with Carter's own birthday, 10/13) that has recurred throughout the series.

Anderson's stand-in, Bonnie Hay, plays the hospital nurse, representing her fifth appearance on the show. Hay also portrayed a nurse in "D.P.O.," a doctor in the "Colony"/"End Game" two-parter, and a therapist in "Oubliette." When it's pointed out that she seems to keep finding herself playing some sort of health-care provider, Hay concludes with a shrug, "I guess I look caring and helpful."

Several key references in "Talitha Cumi" relate back to earlier episodes, most obviously "Colony"/"End Game." X's statement that those who oppose Mulder would risk killing him and turning him into a martyr also refers to an exchange in "Ascension" (part two of the "Duane Barry" mythology episodes earlier in the second season) when the Cigarette-Smoking Man explains that fear of allowing Mulder's work to become a crusade is what prevents the forces with which he's aligned from killing the agent.

By sheer coincidence, the season finale of NBC's *Homicide: Life on the Street*—which aired on the same night in the hour immediately after *The X-Files*—opened with the aftermath of a multiple shooting in a fast-food restaurant.

Spotnitz, a journalist and filmmaker who joined the show in the midst of its second season, acknowledges that Carter is demanding but says he prefers that to the alternative. "I often think the only thing worse than having somebody with such a clear idea of what he wants as your boss would be to have somebody who had no idea of what he wants," he says. "Chris has an exceptionally good sense of how a story should be told, what's scary, how to make a moment scarier, how to sharpen the drama. It's kind of amazing to watch

WRITING THE X-FILES

Everybody with a computer, word processor, or typewriter seems to think they can do it, but those who do it for a living find themselves in accord on one salient point: Writing *The X-Files* is a lot more difficult than most people would probably imagine.

"That, I think, is the biggest misconception: People just don't realize it's not easy writing this show. It takes a lot of time and emotional anguish," says story editor Frank Spotnitz, one of several writers for whom *The X-Files* represents their first TV series. That also includes staffers John Shiban and Vince Gilligan, who, along with Spotnitz, return to the staff from the third season.

Executive producer–creator Chris Carter is a notorious perfectionist, one so attuned to the rhythms of Mulder and Scully's interaction and the parameters of the show itself that writers always have to be cognizant of keeping the series true to those principles.

Creative consultant, Vince Gilligan.

Co-executive producer Howard Gordon—the only other writer to be with *The X-Files* since its first season—credits Carter with serving as the show's guiding force, while possessing a vision of the series that remains its compass. "I think any successful show has got a voice. It's almost like a novel," Gordon suggests. "The advantage of being a novelist is that you have the words and you put a book out. Chris has the problem of protecting his voice, which is really Mulder and Scully's voices, but also allowing other voices to contribute." In terms of establishing another voice within Carter's universe, Gordon adds, "I think Darin [Morgan] is really the only one who has successfully taken those voices, since [Glen] Morgan and [James] Wong, and done so."

Darin Morgan joined the show during its second season, writing "Humbug," the circus freaks episode. He followed that up during the third season with the darkly comic "Clyde Bruckman's Final Repose," "War of the Coprophages," and "Jose Chung's *From Outer Space*." Morgan's brother Glen and his partner, James Wong, created such characters as The Lone Gunmen and Tooms before leaving during the second season to develop and produce *Space: Above and Beyond*.

According to Darin Morgan, his unique style evolved in part because humor was essentially the only way he knew how to approach the show. With "Humbug," for example, he pitched Carter the story but didn't *exactly* convey the droll manner in which he was going to write it, since he didn't entirely know himself. "In a TV show, staff writers have to write in the style of the show," he says. "I did it the only way I could. I was just trying to write the damn thing."

The popularity of "Humbug" helped provide Morgan with the latitude to explore such flights of fancy in his subsequent episodes, but the writer stresses that despite the comedic undercurrents he felt compelled to stay within the show's parameters. "I was always very conscious of having it still be an X-file," he suggests. "I wasn't trying to do parody. You make some jokes at the show's expense, but I never wanted to parody it."

The other writers also express their admiration for Morgan's ability to craft hours that could provide a lighter touch without, in their view, undermining the series' ongoing mission. "Darin's episodes verge on satire—not on parody, but on satire. You can enjoy it and then get back in the game"—without breaching the "implied contract" that exists between a show and its audience, Gordon contends. In his view, "It's almost like an actor talking to an audience for a moment."

Gordon concedes that even with all the time spent on the series, he at times struggles in writing episodes and finds himself turning to Carter for guidance. "I think I understand those characters very well," he says of Mulder and Scully, "but Chris is really the touchstone, and if I cheat a little bit he'll catch it." Using a football analogy, he adds, "I sometimes think that I can get to the ten-yard line, but I need him to get over the goal line."

Spotnitz, a journalist and filmmaker who joined the show in the midst of its second season, acknowledges that Carter is demanding but says he prefers that to the alternative. "I often think the only thing worse than having somebody with such a clear idea of what he wants as your boss would be to have somebody who had no idea of what he wants," he says. "Chris has an exceptionally good sense of how a story should be told, what's scary, how to make a moment scarier, how to sharpen the drama. It's kind of amazing to watch how

his instincts work, and he never seems to be off. Yes, he's very demanding, but he has a coherent vision behind those demands."

Similarly, Gordon notes that Carter has the ability to "find ways to fix things in the eleventh hour" when the show runs into problems. "Ernest Hemingway said a good writer has a bullshit detector—that when you're writing something that isn't propelling the characters or story

From left to right: Vince Gilligan, Frank Spotnitz, and John Shiban.

forward in any way, the bullshit meter would go off," says Gordon. "Chris really has enforced this sort of rigorous kind of thinking, [where] every scene should really mean something, should really propel the story forward. It works very well for the show."

Beyond the discipline Carter imposes, most writers deem working on *The X-Files* to be different from other television programs for a variety of reasons. "What's unique about this show is that it's frankly sort of unlike anything with which I've been involved," says Gordon, who has previously written for such series as *Beauty and the Beast* and *Spenser: For Hire*. "It has no formula. It doesn't have any conventions of soap operas. The idea is to do nothing that you've seen before, so it really forces you to use your imagination and try telling stories in a different way."

The current writers credit Carter, Morgan, and Wong, and Gordon and his former partner, Alex Gansa—the three teams who wrote nearly every episode during the first season—with establishing initially that viewers wouldn't know what to expect each week from the series. "That was sort of bucking the conventional wisdom about television, which is you should be seeing the same show every week," Spotnitz contends. "I think that's actually a virtue in that the show is a surprise, keeping the show fresh."

"I find that's what's exciting about *The X-Files*: Every episode is different," observes producer-director Kim Manners. "The only like factor we have is two actors, with new sets, new everything each week."

That dynamic may also explain in part why writers without a proven track record in television series have sometimes fared better than their more experienced counterparts. "Part of the problem is because *The X-Files* is so different from other shows, the people we brought in at higher levels who had worked on other shows in the business were accustomed to writing a certain way, and there was a certain advantage to hiring people who were inexperienced," says Gordon.

"It's sort of been tougher on some of the people who came from TV, because they're used to working in a different way," agrees creative consultant Vince Gilligan, who had written the movie *Wilder Napalm* before scripting the second season episode "Soft Light"—about a man whose shadow could cause instant death—and then becoming a regular contributor to the series. "It seems on the whole to be easier—'easier' being a relevant term—on people who have written feature scripts, people who have that background, whether they've gotten made or not."

John Shiban was also new to television, and suggests that *The X-Files* provides its writers more creative freedom because of Carter's background and desire to treat each episode like a one-hour movie. "A lot of shows don't even allow you to put camera directions in. We're encouraged to," says Shiban, whose credits include "The Walk" and "Teso dos Bichos." "Chris wants to tell the story visually and he wants us to tell the story visually. Most TV shows, from what I understand, aren't looking for that, they don't like it, and they don't encourage it. That's the director's job.

"Then again, most TV shows have standing sets and they're doing the same type of story every week. We're doing a different mini-feature each week, so I think it serves us well that we had no experience previously and thus no expectations."

Carter also instituted a rare practice in which the writers—who are all based in Los Angeles—go to Vancouver to witness the production process whenever an episode they've written is being shot in an effort to protect their vision and convey that to the director and crew. "It's great, and I think it's smart too," Shiban indicates. "I feel like it's made me a better writer, when you actually have to see how they put the thing together and what problems they encounter, it makes you think of that when you start working on your next episode. You say, 'How can I make this work? How can I make this interesting and yet produceable?'"

In the same vein, those trips help the writers realize what's feasi-

ble from a production standpoint. "You must be conscious of it, you must think of how much you're asking them to do based on the budget and the time they have," Spotnitz says. "That's actually something I know it's taken me several episodes to get a handle on," he adds with a grin, having written epic mythol-

ogy episodes like "Colony"/"End Game" and "Nisei"/"731," which involved submarines, trains, and spaceships—all of which presented unique and sometimes extremely trying challenges in terms of production.

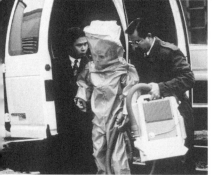

Those major two-part episodes prompt other considerations, such as how much attention the writers have to pay to those over-arching themes when they're followed up with stand-alone episodes that don't explore such cosmic issues. Gordon, for example, thinks "D.P.O."—his episode about a lightning-wielding teenager—may have suffered coming on the heels of the elaborate "Anasazi"/"Blessing Way"/"Paper Clip" trilogy. "We

always worry about that—how much of what we've just been through should we address?" Spotnitz concedes. "You don't want to sort of corrupt 'D.P.O.' by saddling it with all that."

Granted, some fans feel the more intriguing stand-alone episodes will actually be better remembered in the end. While hard-core fans may savor connecting the dots, as it were, in tracking the arc of the program's mythology, the show takes its individual episodes and mandate to provide thrills and chills no less seriously. "Pragmatically speaking," adds Gilligan, "some day years from now in syndication they're going to show these things all out of order anyway."

From a storytelling perspective, *The X-Files* moves in and out of different genres loosely categorized as monsters, strange science, and dark conspiracy/mythology. Yet the show has continuously added other wrinkles, including forays into black comedy and an episode like "Avatar," which shifted the focus from Mulder and Scully to their boss, FBI Assistant Director Walter Skinner. There's also an art of its own to mastering the ongoing banter between the principals.

Although *The X-Files* has done a sort-of werewolf story in exploring myths surrounding the Manitou ("Shapes") as well as a contemporary vampire tale ("3"), the series has steered clear of conventional monsters, which present their own unique problems creatively for a show that constantly endeavors to be different. "If you do too many of them you realize you never get to know these monsters, because they don't talk, they just kind of lumber around," Gilligan suggests. "It becomes more interesting to build a character who happens to be an antagonist. They can interact on some other level beyond chasing one another." Gilligan notes that Tooms, the liver-eating mutant featured twice during the first season, was "an interesting monster because he could interact."

Not surprisingly, finding appropriate ideas for the show remains one of the most significant and daunting challenges the writers face. Gordon cites Gilligan's script for "Pusher" as a prime demonstration of coming across a concept that works for the series—the simple idea of someone who could whisper in a person's ear and make them do exactly what he said. "When Vince told me that idea it was like a light went off in my head. I said, 'This is an unbelievable episode.' I knew in a moment that he'd found something," Gordon says.

Developing such ideas presents its own headaches, and the writers frequently find their inspiration in unlikely places. Sometimes a newspaper article or photograph will be enough to get the ball rolling, as was the case with the "face on the moon" picture that ultimately led to the early episode "Space," or the shot of a submarine conning tower breaking through the ice that spurred "Colony"/"End Game."

Shiban says he spends a lot of time in UCLA's research library in addition to accessing information via the Internet, where he found a helpful home page on astral projection while he was running through ideas for "The Walk."

"It is fairly research intensive," says Gordon, who's repeatedly used his brothers—both of whom are doctors—as resources. Similarly, Spotnitz's brother is a neurologist and his father a doctor, which came in handy when he wrote the episode "Our Town," in which a key plot point hinged on Creutzfeldt-Jacob Disease. "I'll do the research," Gordon says, "but I need my brothers to make it comprehensible."

The writers also say there's an advantage to periodically offering episodes that can be resolved without any obvious paranormal explanation—such as "Grotesque," which appears simply to be a case of work-induced insanity, or potentially "War of the Coprophages," where the cockroach invasion can be easily explained away as a case of mass hysteria. "It's a nice change-up from being in a place where Mulder's

always right," notes Gordon. "Whenever he says it's a blood-sucking vampire or a lightning boy and he's always right, it's a way to say maybe this is a little bit hysterical."

Even though the writers are encouraged to be creative and explore new terrain, *The X-Files* still functions within specific guide-lines. Writers consistently wrestle with certain questions, such as what makes their idea an X-File, how to involve Mulder and Scully in the story, and what differentiates a concept from previous episodes. "That's always the test, is have we done this before, if we have done it is this different enough to justify doing something like it again," says Spotnitz. "You're always trying to figure out, 'When do I have the critical mass here?' Of course you don't have a story fully developed, but when do I have enough to come forward and say, 'Do you like this idea?'"

As an example, Gilligan cites an episode he's been noodling with about psychic photography—someone being able to project their thoughts on a camera and create an image. "It's sort of intangible," he acknowledges of what really clicks in coming up with an episode. "Usually, if you have a pretty well-worked-out teaser scene you can go to Chris and say, 'How does this grab you?'

"That teaser may change as you start to board it, but basically the teaser is not only a way to grab the audience but sometimes a good way to grab Chris. But you have to have something to back it up, some sort of thought behind it. . . . Part of it is you sell him on your own enthusiasm for the story."

Carter also established early on that *The X-Files* generally leaves room for multiple theories regarding what's transpired, and part of a writer's job thus involves telling a story without necessarily doing so in such a definitive manner as to rule out such room for speculation. "The more you give away, the more light you shine on something, the less mysterious it becomes, and therefore the more you reveal the more you're sort of chipping away at what makes *The X-Files* great," Gilligan says. "The less you show the better. People's imaginations are better than anything you can completely give them."

"If you know everything, there's no paranoia," Spotnitz contends.

Writers do try to keep track of what they're all individually working on so as not to duplicate or too closely parallel each other's proposals. Shiban notes that the writing process remains extremely collaborative, and even before ideas get to Carter the writers often bat them around amongst each other. "We do an incredible amount of rewriting and reworking, bouncing things off each other, just to try and make the story as good as possible," he says. Though usually only one writer is credited, scripts frequently get rewritten and massaged by committee, with Carter's always the last typewriter through which the teleplay passes.

Still, all the planning doesn't prevent cases where the producers end up regretting the way an episode is executed, the proximity of one episode to another similarly themed installment, or how the sup-

porting characters get deployed from week to week. "It doesn't work out as neatly as it should," Spotnitz admits, referring to when recurring characters like Skinner, X, or the Cigarette-Smoking Man appear. "We had Skinner absent for most of the early part of the season after 'Paper Clip,' and suddenly, bam. He's in practically every episode."

"If it worked out better, we wouldn't have his ass kicked in, like, three episodes back-to-back," Gilligan adds wryly, echoing an observation made by Mitch Pileggi, who concedes that he began to grumble a bit when Skinner took his third drubbing—from a "scrawny little researcher" under the influence of mind control—in "Pusher."

When to use characters nevertheless remains up to the writers, who must decide whether doing so advances the story and if there's logic in featuring them. "The stories come first," says Spotnitz.

"Chris would never come and say, 'Put X in this story' if it's not essential to the story," agrees Shiban. "The only people who *have* to be there are Mulder and Scully."

"Which we appreciate, not forcing stuff on us," adds Gilligan.

The X-Files has also employed few writing teams—pairs of writers who work together being a fairly standard practice in television—other than Morgan and Wong (often referred to as "the Wongs," for no particular reason) and Gordon and Gansa before the duo split. Gordon thus can offer a perspective on the difference between writing with a partner and toiling alone. "Instead of sort of

sleeping at night and saying the other guy will figure it out, I've had a lot more sleepless nights saying how am I going to solve this," says Gordon, a genuine insomniac whose occasional sleepless fits inspired the episode "Sleepless," about war veterans operated on to eliminate the need for sleep. Writing alone, he concludes, is "a lot more challenging and a lot more lonely than it's been, but it's also a lot more exciting to take responsibility for the whole thing."

Writers don't know in advance which directors are going to do their episodes, but that's largely irrelevant because most of the show's regular directors—especially Rob Bowman and Kim Manners—have had a crack at every kind of *X-Files* episode. Co–executive producer R. W. Goodwin notes that while some shows might call for a flare for drama, suspense, action, or comedy, this one requires a little of everything. "It's hard to pigeonhole them, because they've done all sorts of genres now," says Spotnitz, who adds that the writers are similarly inclined, despite his own seeming penchant for two-parters. "It just sort of happened that my first show ended up being a mythology show," he says.

Directors, of course, bring their own sensibility to the material, as do the performers. Manners, for example, agrees with David Duchovny about the need for Mulder and Scully to evolve as time passes. "We're realizing at the end of the third season that they've got to take on a different dynamic," he contends. "Scully cannot possibly remain so skeptical." Despite those who resist the notion of delving into the characters' personal lives, Manners adds, "We should see Scully with a guy, and we should see Mulder with a woman, or an outside interest, or something. The show has to go in that direction, I think."

Duchovny has his own strong opinions along those lines, and his input frequently finds its way into the episodes—whether it's questioning a line or pushing for Mulder to behave in a manner he thinks consistent with the character. Gordon cites Duchovny's innate intelligence as an enormous asset for the writers, and the understated approach both he and Gillian Anderson bring to their roles as helping make the show believable—that understatement working perfectly "against material that's so fantastic."

Fox executives, meanwhile, have learned to give Carter a relatively wide berth in charting the program's creative direction ("We don't get many notes from the network on this show," he concedes), though the producer still insists that Fox's broadcast standards and practices department—which sets guidelines for program content—is no more lenient or permissive than any of the other networks'. The writers don't specifically look for ways to test those boundaries, they say, merely to tell their stories in the most compelling manner available.

Most of the writers and producers do follow ongoing discussion of the show and individual episodes on the Internet, though they acknowledge that their emphasis on such comments has cooled a bit as the show's audience has grown. Though thousands participate in such chat rooms and online sessions, millions more watch *The X-Files* each week, and its creators want to be cautious not to skew the show based on what might be the opinion of a highly vocal minority. As a result, the truth may not always be in cyberspace.

"I actually read less than I used to," Spotnitz says. "We're all grateful for these hard-core fans who follow every breath and nuance of the show, but at the same time it's a very narrow sample of the audience, and they're interested in some things disproportionate to the larger audience and disproportionate to ourselves. It's a little frustrating that you work on something you think is really interesting in the script that doesn't get commented upon, and instead you get a lot of nitpicking or focusing on the soap-opera aspects of Mulder and Scully's relationship, which is ultimately not that interesting to us."

"You have to realize the greater proportion of people watch the show and enjoy it but don't ever post anything on the Internet," agrees Gilligan. "I remember on 'Soft Light' . . . half the postings were about some really mod pair of sunglasses Mulder was wearing in the funeral scene at the end. I thought, 'What's that about?' It's something that's interesting to read, but not something you base future storytelling decisions on."

At least, not with so much out there to consider, and so many stories to tell.

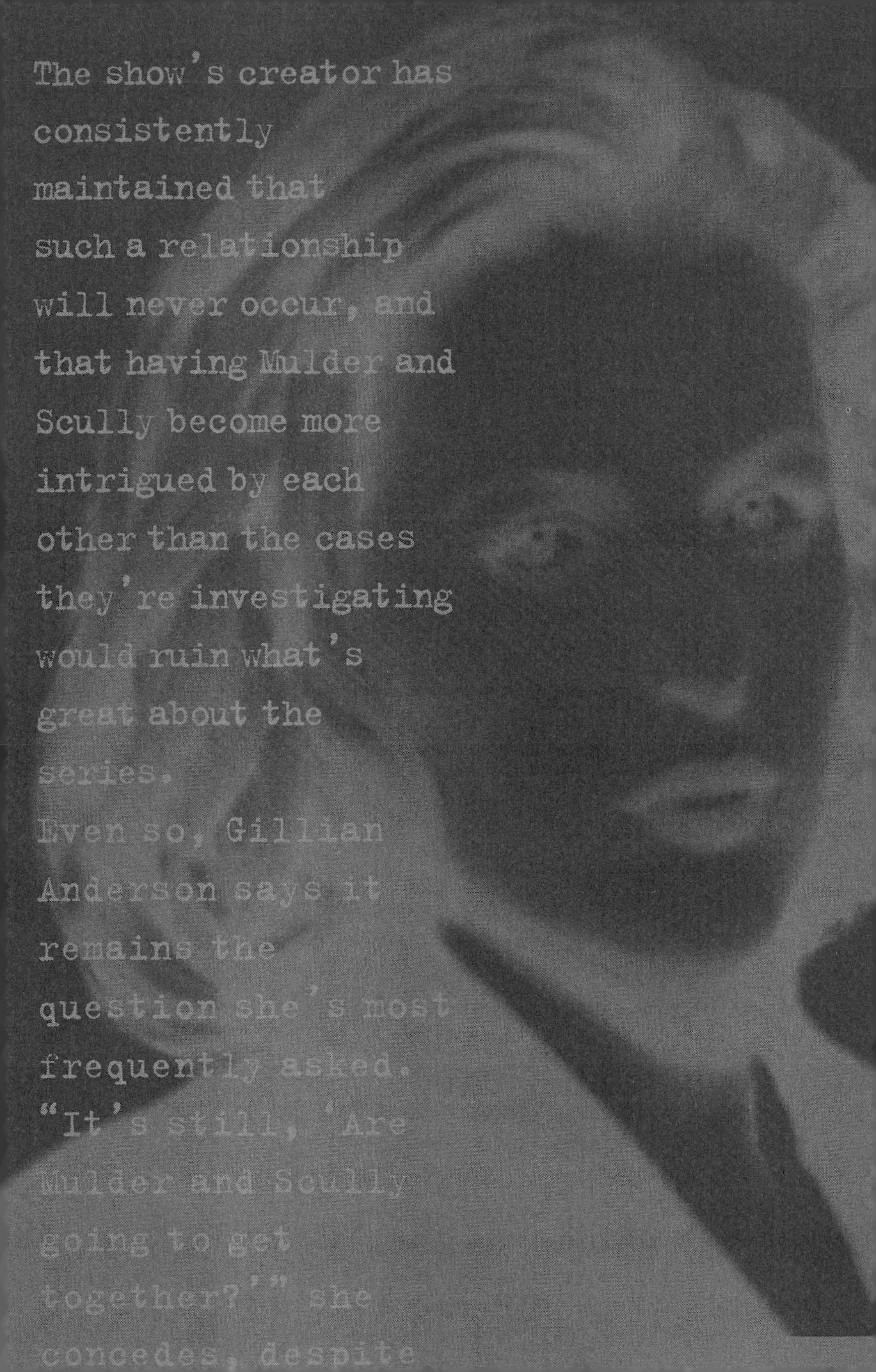

The show's creator has
consistently
maintained that
such a relationship
will never occur, and
that having Mulder and
Scully become more
intrigued by each
other than the cases
they're investigating
would ruin what's
great about the
series.
Even so, Gillian
Anderson says it
remains the
question she's most
frequently asked.
"It's still, 'Are
Mulder and Scully
going to get
together?'" she
concedes, despite

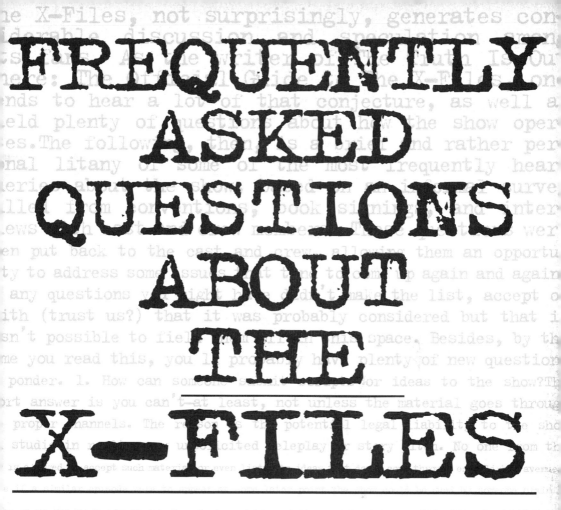

FREQUENTLY ASKED QUESTIONS ABOUT THE X-FILES

he X-Files, not surprisingly, generates considerable discussion and speculation among its fans. As the writer of *The Truth Is Out There: The
Official Guide to The X-Files*, one tends to hear a lot of that conjecture, as
well as field plenty of questions about how the show operates.

The following, then, is a brief and rather personal litany of some of the
most frequently heard questions that I was asked while writing this book, at conventions, book signings, and interviews. I then put these questions back to the cast and
crew, allowing them an opportunity to address some issues that tend to come up again
and again. If any questions you might have didn't make my list, accept on faith that it
was probably considered but that it wasn't possible to field them all in this space.
Besides, by the time you read this, you'll probably have plenty of new questions to
ponder.

1. How can someone submit scripts or ideas to the show?

The short answer is you can't—at least, not unless the material goes through the proper channels. The reason is the potential legal liability to the show and studio in reading any unsolicited teleplay or story pitch. No one from the show is allowed to accept such material or even listen to ideas that don't come through established avenues, since if a similar episode were to appear at some later point the show could be sued by someone claiming that his or her idea had been appropriated.

For that reason, nothing can even be looked at unless it comes through a licensed literary or TV agent, an attorney, or with a signed waiver from the author. Initially, the producers did receive scripts if they met those guidelines, but more recently the show has curtailed accepting any unsolicited screenplays, Chris Carter says, "because we just haven't had time to read it all, and we just don't have the manpower to do it."

The situation is much the same with any popular television show, adds Carter, who enjoys regularly chatting with fans over the Internet but also can't allow them to discuss story ideas in that forum, again, to avoid "the huge legal consequences" that could potentially arise.

2. What's the status of The X-Files movie?

At the time of publication, Chris Carter's deal was done to write and produce the movie, and contracts were being made with the actors. "After that, it's really just a matter of getting a good script," says Carter, as well as figuring out logistically when such an endeavor could occur. The idea would be to shoot the film in the spring—once the show completes production—for a fall or winter release.

When that will happen remains undetermined, based in part on the availability of those involved and deciding whether the movie should be done while the series is still on the air. "Of course, I don't want to do anything that blows the series out of the water, but you have to do something in a movie that's bigger than the TV show, or there's no reason to do it as a movie," Carter declares.

The ideal scenario would be for the movie to be produced after the TV series has run its course, which "would allow the movies to come one after another in a more interesting way," the producer says, rather than having to oscillate between the series and the movie. Carter sees the movie as a means of expanding the *X-Files* franchise in a storytelling way, adding, "Storytelling is what we do best."

3. How and where can I participate in the show online on the Internet, or through other channels?

The official Twentieth Century Fox World Wide Web site is at http://www.thex-files.com. According to the studio, the show receives at least 1,000 visits and postings per day, more than any other television program. Material available online includes an episode guide, merchandise, and a variety of chat rooms. There is also an unauthorized service on America Online.

Those who remain computerphobic can still become involved through such enterprises as The Official *X-Files* Fan Club, which includes a newsletter, membership kit, and various ways to order merchandise. People interested in joining that club can write to:

CREATION "X-FILES"

411 N. Central Avenue, Suite 300

Glendale, CA 91203

4. Do you believe in UFOs and the paranormal?

Depends on who you ask. The cast and crew has its own mix of skeptics and those more open to the notion of paranormal phenomena. Still, the question itself remains remarkably persistent, often to the chagrin of those involved, who—separating reality from

the roles they play—don't see the answer as being particularly germane to what they do for a living. "I don't think it will go away," sighs David Duchovny of the question itself, adding rather pointedly, "They don't ask Jimmy Smits [of *NYPD Blue*] if he believes in law enforcement."

5. Will Mulder and Scully ever become romantically involved?

Not if Chris Carter has anything to say about it. The show's creator has consistently maintained that such a relationship will never occur, and that having Mulder and Scully become more intrigued by each other than the cases they're investigating would ruin what's great about the series.

Even so, Gillian Anderson says it remains the question she's most frequently asked. "It's still, 'Are Mulder and Scully going to get together?'" she concedes, despite Carter's repeated and much-publicized denials, which have also included jokingly nixing the notion of Scully and Skinner becoming romantically intertwined or, for that matter, Mulder and Skinner. "I swear people have heard it, they've read it, but they still ask," Anderson shrugs, admitting that the *Rolling Stone* cover may have fueled that fantasy in some people's minds— causing easily suggestible folk to think that either she and Duchovny were sleeping together or that Mulder and Scully would be.

6. Why are there so many repeats of the show during the season?

Ultimately, it comes down to a matter of mathematics and network economics. Because of time constraints, the show can, in a 10-month production period, produce 24 episodes a year, about standard for a one-hour drama. (Most successful TV shows produce 22 to 25 episodes each season, with the exception of prime-time soaps like *Melrose Place*, which can churn out as many as 34 episodes and which try to stay original, because they don't do well in reruns. David Duchovny has in fact publicly lobbied to reduce the number to 22, the industry standard, to provide the stars with more time off to pursue features or at least shorten the 10-month production grind. Since *The X-Files* is such a successful program for the network, Fox is so far holding fast to the 24-per-year equation.)

As for the math, the official television season runs from mid-September through May, a span of about 35 weeks. In addition, the networks try to air new episodes of their highest-rated series each week during November, February, and May, which are sweeps periods—key months to network affiliates because they are used to help determine local advertising rates.

A dozen episodes, then, air during those periods, following the flurry that usually opens the new season. In order to stretch the supply of original episodes through May, most series consequently have to offer a number of repeats during the months of December (when many people are on vacation anyway, so viewing levels drop), March, and April. That may not help X-Philes in need of a fix during those arid periods, but if it's any consolation, fans of shows like *ER* and *Friends* complain about the same problem.

7. When and where will repeats of the episodes be shown?

The fX cable network will begin airing *The X-Files* show Monday through Friday in September 1997. Separate deals have been made with local TV stations to start televising the show on the weekends at that time as well in what's known as off-network syndication, meaning time periods will vary from city to city. So, as they say in television, check local listings.

8. Where do the writers get their ideas?

From anywhere and everywhere, including magazine articles, news reports, old movies, and virtually anything else they encounter that might have an X-File in it. "That's always the first question," states writer John Shiban, who, when asked how he comes up with ideas himself, says he likes to respond, "Years of training."

9. Why are the episode titles so arcane and confusing?

Because they're meant to be. Part of the fun for hard-core fans has become deciphering the titles, and the writers enjoy thinking up appropriately impenetrable labels. "Not that much work goes into them," according to writer Vince Gilligan, "and Chris is cool, because ninety-nine percent of the time he lets it stay."

"He encourages us to be as obscure as possible," adds story editor Frank Spotnitz.

10. What's the collectible market like related to the series?

Booming. That Australian *Rolling Stone* cover, for example, is fetching at least $100 per copy. An issue autographed by the two stars went for $475 at a convention. At another convention in San Diego, two autographed shooting scripts were auctioned off for $650 each, and a poster signed by David Duchovny and Gillian Anderson went for $240. An issue of the *X-Files* comic book autographed by Chris Carter commanded $160.

Each convention features a charity auction benefiting the Eras Center for Autism, which provides help for autistic children. The charity was brought to Chris Carter's attention by a Fox executive who has an autistic child.

11. Does the Cigarette-Smoking Man really smoke?

No. William B. Davis, who plays the character, gave up smoking years ago, so now he puffs away on special herbal cigarettes.

12. Is the truth really out there?

Sure. Maybe. Keep watching.

the entire story,
however, inasmuch as
The X-Files ranks
third—behind only ER
and NYPD Blue—among
one-hour drama series
within the broad
demographic segment
of adults age 18-49,
the most highly prized
group among national
advertisers and thus
the principal factor
in determining the
cost of commercial
time. In fact, the
show won its time
period by the most
important sales
demographics all 35
weeks of the 1995-96
season and emerged as
Fox's top-rated

RATINGS

SEASON 3

"X" signifies an unknown quantity, then The
Files has in many respects become something of
misnomer. The third season witnessed the Fox
oadcasting Company series experience audience
owth both in the United States and abroad, while
rious cottage industries surrounding the program
other media have flourished as well. In terms of
ewing levels for the primetime TV season that
ns from September through May, the show's total
grew by 7% compared to the previous year,
the average episode (including repeats during
at period seen by more than 15.4 million viewers up fro
average of 14.5 million over the 1994-95 campaign. Tha
rformance bucked a trend in network television that sa
tings for the major broadcast networks drop practically
ross the board. Granted, that's still about half the audi
ce of primetime's biggest hits, shows like ER and Seinfeld
se figures don't tell the entire story, however, inasmuch as The X
es ranks third-behind only ER and NYPD Blue-among one-hour dram
ies within the broad demographic segment of adults age 18-49, the mos
hly prized group among national advertisers and thus the principal fac
in determining the cost of commercial time. In fact, the show won its time period by the mo

If "X" signifies an unknown quantity, then *The X-Files* has in many respects become something of a misnomer. The third season witnessed the Fox Broadcasting Company series experience audience growth both in the United States and abroad, while various cottage industries surrounding the program in other media have flourished as well.

In terms of viewing levels for the primetime TV season that runs from September through May, the show's total audience grew by 7% compared to the previous year, with the average episode (including repeats during that period) seen by more than 15.4 million viewers, up from an average of 14.5 million over the 1994–95 campaign. That performance bucked a trend in network television that saw ratings for the major broadcast networks drop practically across the board.

Granted, that's still about half the audience of primetime's biggest hits, shows like

ER and *Seinfeld*. Those figures don't tell the entire story, however, inasmuch as *The X-Files* ranks third—behind only *ER* and *NYPD Blue*—among one-hour drama series within the broad demographic segment of adults age 18–49, the most highly prized group among national advertisers and thus the principal factor in determining the cost of commercial time. In fact, the show won its time period by the most important sales demographics all 35 weeks of the 1995–96 season and emerged as Fox's top-rated program.

That's despite airing on Friday night, when the number of available viewers—especially those in younger age brackets—tends to be lower, ranking ahead of only Saturday night in terms of the percentage of sets in use during primetime. Indeed, that success despite such factors is what prompted Fox to make the stunning decision, when setting its new schedule in May, to move the program to Sundays—when TV viewing levels are as much as 20% higher than Fridays—opposite movies on the Big Three networks.

The X-Files also has the advantage of commanding one of the most loyal audiences in television—what network executives like to call "an appointment show," meaning viewers make an appointment with themselves to watch each week.

The following is a breakdown of viewing levels for each new *The X-Files* episode that aired during the show's third season. Each rating point represents 959,000 homes, 1% of the 95.9 million homes with television in the United States during the third season—a figure Nielsen had since revised up to 97 million. The total U.S. population is more than 249 million. The share represents the percentage of homes viewing television in that particular hour. The list also includes the number of total viewers for each episode, as measured by Nielsen's people-meter ratings service, which draws its figures from a small sample designed to represent of all television viewers in the United States.

AIRDATE	EPISODE	RATING/SHARE	VIEWERS (IN MILLIONS)
9/22/95	The Blessing Way*	12.3/22	19.94
9/29/95	Paper Clip	11.1/20	17.20
10/6/95	D.P.O.	10.9/20	15.57
10/13/95	Clyde Bruckman's Final Repose	10.2/18	15.38
10/20/95	The List	10.8/19	16.72
11/3/95	2Shy	10.2/17	14.83
11/10/95	The Walk	10.4/18	15.91
11/17/95	Oubliette	10.2/17	15.90
11/24/95	Nisei	9.8/17	16.36
12/1/95	731	12.0/21	17.68
12/15/95	Revelations	10.0/17	15.25
1/5/96	War of the Coprophages	10.1/16	16.32
1/26/96	Syzygy	10.8/17	16.04
2/2/96	Grotesque	11.6/18	18.32
2/9/96	Piper Maru	10.6/18	16.44
2/16/96	Apocrypha	10.8/18	16.71
2/23/96	Pusher	10.8/18	16.20
3/8/96	Teso dos Bichos	10.7/18	17.38
3/29/96	Hell Money	9.9/17	14.86
4/12/96	Jose Chung's *From Outer Space*	10.5/19	16.08
4/26/96	Avatar	9.3/16	14.62
5/3/96	Quagmire	10.2/18	16.00
5/10/96	Wetwired	9.7/17	14.48
5/17/96	Talitha Cumi	11.2/21	17.86

* Highest rating, share, and total audience through the first three seasons.

Each rating point equals 959,000 homes, or 1 percent of all TV households in the U.S. Share is based on the percentage of TV sets in use within the time period.

Source: Nielsen Media Research

— Winner, outstanding
guest actor in a drama
series — Peter Boyle
as Clyde
    Bruckman ("Clyde
Bruckman's Final
Repose")
— Winner, outstanding
writing in a drama
series — Darin Morgan
("Clyde
    Bruckman's Final
Repose")
— Winner, outstanding
achievement in cine-
matography for a
series —
    John Bartley
("Grotesque")
— Nominee, outstand-
ing individual
achievement in art
direction for a series

Awards and Honors

PRIME-TIME EMMY AWARDS

- Winner, Outstanding Writing in a Drama Series—Darin Morgan for "Clyde Bruckman's Final Repose"
- Winner, Outstanding Guest Actor in a Drama Series—Peter Boyle as Clyde Bruckman in "Clyde Bruckman's Final Repose"
- Winner, Outstanding Individual Achievement in Cinematography for a Series—John Bartley for "Grotesque"
- Winner, Outstanding Sound Editing for a Series—Thierry J. Couturier for "Nisei"
- Winner, Outstanding Sound Mixing for a Drama Series— Michael Williamson, Production Mixer; David J. West, Nello Torri, Doug Turner, Re-recording Mixers "Nisei"
- Nominee, Outstanding Drama Series
- Nominee, Outstanding Lead Actress in a Drama Series— Gillian Anderson
- Nominee, Outstanding Individual Achievement in Art Direction for a Series — Graeme Murray, Art Director; Shirley Inget, Set Decorator for "Jose Chung's *From Outer Space*"

GOLDEN GLOBE AWARDS

- Nominee, Outstanding Performance by an Actress in a Drama Series— Gillian Anderson
- Nominee, Outstanding Performance by an Actor in a Drama Series— David Duchovny

SCREEN ACTORS GUILD AWARDS

- Winner, Outstanding Performance by an Actress in a Drama Series—Gillian Anderson
- Nominee, Outstanding Performance by an Actor in a Drama Series—David Duchovny

DIRECTORS' GUILD OF AMERICA AWARDS
- Nominee, Best Direction in a Dramatic Series—Chris Carter for "The List"

WRITERS GUILD OF AMERICA AWARDS
- Nominee, Best Writing in a Dramatic Series—Chris Carter for "Duane Barry"

PRODUCERS GUILD OF AMERICA AWARDS (GOLDEN LAUREL AWARDS)
- Nominee, Outstanding Series

AMERICAN SOCIETY OF CINEMATOGRAPHERS AWARDS
- Nominee, Outstanding Achievement in Episodic Television— John Bartley for "731"

CINEMA AUDIO SOCIETY AWARDS
- Nominee, Outstanding Series—"Humbug"

MYSTERY WRITERS OF AMERICA (EDGAR ALLAN POE AWARDS)
- Nominee, Best Episode in a Television Series—Darin Morgan for "Humbug"

ACADEMY OF SCIENCE FICTION, FANTASY & HORROR (SATURN AWARDS)
- Nominee, Best Genre TV Series

ENVIRONMENTAL MEDIA AWARDS
- Nominee, Outstanding Episodic Television (Drama) — Kim Newton for "Quagmire"

NEW YORK FESTIVAL AWARDS
- Nominee, Best Drama Series

THE INTERNATIONAL MONITOR AWARDS
- Winner, Best Director—Chris Carter for "The List"
- Winner, Best Audio Post Production—Thierry J. Couturier & David West for "Nisei"
- Nominee, Best Achievement for "731"

- Nominee, Best Editing—Heather MacDougall for "The List"
- Nominee, Best Electronic Special Effects—Mat Beck for "Paper Clip"
- Nominee, Best Color Correction—Phil Azenzer for "The List"

TELEVISION CRITICS ASSOCIATION (TCA) AWARDS
- Nominee, Best Drama Series

1994-95

PRIME-TIME EMMY AWARDS
- Nominee, Outstanding Drama Series
- Nominee, Outstanding Writing in a Drama Series—Chris Carter for
     "Duane Barry"
- Nominee, Outstanding Guest Actress in a Drama Series—CCH Pounder as
     Agent Kazdin in "Duane Barry"
- Nominee, Outstanding Individual Achievement in Editing for a Series—
     Single Camera Production—James Coblentz for "Duane Barry"
- Nominee, Outstanding Individual Achievement in Editing for a Series—
     Single Camera Production—Stephen Mark for "Sleepless"
- Nominee, Outstanding Individual Achievement in Cinematography for a
     Series—John Bartley for "One Breath"
- Nominee, Outstanding Sound Editing for a Series—Thierry J. Couturier,
     Supervising Sound Editor for "Duane Barry"

GOLDEN GLOBE AWARDS
- Winner, Best Dramatic Series

ENVIRONMENTAL MEDIA AWARDS
- Winner, Outstanding Episodic Television (Drama)—Steve DeJarnett for
     "Fearful Symmetry"

THE INTERNATIONAL MONITOR AWARDS
- Nominee, Best Editing—James Coblentz for "Duane Barry"

TELEVISION CRITICS ASSOCIATION (TCA) AWARDS
- Nominee, Best Drama Series
- Nominee, Program of the Year

VIEWERS FOR QUALITY TELEVISION (VQT) AWARDS
- Nominee, Best Drama Series
- Nominee, Best Actor in a Drama Series—David Duchovny
- Nominee, Best Actress in a Drama Series—Gillian Anderson

ACADEMY OF SCIENCE FICTION, FANTASY & HORROR (SATURN AWARDS)
- Winner, Outstanding Television Series

DIGITAL HOLLYWOOD AWARDS
- Winner, Best Digital Writer—James Wong and Glen Morgan for "Beyond the Sea"
- Nominee, Best in Digital Television Series

MYSTERY WRITERS OF AMERICA (EDGAR ALLAN POE AWARDS)
- Nominee, Best Episode in a Television Series—Chris Carter for "The Erlenmeyer Flask"

AMERICAN SOCIETY OF CINEMATOGRAPHERS AWARDS
- Nominee, Outstanding Achievement in Cinematography (Series)—John Bartley for "Duane Barry"

1993-94

PRIME-TIME EMMY AWARDS
- Winner, Outstanding Individual Achievement in Graphic Design and Title Sequences—James Castle, Bruce Bryant, Carol Johnsen
- Nominee, Outstanding Achievement in Main Titles Theme Music—Mark Snow

ENVIRONMENTAL MEDIA AWARDS
- Winner, Outstanding Episodic Television (Drama)—Chris Carter for "Darkness Falls"

NEW YORK FESTIVAL FOR TELEVISION PROGRAMMING AND PROMOTION
- Finalist for Best Writing—Chris Carter for "The Erlenmeyer Flask"
- Finalist for Best Writing — James Wong and Glen Morgan for "Beyond the Sea"

PARENT'S CHOICE AWARDS
- Winner, Best Series

AMERICAN SOCIETY OF CINEMATOGRAPHERS AWARDS
- Nominee, Outstanding Achievement in Episodic Television—Tom Del Ruth for "Pilot"

THE INTERNATIONAL MONITOR AWARDS
- Winner, Best Editing—James Coblentz for "Beyond the Sea"

Appendix

SEASON 1

PILOT 1X79

FBI Agent Dana Scully is paired with maverick agent Fox Mulder, who has made it his life's work to explore unexplained phenomena. The two are dispatched to investigate the mysterious deaths of a number of high school classmates.

DEEP THROAT 1X01

Acting on a tip from an inside source (Deep Throat), Mulder and Scully travel to Idaho to investigate unusual disappearances of army test pilots.

SQUEEZE 1X02

Mulder and Scully try to stop a mutant killer, Eugene Tooms, who can gain access through even the smallest spaces and awakens from hibernation every 30 years to commit murder.

CONDUIT 1X03

A teenage girl is abducted by aliens, compelling Mulder to confront his feelings about his own sister's disappearance.

THE JERSEY DEVIL 1X04

Scully and Mulder investigate murders thought to be the work of the legendary man-beast living in the New Jersey woods.

SHADOWS 1X05

Mulder and Scully investigate unusual murders committed by an unseen force protecting a young woman.

GHOST IN THE MACHINE 1X06

A computer with artificial intelligence begins killing in order to preserve its existence.

ICE 1X07

Mulder and Scully and a small party in the Arctic are trapped after the unexplained deaths of a research team on assignment there.

SPACE 1X08

A mysterious force is sabotaging the United States' space shuttle program and Scully and Mulder must stop it before the next launch.

FALLEN ANGEL 1X09
Scully and Mulder investigate a possible UFO crash site, which Mulder believes the government is covering up.

EVE 1X10
Two bizarre, identical murders occur simultaneously on different coasts, each involving a strange young girl.

FIRE 1X11
Mulder and Scully encounter an assassin who can start fires with the touch of his hand.

BEYOND THE SEA 1X12
Scully and Mulder seek the aid of a death-row inmate, Luther Lee Boggs, who claims to have psychic abilities, to help them stop a killer who's on the loose.

GENDERBENDER 1X13
Scully and Mulder seek answers to a bizarre series of murders committed by one person who kills as both a male and a female.

LAZARUS 1X14
When an FBI agent and a bank robber are both shot during a bank heist, the robber is killed but the agent begins to take on the criminal's persona.

YOUNG AT HEART 1X15
Mulder finds that a criminal he put away who was supposed to have died in prison has returned, taunting him as he commits a new spree of crimes.

E.B.E 1X16
Scully and Mulder discover evidence of a government cover-up when they learn that a UFO shot down in Iraq has been secretly transported to the U.S.

MIRACLE MAN 1X17
The agents investigate a young faith healer who seems to use his powers for both good and evil.

SHAPES 1X18
Mulder and Scully travel to an Indian reservation to examine deaths caused by a beast-like creature.

DARKNESS FALLS 1X19

Mulder and Scully are called in when loggers in a remote Pacific Northwest forest mysteriously disappear.

TOOMS 1X20

Mulder becomes personally involved when Eugene Tooms, the serial killer who extracts and eats human livers, is released from prison.

BORN AGAIN 1X21

A series of murders is linked to a little girl who may be the reincarnated spirit of a murdered policeman.

ROLAND 1X22

Mulder and Scully investigate the murders of two rocket scientists apparently linked to a retarded janitor.

THE ERLENMEYER FLASK 1X23

Working on a tip from Deep Throat, Mulder and Scully discover that the government has been testing alien DNA on humans with disastrous results.

SEASON 2

LITTLE GREEN MEN 2X01

With the X-Files shut down, Mulder secretly journeys to a possible alien contact site in Puerto Rico while Scully tries to help him escape detection.

THE HOST 2X02

Mulder stumbles upon a genetic mutation, the Flukeman, while investigating a murder in the New Jersey sewer system.

BLOOD 2X03

Several residents of a small suburban farming community suddenly turn violent and dangerous, prompted by digital readouts in appliances telling them to kill.

SLEEPLESS 2X04

Mulder is assigned a new partner, Alex Krycek, and they investigate a secret Vietnam-era experiment on sleep deprivation that is having deadly effects on surviving participants.

DUANE BARRY (PART 1 OF 2) 2X05

Mulder negotiates a hostage situation involving a man, Duane Barry, who claims to be a victim of alien experimentation.

ASCENSION (PART 2 OF 2) 2X06

Mulder pursues Duane Barry in a desperate search for Scully.

3 2X07

Mulder investigates a series of vampiresque murders in Hollywood and finds himself falling for a mysterious woman who is a prime suspect.

ONE BREATH 2X08

Scully is found alive but in a coma, and Mulder must fight to save her life.

FIREWALKER 2X09

Mulder and Scully stumble upon a deadly life form while investigating the death of a scientist studying an active volcano.

RED MUSEUM 2X10

Mulder and Scully investigate a possible connection between a rural religious cult and the disappearance of several teenagers.

EXCELSIUS DEI 2X11

Mulder and Scully uncover strange goings-on in a nursing home after a nurse is attacked by an unseen force.

AUBREY 2X12

Mulder and Scully investigate the possibility of genetic transferring of personality from one generation to another in connection with a serial killer.

IRRESISTIBLE 2X13

A psycho who collects hair and fingernails from the dead steps up his obsession to killing his soon-to-be collectibles himself.

DIE HAND DIE VERLETZT 2X14

Mulder and Scully journey to a small town to investigate a boy's murder and are caught between the town's secret occult religion and a woman with strange powers.

FRESH BONES 2X15

Mulder and Scully journey to a Haitian refugee camp after a series of deaths, finding themselves caught in a secret war between the camp commander and a Voodoo priest.

COLONY (PART 1 OF 2) 2X16

Mulder and Scully track an alien bounty hunter, who is killing medical doctors who have something strange in common.

END GAME (PART 2 OF 2) 2X17

Mulder tracks an alien bounty hunter who has taken Scully prisoner while discovering that his sister may not be who she seems.

FEARFUL SYMMETRY 2X18

Mulder and Scully investigate animal abductions from a zoo near a known UFO hot spot.

DOD KALM 2X19

Mulder and Scully fall victim to a mysterious force aboard a navy destroyer that causes rapid aging

HUMBUG 2X20

Mulder and Scully investigate the bizarre death of a retired escape artist in a town populated by former circus and sideshow acts.

THE CALUSARI 2X21

A young boy's unusual death leads Mulder and Scully to a superstitious old woman and her grandson, who may be possessed by evil.

F. EMASCULATA 2X22

When a plaguelike illness kills 10 men inside a prison facility, Scully is called to the quarantine area while Mulder tracks two escapees.

SOFT LIGHT 2X23

An experiment in dark matter turns a scientist's shadow into a form of instant death.

OUR TOWN 2X24

Mulder and Scully investigate a murder in a small Southern town and its strange secrets surrounding a chicken processing plant.

ANASAZI 2X25

Mulder and Scully's lives are jeopardized when an amateur computer hacker gains access to secret government file providing evidence of UFOs.

About the Author

BRIAN LOWRY reports on television for the *Los Angeles Times*, which he joined in May 1996, in the midst of writing this book. He is also the author of the first *X-Files* companion book, *The Truth Is Out There: The Official Guide to The X-Files*, which was released in 1995. Lowry previously served as the Los Angeles television editor for *Daily Variety*, the show-business trade newspaper, covering the TV industry in addition to writing reviews and a weekly column, "Changing Channels." A native of Los Angeles, he is a graduate of UCLA.

THE TRUTH IS OUT THERE™: THE OFFICIAL GUIDE TO THE X-FILES™
by Brian Lowry

The New York Times Bestseller

The only official viewer's guide to America's hottest TV series. Includes scores of incredible photos.

THE X-FILES™ POSTCARD BOOK

A full-color collection of the bizarre and unforgettable adventures of agents Scully and Mulder.

THE A–Z OF THE X-FILES™ by Jane Killick

An encyclopedic, alphabetically organized list of facts, characters, places, dates, and virtually everything else a devoted fan of The X-Files would ever want.

TRUST NO ONE™: THE OFFICIAL GUIDE TO THE X-FILES™, VOLUME II
by Brian Lowry

The official companion guide to the third smash season of The X-Files.

THE OFFICIAL MAP OF THE X-FILES™

See where the truth is. This full-color map highlights areas where bizarre occurrences of The X-Files have taken place and includes intriguing facts about specific episodes as well as real-life supernatural phenomena.

A N D   C O M I N G   S O O N . . .

THE X-FILES™ BOOK OF THE UNEXPLAINED, VOLUME TWO

THE ⓧ FILES ™

For complimentary information on the
official fan club and conventions,
please send a self-addressed stamped
envelope to:

CREATION-XF
411 North Central Ave. #300
Glendale, CA 91203